religious discovery,

faith,

and knowledge

James Kellenberger

religious discovery, faith, and knowledge

Prentice-Hall, Inc.
Englewood Cliffs, New Jersey

ISBN: P 0-13-773283-X
        C 0-13-773219-0

Library of Congress Catalog Card Number 76–37362

10 9 8 7 6 5 4 3 2 1

Printed in the United States of America

Prentice-Hall International, Inc., London
Prentice-Hall of Australia, Pty. Ltd., Sydney
Prentice-Hall of Canada, Ltd., Toronto
Prentice-Hall of India Private Limited, New Delhi
Prentice-Hall of Japan, Inc., Tokyo

Several of the chapters of this volume are revised versions of articles that have
appeared or will appear in various journals. They are reprinted here by the kind
permission of the editors of those journals. I wish to thank Professor H. D. Lewis, the
editor of *Religious Studies,* for permission to reprint "The Falsification Challenge"
and "More on the Falsification Challenge," from Vol. V, 1969; to thank Professor
M. J. Charlesworth, the editor of *Sophia,* for permission to reprint "We No Longer
Have Need of That Hypothesis" from Vol. VIII, 1969, and "Religious Discovery"
from Vol. IX, 1970; to thank Professor H. B. Acton, the editor of *Philosophy,* for
permission to reprint "The Ontological Principle and God's Existence" from Vol.
XLV, 1970; and to thank Professor Gilbert Ryle, the editor of *Mind,* for permission
to reprint "On Necessary and Sufficient Conditions for Knowledge," forthcoming.

I also wish to gratefully acknowledge permission to use the published material of
the following:
Professor Peter Winch, the editor of *Analysis,* Blackwell, Oxford, and Edmund L.
Gettier for material from "Is Justified True Belief Knowledge?" SCM Press Ltd.,
London, and The Macmillan Company, New York, for material from *New Essays
in Philosophical Theology,* Antony Flew and Alasdair MacIntyre, editors. The

acknowledgments

Macmillan Company, New York, for material from *Belief and Unbelief* by Michael Novak. Hutchinson, London, and Harcourt Brace Jovanovich, Inc., New York, for material from *God and Philosophy* by Antony Flew. Harcourt Brace Jovanovich, Inc., for material from *Religious Belief and Philosophical Thought*, William P. Alston, editor. Collier Books, New York, for material from *The Rise of Silas Lapham* by William Dean Howells. Campus Crusade for Christ and James F. Engel for material from "Let's Get Serious!" *Student Action*. St. Martin's Press, Inc., Macmillan & Co., Ltd., New York, for material from Immanuel Kant's *Critique of Pure Reason*, edited by Norman Kemp Smith; *Faith and the Philosophers*, John Hick, editor; and *The Problem of Knowledge* by A. J. Ayer. The Aristotelian Society for material from "Gods" by John Wisdom. P. J. Kenedy & Sons, New York, for material from *Butlers Lives of the Saints*, edited by Herbert Thurston, S. J., and Donald Attwater. Professor H. B. Acton, the editor of *Philosophy* and Kai Nielsen for material from "Wittgensteinian Fideism." George Allen & Unwin Ltd., London, for material from *Faith and Logic*, Basil Mitchell, editor. Cornell University Press, Ithaca, N. Y., for material from *Faith and Logic* by John Hick. Doubleday & Company, Inc., Garden City, N. Y., for material from *The Ontological Argument*, Alvin Plantinga, editor. Dickenson Publishing Company, Inc., Encino, California, for material from *Judaism:*

Development and Life by Leo Trepp. Princeton University Press, Princeton, N. J., for material from Soren Kierkegaard's *Concluding Unscientific Postscript,* translated by David F. Swenson and Walter Lowrie. The editors of *Encounter* for material from "Ludwig Wittgenstein" by Stephen Toulmin. The Bobbs-Merrill Company, Inc., Indianapolis, Indiana, for material from Rene Descartes' *Meditations on First Philosophy,* translated by L. J. Lafleur. The Bobbs-Merrill Company, Inc., Indianapolis, Indiana, and William Hamilton for material from *Radical Theology and the Death of God* by Thomas J. J. Altizer and William Hamilton. David McKay Company, Inc., New York, for material from John Henry Cardinal Newman's *An Essay in Aid of A Grammar of Assent,* edited by Frederick Harrold. Random House, New York, for material from *Basic Writings of Saint Thomas Aquinas,* edited by Anton C. Pegis. Prentice-Hall, Inc., Englewood Cliffs, N. J., for material from *Knowledge and Certainty* by Norman Malcolm. Russell & Russell, New York, for material from *The Correspondence of Spinoza,* translated and edited by A. Wolf.

In writing this book I have been helped by many people in many ways; to all of them I am grateful.

They include Mrs. Dorothy Johnson and Mrs. LuAnne Rohrer, the secretaries of the Department of Philosophy at San Fernando Valley State College, who helped by getting material duplicated, typing letters, etc. (and the etc. is vast). And they include Mrs. Hannah Hawkes and Miss Linda Mintz, who typed the manuscript in its final form. I am also grateful to my colleagues at San Fernando Valley State College for their criticism and suggestions; several of the chapters in one form or another were discussed with John Kekes; and Donald F. Henze's persistent questions helped me greatly in thinking about the falsification issue. I also owe much to my former fellow students and teachers at the University of Oregon who helped me to think through certain thoughts on knowledge and religious knowledge, as well as on other subjects. And, too, I am grateful to Professor John Wisdom for his redolent writings on religious epistemology and their abiding stimulation.

My greatest debt of gratitude, though, is to Frank B. Ebersole, my thesis advisor and more, who lavished on rocky ground the seeds of philosophy and to whom I hope these thoughts will seem worthy of the sowing.

contents

I

rationality and discovery

I

II

religious knowledge

II

appendix: meaning

introduction

The purpose of this book is to raise the possibilities of religious knowledge and religious discovery. By *religious* knowledge and discovery I mean knowledge and discovery of God, and by *possibility* I mean a viable possibility, the kind that a new look under a new light finds; I do not mean a minimal or a "logical" possibility.

In trying to raise the possibility of religious discovery, I first distinguish between two kinds of evidence: hypothetical and nonhypothetical. Hypothetical evidence is clearly evidence, but the latter may not be seen to be evidence at all. Then I discuss two models of discovery. The latter sort of evidence has significance for religion in that it plays a role in a model of discovery which, in its religious application, may very possibly lead to a religious discovery. This "nonhypothetical" model of discovery applies to those situations where we finally discover what was really before us all the time even though we did not or could not see it. For example, a young man suddenly realizes that, contrary to what he himself believed, he *does* have feelings of affection for a young woman he thought beneath him and for whom he thought he did not care, as he frequently told all his friends. This is a secular situation where a nonhypothetical discovery of one's relationship to another person is made, but religious situations share some of the aspects of such secular situations. Whether they share all the aspects is another question. To ask this question is to ask if there *are* religious discoveries of the nonhypothetical type, and to ask this question is to come a step toward seeing that there possibly could be.

The same approach will be followed for religious knowledge (other than that knowledge possibly gained through nonhypothetical discoveries). That is, certain ignored secular situations in which men have knowledge, or very possibly have knowledge, will be developed, and then a parallel will be drawn to establish the possibility of analogous religious knowledge.

At the same time that we raise the possibilities of religious knowledge and discovery, we will call into question certain dominant philosophical models of discovery and knowledge. Indeed, to do the one thing is to do the other. The dominant model of discovery that we will examine in its relation to religion is the hypothetical model of discovery, which construes factual discoveries (as opposed to mathematical or logical discoveries) as discoveries that confirm a hypothesis. And the model of knowledge that we will examine in its relation to religion is the model of knowledge that construes knowledge as true, justified belief, or belief of which one is sure with the right (adequate justification) to be sure. I mean by a "philosophical model" not a model only philosophers have, but a model anyone might have. It is a picture or view of what, say, knowledge is, which is perhaps not articulated but lies beneath the surface of our thinking as an assumption. Such models may derive from a selection of certain examples of knowledge or discovery which are taken to be crucial or paradigmatic and to exhibit the nature of the concept. When philosophers talk about what knowledge is conceptually or what it is by its very nature, they are drawing upon such a philosophical model or picture. This is not to imply that all such models are completely wrong and have no application, but it does seem that these dominant philosophical models of knowledge and discovery have tended to blind us when applied to religion.

Let me point out one way in which these models blind us. It is indicative of the way many of us tend to view knowledge, discovery, and the possibility of religious knowledge and discovery, that we would concentrate on the arguments for God's existence. We tend to think that to have religious knowledge—to know that there is a God—we must be able to prove, deductively or inductively that there is a God. This perspective, I suggest, is a paramount reason why we fail to appreciate the possibility of religious knowledge and discovery—a possibility which I hope will be made evident in what follows. From this perspective our view is dominated by those models of discovery and knowledge just noted, which are more appropriate to scientific discovery and the testing of knowledge claims. As a consequence we fail to appreciate quite another model of discovery, the nonhypothetical model, and its possible application to religion, and we tend to construe knowledge extremely narrowly. We then think that if there is to be a religious discovery of God and religious knowledge they will come only when the God hypothesis has been conclusively verified by a proof. There are ways, however, of overcoming the domination of these models. Hopefully this book, by focusing upon largely neglected examples of discovery and knowledge, will facilitate the exorcism.

"Exorcism" is not a wholly inappropriate word in this connection. The question of whether there is religious knowledge or religious discovery is more than a difficult question. It is more because certain aspects of it touch those parts of us that so often evade scrutiny; those parts of us in which we find self-deception. This may sound ominous, but perhaps it should. The way in which self-deception relates to religious discovery will emerge in the discussion of religious discovery found in Chapter 2. It will also become evident that while these matters can be discussed, it may be that they cannot be settled by reasoned discourse alone. It may be that possibilities can be delineated, but beyond that the limits of the sayable are reached. If, however, the limits of the sayable are reached, it is *after* the emergence of the possibility of religious discovery, and it is in an understandable way—a way encountered in the secular as well as in the religious sphere. We will further discuss this in Chapter 3.

A book that raises possibilities also raises questions. The primary questions that are raised here are the obvious ones: 1) Is there a sort of discovery, unlike that which relates to hypotheses, that applies to religion? and 2) Can there be religious knowledge? A more specific form of this last question is: Can religious people come to know that there is a God from the Bible? Other questions that are raised are: Does one have to be "inside" religion to make a religious discovery (if there are any) or to understand religion? What is the relation between knowledge and faith? Does knowledge make faith impossible? Or does faith lead to knowledge?

A note on my use of the word "religion." Unless the context indicates otherwise it means religion that involves belief in God, specifically religion within the Judaeo-Christian tradition. Of course, Judaism and Christianity are only two among many religions, but since the discussion will be conducted in terms of Judaeo-Christian concepts and belief, it is useful to limit the scope of the term.

One other note. Many might feel as I do that an issue logically prior to questions about religious discovery and knowledge is the issue of the meaning of religious statements. For those who further feel that this logically prior issue demands treatment before entering into the discussion of religious discovery the Appendix is provided; Parts A and B treat the issue of the meaning of religious statements.

to my father and mother,

and to my students, teachers,
and colleagues

religious discovery,

faith,

and knowledge

I

rationality
and discovery

I

1

we no longer

have need of

that hypothesis

1

I

Some years ago there appeared in the literature of the philosophy of religion a parable that has proven particularly provocative: John Wisdom's parable of the garden.

> Two people return to their long neglected garden and find among the weeds a few of the old plants surprisingly vigorous. One says to the other "It must be that a gardener has been coming and doing something about these plants." Upon inquiry they find that no neighbor has ever seen anyone at work in their garden. The first man says to the other "He must have worked while people slept." The other says "No, someone would have heard him and besides, anybody who cared about the plants would have kept down these weeds." The first man says "Look at the way these are arranged. There is purpose and a feeling for beauty here. I believe that someone comes, someone invisible to mortal eyes. I believe that the more carefully we look the more we shall find confirmation of this." They examine the garden ever so carefully and sometimes they come on new things suggesting that a gardener comes and sometimes they come on new things suggesting the contrary and even that a malicious person has been at work.[1]

From this parable Antony Flew draws the principle that every genuine factual statement must deny certain specific empirical conditions, or else it really asserts nothing.[2] To do this he gives the parable a bit of a twist. In Professor Flew's version two explorers come upon a clearing in a jungle. One explorer says "Some gardener must tend this plot." The other disagrees. They decide to set a watch, but no gardener comes. Then they rig electrified fences and bring in bloodhounds, for, the first explorer maintains, the gardener might be invisible. Still no gardener is detected. "Perhaps he is also intangible," the first explorer suggests. At this point, the second explorer and Flew ask what remains of the original assertion that there is a gardener? What is the difference between an invisible, intangible, and completely undetectable gardener and no gardener at all? Flew's lesson is this: What starts as an intelligible hypothesis may be qualified out of existence until nothing at all is asserted. And this is the case with what religious persons say they believe: that there is a God or that God is good. It ends up, Flew suggests, that there is nothing whatsoever that will count against their assertion; there is nothing that their assertion denies and therefore nothing that it asserts.

There is an answer or at least a partial answer to Flew in his own terms, however. That answer is provided by Basil Mitchell.[3] Professor Mitchell introduces a different parable—one which contains an element lacking in Flew's —that of commitment. His parable is that of the partisan and the Stranger. The partisan, a member of a resistance movement, one evening meets a man he presumes is a fellow member of the resistance. This man is the Stranger. Though they meet only once, the partisan is deeply impressed and moved by the Stranger. Then in the weeks following their meeting the Stranger begins doing things that indicate he is not on the side of the resistance. Yet in spite of these things the partisan continues to maintain to his comrades that the Stranger is on their side. He is bothered by the things the Stranger does that indicate he is helping the enemy, but feels they do not and cannot count *decisively* against his being on their side; they may count against his belief, but they cannot show it to be false, he feels. The point Mitchell makes to Flew, then, is this: Unlike the explorer who maintains there is a gardener, one who believes in God will allow things to count against for instance God's goodness, but he will not allow anything to count decisively against it.

Flew rejects Mitchell's point, for, he argues, it only holds true if the Stranger is a man and not God. However, even if Mitchell's parable and point are accepted, they are small consolation to defenders of religion as an account of religious belief. The partisan emerges as essentially irrational; he will allow various things to count against the Stranger being on his side, but he will allow nothing to count decisively against it. So far as recognizing negative evidence against his hypothesis is concerned he is answerable to reason—but only to a point. He will not in any circumstances reject his hypothesis—he has *resolved* not to let anything count decisively against it.

At this point one might ask: *Is* religious belief—at bottom—belief in nothing (as Flew suggests) or irrational (as Mitchell suggests)? What I hope to bring out is that Flew is wrong in taking hypotheses as models for religious statements and Mitchell is wrong in allowing hypotheses and the holding of hypotheses to operate in the background as the model for religious belief and the holding of a religious belief. This will be accomplished, hopefully, by bringing out the essential differences between hypotheses and religious beliefs. This may sound a bit like what the earlier Alasdair MacIntyre said,[4] and in a way it is, but in essential respects I mean something quite different. What MacIntyre said is this: A religious belief is not held tentatively and provisionally, as a hypothesis is. To the extent that theism is treated as a hypothesis, it is either false or fantastic; consequently it is not a hypothesis. Each religion has its authority, e.g., the Bible for Protestant Christianity, and religious belief is justified in terms of these authorities; evidence is not offered for what is believed.

MacIntyre has been criticized for not recognizing natural theology, which is an attempt to argue for the existence of God on the basis of evidence.[5] This criticism seems to be well aimed, but misguided, for while MacIntyre failed to recognize a very real role of evidence in supporting religious belief, he was essentially right in distinguishing religious beliefs from hypotheses. To bring out the contrast between hypotheses and religious belief and the role of evidence vis-à-vis religious belief, let us examine an instance of a hypothesis and an instance of a religious belief. The hypothesis we shall examine concerns the doings of M; the religious belief is that of a Job-like man, whom I shall call JB. First the hypothesis.

II

It is a hypothesis held by a newspaper editor who was investigating the slums of his city. His hypothesis, which he came by nearly accidentally, was that many of the slum tenements were owned by a respected community leader named M. While doing a story on a charity to which M had contributed a large sum, he was struck by how active and influential M had become in community matters though still a newcomer to the community; he was also struck by how M's business concerns, though substantial, belied his actual wealth. It was only later, faced with the fact that slum ownership was for the most part a carefully guarded secret, that he saw the possible significance of the mystery of M's wealth. Making inquiries he found that M's acknowledged business enterprises did not account for half the money he obviously had; the other sources he kept secret. The editor thus began to investigate the ownership of the slums with the hypothesis that M owned them or at least a good part of them.

At first the evidence the editor discovered pointed to another man as the primary owner of the slums. Many documents relating to the slums, e.g., bills of sale, had another man's name on them and not M's. In the light of this evidence the editor discounted his hypothesis and very nearly abandoned it. Then, however, the editor discovered letters linking this man whose name so often turned up to M. In fact, as one letter made clear, the man was an officer in one of M's corporations—this corporation, and hence M, being the real owner of the tenements. The editor located several documents indicating that this was the case. On the basis of these documents the editor concluded that his hypothesis was correct.

III

The second case is that of JB and his faith in God and His goodness. I imagine JB to be rather like Archibald MacLeish's JB, but more Job-like.[6] He too is a contemporary, let us say, although it is not essential that he be. Like Job and like MacLeish's JB, he is visited with adversity and affliction. His business fails, he receives news that his sons have been killed, his wife leaves him; all that he has, even his health, he loses. Yet he continues to believe in God and His goodness—at least he does for some time. During this time some think him a fool while others see his faith as great, and he thanks God for his sustained faith.

Seeking escape or distraction he rereads the few books he yet possesses. Among them is Dostoyevsky's *The Brothers Karamazov,* and in rereading it he finds a particular fascination with the older brother, Ivan Karamazov. He sees Ivan's questioning with new eyes. Alyosha now appears to him to be foolishly infantile and blind to his brother Ivan's sensitivity. When he reads again Ivan's catalogue of the suffering of children it registers as it never did before. He sees it as indicative of the world and the lot of men. Seeing it thus, he cries out as Job did not: "Where is the goodness of the Lord if there is indeed the God I have believed in?"

So JB may lose his faith in God. Also of course he may not. Rereading *The Brothers Karamazov* may not lead him to see suffering anew and so may not cause him to cry out against God. And, also, if he loses his faith he may regain it. A friend who knew JB as a man of great faith, hearing that he no longer has that faith, might resolve to talk with him to help him see again what he no longer sees. What could he say to help him regain his faith? Perhaps he could say this: "Remember how you started with nothing but your two hands, JB—the two hands God gave you; you still have those two hands." This might return JB's faith and hope to him or it might not. As his friend would say, he might see the significance of that fact or he might not.

The contrast between hypotheses and religious belief, as they are exemplified by the M hypothesis and JB's belief, may be drawn under two headings: First, under the heading of evidence; and second, under the heading of how they are held.

Evidence. Clearly there is evidence in the case of the M hypothesis. M's financial figures and the letters the editor collected were evidence for this hypothesis. The bills of sale on which M's name did not appear were evidence against it, taken by themselves. The hypothesis was established because the overwhelming evidence supported it.

In the case of JB's belief there also was evidence. The evils done to children catalogued by Ivan Karamazov comprised evidence against JB's belief, or so he saw such evils. The fact that he was left the use of his two hands was evidence for his belief, or so at least his friend saw it.

To be sure, there are important differences between the evidence that figures in the hypothesis case and that which figures in the case of JB's belief. These differences may be hit off thus:

In the case of the hypothesis:

(1) *The evidence was collected or gathered.* (The editor gathered documents and letters.)
(2) *The evidence clearly applied.* (There was no question about whether the incriminating letters were in fact incriminating and supported the hypothesis.)

In the case of JB's belief:

(1) *The evidence was already before JB.* (JB did not learn from his reading or rereading *The Brothers Karamazov* that children are beaten and made to suffer; nor of course did he discover that he had two hands.)
(2) *It had a relevance and significance that might or might not be seen.* (While JB did not discover that he had two hands, seeing the significance of his having two hands would involve a discovery; similarly he had to come to see the significance, or what he took to be the significance, of the evil around him for it to challenge his belief. The significance of evil for belief in God, of course, is something that can be argued for either way, but this is so precisely because there is a sensible issue about the significance of evil as evidence against there being a God concerned with men.)

How Hypotheses and Belief in God are held:

Regarding hypotheses, taking the M hypothesis as representative:

(1) *The hypothesis was accepted only when well supported, and it would have been rejected in the light of substantial negative evidence.*
(2) *There was a clear idea beforehand of test conditions that would show it to be false.*
(3) *The hypothesis was tentatively held; the effort was to be reasonable and to investigate.*

Regarding belief in God and taking JB's belief as representative:

(1) *It was accepted as a matter of faith; it may have been held only on the basis of the Bible (as MacIntyre saw and stressed) and was held at*

first in the face of much that many claimed counted against it—namely suffering and evil—this being considered a test of faith; he who believed, in this case JB, came to see evil and suffering as evidence against his belief, and he then abandoned his belief, this coinciding with a loss of faith.

(2)   *It was not clear beforehand what specified conditions would show the belief to be false.*

(3)   *It was not tentatively held; the effort was to believe.*

The sort of evidence just described that relates to religious belief should be distinguished from what some philosophers have called "internal evidence."[7] "Internal evidence" is evidence 1) such that only believers know what constitutes it, 2) which would not convince a nonbeliever, and 3) which is not empirical. The evidence that would go to reestablish JB's belief clearly does not meet any of these conditions (with perhaps some question about the third). Let us say JB does come to see the significance of his having two hands, of his being alive, and of all else for which he might be thankful to God.

Is it the case that only JB or another believer knows what constitutes this evidence? Not at all. The atheist may be able to correctly indicate why JB would thank God. The difference between the atheist and the believer is not that the believer knows what to point to and the atheist does not; the difference is that the believer sees what is pointed to as evidence of God's concern and the atheist does not.

Nor need it be the case that the atheist never recognizes the indications of God's goodness for what they are. He might recognize them, as JB might while disbelieving, and if he does, he might then come to believe in God. Conversions sometimes happen precisely when one believes he has come to see signs of God's goodness and concern for what they are.

Finally, is the kind of evidence that relates to religious belief empirical? It is in that it is there in the world to be seen by any who have eyes to see it. This is not to say that it can be seen by anyone who has eyes in his head; although one who fails to see the significance of what is before him *may* come to see it—if it is there to be seen.

I think that we are now in a position to observe one or two things. If one confuses holding a belief in God (as did JB before he lost his faith) with holding a hypothesis, then it is understandable that he should conclude that such a belief is irrational. For it does seem that it is irrational to hold a hypothesis in the face of overwhelming evidence against it, or to accept it when there is no or little evidence for it, as JB would seem to be doing if he were thought to be holding a hypothesis. This comes to holding a tentative belief tenaciously or to accepting without substantiation a belief that by its very nature is accepted only with substantiation. However, it is a mistake to think of JB's belief in God as a hypothesis. This in itself does not mean that JB's or anyone's religious belief is rationally held; but it does point out that, if religious beliefs are not rationally held, it is not because believers have accepted a hypothesis without substantiation or because they tenaciously hold beliefs that by their very nature should be tentatively held.

A basic confusion between hypotheses and religious belief, it seems, can lead one to correctly deny that religious belief is a hypothesis, but can also lead him to deny too much. JB, before he lost his faith, might have seen evidence of God and His goodness all around him. If we think that hypothetical evidence is the only kind, we will think that saying a) that there is evidence for there being a God, is equivalent to saying b) that the belief that there is a God is a hypothesis and thus requires a tentative adoption by rational men. It was perhaps reasoning thus that MacIntyre concluded it was as much a mistake to think that there was evidence for there being a God as it was to think that belief in God was a hypothesis.

Finally let us return to the lessons of Flew and Mitchell.

Flew suggested that belief in God is in fact a belief in nothing—that is, belief with no content. It denies nothing, so it asserts nothing, he thought. However, belief in God does deny something, although it may not have the sort of denial a hypothesis does; it denies that God is unconcerned with men and it denies the triumph of the Devil. It is true no specified test conditions are denied, as is the case with hypotheses. But this does not mean that there are no conditions under which one would give up his belief: a believer can lose his faith in God. When he does, he does so precisely because he thinks he has discovered what his belief denies: for instance, that God is unconcerned with men.[8]

Mitchell's suggestion, on the other hand, was that belief in God or God's goodness was irrational. His partisan apparently had irrationally resolved not to allow anything to count decisively against his hypothesis that the Stranger was on his side. Mitchell's suggestion stems from his imagining belief in God and His goodness to be a kind of cosmological hypothesis. Flew encouraged us to do just this by giving us a new version of the garden parable in which two explorers discover a spot in the jungle. When one offers an explanation of why the spot appears as it does, we can only understand his explanation as a hypothesis. Mitchell follows along this line, although he is aware that religious belief is not tentatively held and that people who believe in God often feel their faith challenged by what they find in the world. He tries to take both these elements into account in his parable of the partisan and the Stranger by making the partisan committed to the Stranger and by allowing things to count against his belief—but nothing decisively. Thus the partisan appears to be holding a hypothesis against which things count, but against which nothing will count decisively. Mitchell's explanation for the scales never tipping is that the partisan will not allow them to; he has irrationally resolved not to allow anything to disrupt his hypothesis. We would have had another instance of the kind of belief the partisan has in Mitchell's parable if the editor had hated M and had been so attached to his M hypothesis that, while recognizing evidence against it, he would not have relinquished it even had it been disproved.

To put Mitchell right let us note again several features of JB's belief. While JB retains his faith in God he does not see the evil things that happen to him or to others as evidence against God and His goodness. When he loses his faith, he sees evil differently; then it counts *decisively* against his belief. In contrast with Mitchell's account, then, at no time does JB allow evil or anything else to count against his belief but just not decisively; it either is not seen as evidence or, if it is seen as evidence, it can count decisively against his belief. Continuing to believe in God and His goodness hinges on a retention of faith—not a resolution not to let anything count against one's belief, as Mitchell suggests. It is true that one might never lose his faith, regardless of the test to which his faith is put. And such a Job-like man does bear a superficial resemblance to Mitchell's partisan. It is also true, however, that even the Job-like man can lose his faith. It is for this reason that there is the prayer for strengthened faith—a prayer that is not always answered. This does not in itself make JB's belief in God rational, but it does show how it is not irrational in the way the partisan's belief in the Stranger apparently is.

Notes

[1]John Wisdom, "Gods," *Proceedings of The Aristotelian Society* 45 (1944-45): 91. Reprinted in John Wisdom, *Philosophy and Psychoanalysis* Oxford: Blackwell, 1944); and in Antony Flew, ed., *Logic and Language* (First Series, Oxford: Blackwell, 1960).

[2]In "Theology and Falsification," *New Essays in Philosophical Theology,* eds. Antony Flew and Alasdair MacIntyre (New York: The Macmillan Company; London: SCM Press, 1955).

[3]In his contribution to "Theology and Falsification," *New Essays in Philosophical Theology.*

[4]Cf. his "The Logical Status of Religious Belief," *Metaphysical Beliefs,* 2nd ed., ed. Alasdair MacIntyre (London: SCM Press, 1970).

[5]By Frederick Ferré, *Language Logic and God* (New York: Harper & Row, Publishers, 1961), p. 142. See also William T. Blackstone, *The Problem of Religious Knowledge* (Englewood Cliffs, N.J.: Prentice-Hall, 1963), pp. 104–5.

[6]Archibald MacLeish, *JB* (Boston: Houghton Mifflin, 1958).

[7]See for instance D. Z. Phillips, "Faith, Scepticism and Religions Understanding," *Religion and Understanding,* ed. D. Z. Phillips (Oxford: Blackwell, 1967), p. 63.

[8]In *God and Philosophy* (New York: Harcourt Brace Jovanovich; and London: Hutchinson, 1966) Flew, it should be noted, seems to qualify the point he argued for in "Theology and Falsification." In *God and Philosophy* he says, "The fact, *if it be a fact,* that some of its [Christian theism's] teachings are not even in principle exposed to falsification in this world has no tendency to show that its claims about eternity are empty," p. 22 (my emphasis). This seems to qualify Flew's original

point in two ways: 1) it indicates that it may be the case that something in this world could count in principle against Christian teachings, and 2) it suggests that even if nothing in this world could, something in the next world conceivably might. Regarding the second point, see Flew's reply to D. R. Duff-Forbes, especially on I. M. Crombie's position, in "Falsification and Hypothesis in Theology," *The Australasian Journal of Philosophy* 40 (1962).

2

religious discovery

2

If the primary point of the last chapter is correct, then religious beliefs such as JB's, as they are most often held, differ in important respects from hypotheses, such as the hypothesis about M proposed by the editor. One important respect in which they differ has to do with two kinds of evidence: evidence that relates to hypotheses and evidence that relates to religious belief. The first kind needs to be collected or gathered, and once gathered clearly applies to the hypothesis. The second kind is already before us, but its significance might or might not be seen. Even if this point about different kinds of evidence is recognized, there is still an important question to be asked about the relation of evidence to religious belief. It is this: Is there in fact *decisive evidence* for the belief in God and other religious beliefs, or is it that most of the evidence is against these beliefs, or so balanced that to be rational one must reserve judgment? Noting what we have about the kind of evidence that relates to religious belief does nothing in itself to answer this question about the rationality of religious belief. It is to this concern that we now turn. To phrase the question more simply: Is there decisive evidence for religious beliefs or are they all held irrationally? If one asks this question, though, he might well be misled into looking for hypothetical evidence and so miss the possibility of there being decisive evidence of the other kind for religious beliefs. The point here, of course, is not that the person who asks this question will miss seeing the rationality of religious belief because he is looking for evidence and religious belief is rational on pragmatic or other nonevidential grounds; the point is that there may be decisive evidence for religious belief and this question, paradoxically, may blind him to it. It may blind him because this question may be allowed to become another question: What evidence does an investigation of the proposition "There is a God" reveal? And this question automatically construes religious belief as a hypothesis. It starts one looking for evidence that clearly applies, for or against religious belief; and the sort of evidence that relates to religious belief will not or may not be like this at all.

To correct for the misleading thrust of this question, let us introduce a different question: Is there any possibility that there are religious discoveries such as the discovery of God's existence, or of His concern and His love? This question need not displace the rationality question, but may be asked along with it. In fact it is intended that this question should actually shed light on the rationality question. Discoveries are unlike beliefs in that while they may be lucky or unlucky, they are neither rational nor irrational. So long as our question concerns rationality our eyes will be turned away from discoveries *per se* and our concern will be with beliefs and evidence for beliefs. Thus this new question may widen our field of vision and, hopefully, our perception of the subject.

Of course if one's chief concern is with the rationality of religious belief and evidence that clearly applies to religious belief, he still might allow for the possibility of certain kinds of religious discoveries; but if he does, given his perspective, he will look for discoveries that are like the discovery that a hypothesis is decisively supported and confirmed and so is correct. Religious discoveries, however, will not be like this. Perhaps at one time certain religious discoveries were of this nature—but no longer. It has been observed that the question of God's existence is no longer an experimental question in the way it used to be.[1] In the Old Testament, Elijah on Mt. Carmel tests the power of God against the power of Baal.[2] When God succeeds in lighting the water soaked wood set out for the burnt offering, and Baal fails, this is taken as proof of God's superiority. Actually, Elijah was demonstrating God's superiority, not that He exists. In any case, discovering that there is a God is no longer like this. Today it seems that there are no experiments like the Mt. Carmel experiment by which contemporary religious people can discover that there is a God—or make any other religious discovery. However, it should

not be concluded from this that there can be no discovery that there is a God
or of His love. To draw this conclusion is to assume that the only possible
way to make a discovery is by conducting an experiment or by gathering data
in some other way. It may be right that to confirm a hypothesis one has to
conduct an experiment or in some way gather data. But religious beliefs
are not hypotheses and this model of discovery may not be the one crucially
applicable to religious discoveries.

Interestingly enough, religious people often support the notion that an
experiment or the gathering of data is the means to confirm the existence
of God, or some other religious belief, and this is how religious discoveries
are made. If an atheist were to stand up in the middle of a church service
and loudly challenge God to strike him down, and if he were struck down, no
doubt some of the parishioners would take this as proof that there was a God.
However, if some parishioners would, some would not; and many outside the
congregation would consider it simply a coincidence. Also, if he were not
struck down, these same parishioners would not take this as any indication
that there was no God. This does not mean that they would necessarily be
wrong to take his being struck down as an indication of God's existence, but
it does mean that what would take place would not be an experiment. These
parishioners could not specify what would count as a positive, confirming
outcome nor what would count as a negative, disconfirming outcome. Consider the following taken from an evangelical publication:

> What do you say about Christ? Can He do what He claimed and bring real
> purpose into your life by totally forgiving all your sins and bringing you into a
> vital relationship with God? If you ignore the facts, you are being intellectually
> dishonest. A scientist *tests* a hypothesis to see if it is true. If what Christ said
> is true, consider what it will mean to you—peace, purpose, power, pardon and
> eternal life.
> This hypothesis is tested by saying to God, "O.K. I know something is wrong
> inside me. You said Christ will change me if I invite Him into my heart and
> ask Him to take full control. This is what I want, so come in now and change
> me."
> I challenge you to talk to Christ in this way now, in your own words, if you like.[3]

Here, too, a test seems to be set up, but if so, there should be two possible
outcomes of the experiment: one clearly positive and one clearly negative.
If these are not clear, then it becomes difficult to know how to evaluate the
results of the experiment and so the whole procedure is pointless as a test
of a hypothesis. One might think that if the life of the one issuing the invi-
tation is changed, the hypothesis has been confirmed. But this is not so, for at
this point the key question is asked, not answered. The skeptic asks it: Why
is my changed life thought to be due to God? Similarly, if the life of the
petitioner is not changed, we should not expect this to cause the religious man
to abandon, or even doubt, his belief. Such unanswered prayers would not

show or even tend to show that there is no God. Thus what would count as a positive, hypothesis confirming result is unclear, and also what would count as a negative, hypothesis disconfirming result is unclear. Consequently, what looks and sounds very much like a test of a hypothesis in fact is not. The author of the above passage says, "I challenge you to talk to Christ . . . ," and so he can, but in doing so—despite his implication—he is not challenging anyone to conduct an experiment to test a hypothesis.

There are several points made by Professor H. H. Price in his Gifford Lectures that we ought to note at this point.[4] Professor Price is aware that entertaining a hypothesis is far from holding a religious belief with conviction. But still, he says, a nonbeliever might entertain and test the "Theistic hypothesis." Now I think we have to acknowledge that one *can* entertain as a hypothesis the proposition "There is a God" (although doing so seems far from religious practice). What one cannot do, though, I submit, is test this hypothesis and confirm it, thereby discovering that there is indeed a God. Price says that the nonreligious person has been told that if he assumes the role of the religious person and addresses God in his own heart—and persists in his endeavor—then he will become a changed person and will begin to have new experiences. This, says Price, is the hypothesis open to the nonreligious person's test. Unfortunately, while *this* proposition may be open to a straightforward test, its confirmation leaves open the skeptic's question "Are these experiences and changed life from God?" The test Price suggests fares little better than the atheist's challenge in church or the "test" of inviting Christ into one's heart. Nevertheless, I think that Price does remind us of something very important about religious discovery: the nonreligious person need not be passive; he can assume the religious role and try to believe, and he can incline his heart and open his mind. But if he does then discover God and that he is in His domain, it will be by a discovery whose nature is different from that of a hypothetical discovery.

ii

Seeing that there is a God and discovering God's love are not a matter of disinterestedly (or interestedly) conducting an investigation and discovering that a hypothesis being held or entertained is confirmed. Trying to bring out what is involved in religious discoveries, if there are any, is not altogether easy. However, the differences between evidence relating to hypotheses and evidence relating to religious belief, as exemplified by JB's belief, have already been drawn out; and so some of the work has been done. The next all-important step is to illustrate how the kind of evidence that relates to religious belief fits into a model of discovery very different from the model of discovery appropriate to hypotheses. I think that this can be done, and what is more, I think that this model of discovery, while involved in religion, is found in other areas of life as well. Relying upon those areas as a complement, hopefully this model can be successfully illustrated.

If one suspects that a friend is jealous of his son he may watch him carefully over some time and confirm his suspicions; in doing so he discovers that his suspicions were correct and that his hypothesis—that his friend is jealous of his son—is right. Contrast this with what might be involved in his discovering—not that his friend—but that he himself is jealous of *his* son. In such a case, perhaps, he might suspect that he himself is jealous, just as he suspected his friend was, and again investigate and confirm his suspicions, although this time in a more introspective way. Other times, however, the nature of the discovery that he himself is jealous will be very different, and in these instances quite another model of discovery emerges; in these instances it will be that he has no suspicion that he is jealous of his son; the thought will never have occurred to him or, if it has, he will have brushed it aside as being ridiculous. Then something happens that brings him up abruptly and causes him to re-examine himself; or nothing of this sort happens, but still, for one reason or another, he begins to see himself and his son with a new sensitivity. And what he discovers is that, despite his previous dismissal of the thought, he is in fact jealous of his son. Let us call this sort of discovery a nonhypothetical discovery (but without meaning that every discovery that is not a hypothetical discovery is of this sort).[5] A nonhypothetical discovery is in a number of respects importantly different from a discovery that a hypothesis is confirmed (a hypothetical discovery). Some of these respects should be made prominent at this point. They correlate with the points already noted about the kind of evidence that relates to hypotheses and the kind that primarily relates to religious belief. First, one who discovers that his hypothesis is confirmed does so by investigating and gathering new data which will either confirm or disconfirm his hypothesis. He knows what will count as confirming evidence and what will count as disconfirming evidence—there is no question about this. His entire task consists in gathering data to see which evidence preponderates. In terms of our example, he does so by learning how the person he suspects to be jealous reacts in the presence of his son or when his son's name is mentioned. On the other hand, when a discovery of the nonhypothetical sort is made no investigation is conducted and no data are gathered. No data are gathered because they need not be. They are already at hand and familiar; although they are not seen in their significance as evidence. In terms of our example, the one who makes this sort of discovery does not need to learn that he is often uneasy about his son; he knows this. What he fails to see is that his uneasiness is any indication that he is jealous of his son. Another respect in which these two types of discovery differ is that when a hypothesis is discovered to be confirmed it is because sufficient data have been gathered to confirm it in accordance with a recognized positive, hypothesis confirming condition; but when a discovery on the nonhypothetical model is made it is because the significance of the already familiar facts is seen for the first time. To sum up these points: what is required to discover that a hypothesis is confirmed is the gathering of evidence the significance of which is clear beforehand in accordance with recognized hypothesis confirming and disconfirming conditions; what is required to make a discovery according to the nonhypothetical model is to see for the first time the significance of familiar facts which are already before one.[6]

In outline form the just noted differences between the two sorts of discovery are these:

Hypothetical Discovery	Nonhypothetical Discovery
Example: A discovers that B is jealous of his son.	Example: A discovers that he is jealous of his own son.
1. A *suspects* that B is jealous of his son.	1. A dismisses the thought that he is jealous of his son (if it occurs to him).
2. He *investigates*.	2. No investigation.
3. He collects evidence.	3. No collection of evidence; it is already familiar, although not seen as evidence.
4. He knows what will establish his suspicion or hypothesis and investigates to see if there is such evidence.	4. The discovery is made when what is familiar is seen in its significance as evidence.
5. The discovery is made when a clear hypothesis confirming condition is seen to be met.	

Regarding specifically religious discoveries, discovering God's love and His concern, or the existence of God, may never involve bringing forward new decisive evidence, or conducting a crucial experiment; it may only involve seeing the significance of what has been around us all the time. Thus one may come to discover God's concern and goodness by coming to see all or much in the world in a certain way, namely in its significance as indications of God's concern and goodness. Of course some particular dispensation may stand out, but if it does, under the nonhypothetical model it will have the role of a catalyst that opens one's eyes to the significance of familiar facts, and less the role of crucial evidence that on its own establishes or confirms a hypothesis. Given that religious discoveries have or often have this nature, it should be fairly plain why the believer cannot show the nonbeliever that his belief in God's goodness is a true belief or that his belief is confirmed. He cannot do this, for perhaps everything that he would point to, the nonbeliever is incapable of seeing as indications of that goodness. The nonbeliever is in the position of the believer before he saw the significance of the familiar facts surrounding him. What this further points out is that a change in the viewer is crucial to religious discovery. As it might appropriately be put in this context, he must be given eyes that he might see.

There are, however, noteworthy differences between the father's discovery that he is jealous of his son and the religious discovery of God's concern and goodness. First, when one makes the discovery of God's concern (if there is such a discovery) he discovers thereby that there is a God, while the father, of course, does not discover that he has a son. But while there is this dis-analogy, it is not crucial, for even in human relationships we can understand someone discovering that a relationship exists between himself and another and *thereby* that this other person exists. One who thought himself alone on an island and then discovered that he was being helped by someone who left food and helped in other ways without ever being seen would discover not only his relationship to this benefactor, but also that there was someone to be a benefactor; and such a discovery could be nonhypothetical in nature. A second difference is this: Others besides the father, acting as neutral observers, could confirm his discovery by confirming their own hypothesis that he was jealous of his son, but there are no neutral observers with an analogous hypothesis so far as our religious discovery is concerned. While this difference also is noteworthy, again it is not crucial. If one has indeed made the religious discovery of God's concern and goodness, then he has made that discovery. His discovery is not contingent on another making it or even on another being able to make it. One might say here that, while this is true, nevertheless another must *in principle* be able to make the same discovery for there to be a discovery. This point may be correct. Whether it is or not, so far as the religious discovery is concerned, another *can* in principle make it, for another can come to see what surrounds him in its significance as an indication of God's concern and goodness, just as the first man did (if he did). What another cannot do is test the hypothesis that God is concerned with men before he is able to see the indications of that concern for what they are.

The reason why there can be no discovery on the hypothetical model of God's concern is, again, that there is no commonly accepted hypothesis con-firming condition. There is none because such a condition is by its very nature commonly accepted, and its being commonly accepted presupposes that there is no question about the significance of the data. But all nonbelievers, and possibly many believers, are, or may be, in the position vis-à-vis God that the father who could not see that he was jealous of his son was in vis-à-vis his son. So in the religious situation there are or may be no neutral observers with their hypothesis as there could have been in the case of the father who was jealous of his son; in the religious situation everyone may be involved. This of course does not mean that there is no condition that establishes that there is a God concerned with man. There is, and one makes the discovery that God is concerned with man precisely when he sees that it is met. But one sees that it is met (if it is) only when he sees the significance of what surrounds him, if that significance is there to be seen. One does not see that it is met by gathering new crucial evidence to meet an agreed upon hypothesis confirming condition.

Mystical experiences, or at least some, are to be distinguished from religious discoveries of this nature. Some of the mystical experiences of St. Teresa, for instance, are not, or might not be, instances of religious discovery. William James allows that there is a noetic element in every mystical experience,[7] and perhaps St. Teresa did come to realizations from some of her experiences. She tells us that due to her mystical experience she came to realize that there was a place in hell reserved for her.[8] If so, or even if she only came to realize this or other things more acutely, then perhaps discovery was involved in her experiences (although there may be some question as to the model or nature of the discovery). But to the extent that St. Teresa's mystical experiences were ecstatic experiences of oneness with God, and not discoveries, they are distinct from what is before us here. Also, while often the discovery—or what in the eyes of the believer is a discovery—that there is a God may be precipitated by something dramatic, for instance a miraculous cure, which opens one's eyes to what is around him, this need not be so. Often there may be nothing dramatic in the discovery: one may come to see that God's influence is all about him by realizing, perhaps slowly, that he and others are supported in their lives by Him.

III

As was stated previously, the nonhypothetical model of discovery applicable to religion is not limited to religious discovery. If it were, perhaps any understanding of it would be hopeless. We have already drawn upon one other area of its application, namely that of human relationships, and there are others, one of which might be noted at this point. In the last century, evidence for evolution was often dismissed as not being evidence at all. Even scientists of repute failed to see the support for evolution; they saw only pattern and detail which they took to be in specially created species. This was so even though they were familiar with what others took to be such evidence. Indeed, they could point it out perhaps as well as any. But in doing so they would be pointing out what others, not they, took to be evidence for evolution. Some of these scientists, I believe, finally did come to see that there was indeed evolution. They did not come to this conclusion by finally gathering enough evidence to meet the hypothesis confirming condition of the evolutionary hypothesis. They had been in a position to see that this condition was met for years; yet they had not during that time come to see that evolution existed. What finally brought these recalcitrant scientists to the discovery that evolution existed was, rather, in accordance with the other model of discovery, their eyes being opened to the evidence on every side of them with which they were already familiar.

For our purposes, though, it is most significant that the model of discovery applicable to religion also applies to discoveries of human relationships, for between discoveries in these two areas the analogy is the closest. In three related aspects is the analogy particularly close. The first has to do with what is discovered. Examples of a religious discovery would be the discovery that there is a God and of His love, or that Christ is our Redeemer. If these discoveries were made, much more than an indifferent fact about God would have been discovered; a relationship of love or of redemption between God and one-self would have been discovered, a relationship which, once it has been discovered, is the antipodes of an indifferent fact. One could not be indifferent to such a relationship in the same way a father could not be indifferent to his jealousy of his son, once it has been discovered. The second aspect in which the analogy between these two kinds of discovery is close has to do with the reason why one, in a very real sense, cannot be indifferent to these discovered relationships. One cannot, because what is at stake is a relationship between himself and another *person;* and this holds true equally for discovered human relationships and relationships discovered between oneself and God. It is thus important for the analogy that God be a *personal* God, a God concerned and loving, merciful, and heedful. The third aspect in which the analogy is close is this: given the application of this model of discovery to human relationships, and that God is a personal God, what is, or may often be, involved in failing to see one's relationship to God is the same blindness with the same sources that sometimes prevents us from seeing our true relationships to other human beings; blindness that, for instance, prevents us from seeing another's concern for what it is and leads us to construe it as malevolence and his love as oppression or indifference.

IV

Those discovery situations in which the model of discovery before us applies have a significant feature that we have yet to note. Always, or nearly always, in those situations something vital is at stake. Thus in the case of evolution, where many have failed to see evolution for what it is, Christian dogma was at stake, namely the dogma of the special creation of species, including the special creation of man. This point is different from that noted before (in section III). There the point was brought out that when many human relationships are discovered, and when one discovers a relationship to God, what is discovered is not an indifferent fact about the world, but a vital relationship to a person. The point here is that, even when what is at stake is a fact about the world to which one might in most circumstances be indif-ferent (e.g., evolution), in the discovery situation, for some reason or reasons, the fact takes on vital significance. The reasons may vary, of course. It may be that church doctrine or some other cherished belief is at stake, or that, as may often be true in matters of human relationships, one's picture of himself is at stake. An appreciation of the variety of these reasons is not imperative for the point. What should be appreciated, though, is that in these discovery situations, because something vital is at stake, there is a possible role for self-deception. One may not be able to bring himself to admit that his or his church's understanding of the Book of Genesis is wrong, and he may not be able to bring himself to admit that he is jealous of his own son. Admitting such things even to oneself can call into question the foundations and shores of one's life. Thus when one finds himself in discovery situations such as these, but fails to make the discovery, the possibility that his failure is due in great part to self-deception should not be lightly dismissed.

The point of self-deception relates to religious discovery in the following way. In a sense, we are all in the religious discovery situation. But, of course, not all of us have made the religious discovery that there is a God and that we stand in a relationship of love to Him. Why is it that most of us have not made this discovery? Some would say it is because there is no such discovery to be made. But, as the apparent role of self-deception in other such discovery situations makes evident, this is not the only explanation. Certainly we need not look far for unconscious reasons not to recognize that one stands in a relationship to God. Notoriously this relationship, though one of love, carries with it burdensome responsibilities. The religious ideal is one of sacrifice, humility, and service; in Christian terms it is expressed as "taking up the cross." In Judaeo-Christian terms it involves subjugating oneself to God's Law. What is involved in recognizing one's relationship to God in the Judaeo-Christian tradition and in subjugating oneself to God's Law is much more than living by a code. It is, if the relationship is fully acknowledged, a giving up of all selfhood to love. This is what Paul tells the Corinthians when he says that he would not have the love they must have if he but gives away all that he owns and but delivers up his body to be burned.[9] As Jesus tells the lawyer, "You shall love the Lord your God with all your heart, and with all your soul, and with all your strength, and with all your mind; and your neighbor as yourself."[10] In a very real sense, it is more convenient to believe there is no God to whom one stands committed, for then one's life is one's own in a way it is not for the religious person.

However, in regard to self-deception, there is another side seen from a different perspective. The obverse is figured essentially with Freud's view of religion. His analysis of religion is that it is, in his words, a "universal neurosis."[11] Believers turn to religion, Freud thought, because they have an unconscious need for a father image to give them security and comfort. In short Freud's suggestion was that it was those who believe in God, not unbelievers, who deceive themselves and who have unconscious reasons for their belief. Freud's analysis is strictly of religious belief and not of religious discovery or alleged discovery; however, his import covers religious discovery as well, I think. At this point, then, a question emerges: Who is a prey to self-deception—the nonbeliever who does not make the discovery of a relationship of love to God, or the believer who thinks that he has discovered that there is a God to whom he has this relationship? This question is one we might never ask, given only a concern about the rationality of religious beliefs. And it is one quite perplexing, once asked; perhaps insurmountably perplexing if asked about the self-deceived *by* the self-deceived, but no less a significant question for that reason. The following may be helpful in answering it.

First, it may be true that some religious people use their religion as a device for various selfish ends, such as evading responsibility, condemning enemies, and even wrapping themselves in a cloak of security, and further, though they would be unaware that this is so, these ends may be the operative but unconscious reasons for their belief. These believers, even if their belief that there is a God is true, are yet the victims of their delusions; and regarding them it can hardly be said that they have *discovered* that there is a God to whom they stand in a relationship of love. It would be myopic to deny that there may be believers in this category. It may well be that certain of the once-born,[12] and the members of Christendom,[13] are believers of this ilk. If so they are self-deceived, and there may be others.

In his article "The Death of God Theologies Today,"[14] William Hamilton, a death of God theologian, tells us that he wishes to defend religionlessness. "Religion" he takes to mean "any system of thought or action in which God or the gods serve as fulfiller of needs or solver of problems." He proceeds to discuss what he calls the "Oedipal believer," or the believer whose religion grows from a sense of sin and who is going through a "crisis of growth" with its attendant problems. As Oedipus was, this kind of believer is incapacitated and immobilized by his concern with himself and his sense of guilt. In contrast to the Oedipal believer there is the Orestean man. Unlike Oedipus, Orestes lacks a crippling sense of sin; he has no self-imposed diffidence. As Hamilton puts it, it is "his own free vow" that binds him. Hamilton thinks of the Orestean man as the antithesis of the religious man. He does so because of his definition of "religion." If one is religious according to Hamilton's definition, he necessarily turns to God as a fulfiller of his needs or as a solver of his problems. In short, according to Hamilton, believers are typified by those he calls "Oedipal believers." I think that there is a large question about the correctness of Hamilton's definition of "religion," and consequently about its implications; but it may well be that at least some believers are "Oedipal believers." If so, then fairly clearly they could be victims of self-deception; they would be if the operative reason for their belief in God was their need, say, for relief from guilt feelings, and they were unaware of this.

But there are believers of quite a different character, who contrast with the once-born, with the members of Christendom, and with the believers Hamilton has in mind. These believers, many of whom are said to have made the religious discovery of their relationship to God, see that relationship as one of active and committed love and do not seek from it their peace of mind, or an escape from responsibility, or a fulfillment of their needs, or a solution to their problems. I have in mind, of course, the exemplars of religion: the saints. As far as they were concerned, convenience and ease were on the side of their not believing in God or on the side of their believing their relationship to God was very different and much less demanding; if the saints were self-deceived, they should have ended by not believing in God or by believing in him as, say, the once-born do.

One might think, though, that every believer, including the saints, has built into his religion an unconscious reason for self-deception, namely, a belief in life after death. But does this belief necessarily provide every believer with an unconscious reason for belief in God? I should think that whether or not it does would depend on, first, the way the life hereafter is viewed (whether in terms of duty or pleasure, for example) and, second, the importance of this belief in the believer's life. Perhaps this belief is peripheral, if the believer is concerned or thinks about it at all; if this is so, this belief could hardly be an unconscious reason for a belief in a relationship to God. This is not to say that unless one thinks about a matter it cannot provide an unconscious reason for self-deception, but it is to suggest that whatever provides such a reason must be of great concern to the individual—as would be, for instance, one's picture of oneself as a father, to refer back to our earlier example. And if one looks at the lives of the saints, one will see, with perhaps some exceptions, that their concern was not with their ease and comfort in a life after this one. Their wish, rather, was typically to "die to the world and to [one] self" and to "begin to live to Christ," as St. Marcarius The Elder expressed it in giving spiritual advice to another.[15] Sometimes, to be sure, certain saints do seem to have been greatly concerned about the next life; some of the martyrs in particular did. One might wonder about the centricity of this concern to their lives, and one might wonder, too, whether their concern was great enough to account for self-deception in their belief in God. But in their case, given this concern, there at least appears to be a candidate for the unconscious reason that might cause them to be self-deceived. For that matter, in certain of the other saints' lives we find different but equally or more abiding concerns that could have played the same role. This is true in the life of St. Julian the Hospitaller, for instance. As Flaubert recounts the story of St. Julian in his version of the legend, and also according to Butler,[16] St. Julian killed his own parents after mistaking them for his wife and a supposed paramour. Upon discovering his terrible mistake, in contrition, he assumed a life of abnegation and humility. Whatever role his guilt feeling played, clearly he had such feelings; and so in his particular case there was what appears to be a candidate for an unconscious reason for self-deception. But in the case of other saints, whose lives reflect completely selfless love, neither satisfaction, nor the wish for escape from responsibility or from guilt, nor anything else, appears as the candidate for an unconscious reason for self-deception. Such selfless love is exemplified in Dostoyevsky's Father Zossima. And it seems to be clearly embodied in the lives of such saints as St. Marcarius The Elder, St. Marcian, St. Theodosius and many others.[17] In regarding such believers as these there *seems* to be no room for self-deception, for there appears to be no candidate for an unconscious reason for self-deception. (Although, to be sure, one might wonder if it is ever possible to see deeply enough into a man's life to eliminate this possibility.)

There is another side to this point. Sometimes men struggle not to believe in God, yet even so their eyes are opened (by the grace of God, some have said), and they discover about them signs of God's goodness and love and thus their relationship to God, or so they believe. Francis Thompson, the author of "The Hound of Heaven," apparently was one such reluctant believer. Again, if convenience, ease and all unconscious reasons are on the side of not believing and one truly struggles not to believe, then it cannot be that one ends by believing because he has deceived himself; rather, as he might say, he ends by believing because his eyes have been opened to what he did not want to see but cannot deny having seen. Doubtless in the minds of many there will remain a question as to whether Francis Thompson or any saint saw what he thought he saw—indications of God's influence and love; but, if whatever unconscious reasons there may be are on the side of *not* believing, it cannot be self-deception that caused them not to see aright if they did not.

What I have tried to point out is this: Even if in the lives of most believers (all or many of the once-born, all of Christendom, all "Oedipal believers," and some of the saints) there is room for possible self-deception, in the lives of at least some saints (those who have led transparently selfless lives) self-deception fairly apparently has no place. While there is *always* room for self-deception in those who do not see a relationship to God, for the recognition of such a relationship requires seeing oneself in a certain way, which in turn requires giving up one's life in a sense (a renouncing of the world, as it has been expressed). And *this* ubiquitously provides room for self-deception on the nonbeliever's side (even though many believers do not live up to the ideal). This, if it is correct, does not mean that all nonbelievers are self-deceived, but it does mean that there is always room for self-deception on the nonbeliever's side, while this is not so on the believer's side.[18] Nor is this to say that a nonbeliever cannot lead a virtuous life; it is to say that only a man who his given up his life in the religious sense stands a chance of leading a saintly life, and only such a life, if truly and transparently selfless, provides no candidates for reasons for self-deception regarding the religious discovery.

From these considerations our conclusions must be circumspect. Our question was: Who is a prey to self-deception, the nonbeliever who does not make the discovery of a relationship of love to God or the believer who thinks that he has discovered that there is a God to whom he has a love relationship? The issue was: Where is self-deception, on the side of believers or on the side of nonbelievers? While we cannot conclude that all, or even any, nonbelievers have been self-deceived in regard to their relationship to God (and for this reason failed to see an existing relationship to God), there is an evident case that some believers, some of the saints, could not have been self-deceived (and so may well have seen what they are said to have seen—their relationship of love to God).

Of course, even if it is clear only in the case of some of the saints that there is no self-deception, we should conclude neither a) that where there are such candidates, as there are for perhaps most believers as well as nonbelievers, there necessarily is self-deception and no discovery, nor b) that where there is self-deception on the part of a believer there is no evidence for the belief in a relationship to God. Also we should not conclude c) that because a saint was not self-deceived he truly saw what he thought he saw, signs of God's love and his relationship to God. Though he was not self-deceived, he still might not have seen aright. It does not follow that one sees aright if he is not self-deceived; although it would follow if it were also true that self-deception were the *only* thing that prevents one from seeing aright. And this may well be the case regarding at least some relationships between persons.

V

It is time now to relate what we have covered to the philosophical concern with the rationality of religious belief. The question with which we started was: Is there decisive evidence for religious beliefs like the belief in God, or are they all irrationally held? This is a perfectly good question, but not the only question; and when asked alone, or as the primary question, often our philosophical eyes are too narrowly fixed. Frequently when it is asked alone the questioner is looking upon religious beliefs as religious hypotheses. This is understandable, considering some of the things religious people themselves say, but nevertheless it misrepresents the nature of religious discovery and prejudices the rationality question. So, given the hypothetical perspective, it is probably thought that a religious belief would be rationally held only if it were confirmed as a hypothesis is confirmed, and this is taken to be equal to saying that a religious belief would be rationally held only if there were decisive evidence for the belief. If it is not confirmed in this hypothetical way, since this is taken to be the same thing as there being no decisive evidence for it, it is concluded that to be rational one must reject the belief or at least suspend judgment.

Hopefully, the foregoing discussion has helped to shed a different light on the rationality concern, a light oblique to the hypothetical perspective. It is hoped that the following points were brought into relief in their relation to the rationality concern and to the issue of religious discovery: 1) if holding a religious belief rationally requires decisive evidence, then religious beliefs are, or may be, rationally held; for 2) there may be evidence, and decisive evidence, for them; 3) if so, this does not mean that they are confirmed as hypotheses are confirmed; 4) the evidence that may exist for religious beliefs is not evidence stateable in confirmation conditions, for confirmation conditions are clear beforehand and agreed upon, and there are no such agreed upon conditions for religious beliefs; rather, if there be such evidence, it is comprised of familiar facts, the significance of which some have seen and some have not; and 5) the possibility that there may indeed be this evidence is seen by reminding ourselves of a nonhypothetical mode of discovery, noting its application to, for instance, discoveries of human relationships, and seeing the possible analogous application of this model to the religious discovery of a relationship to God.

To be sure, questions remain. The paramount one is: Have the scales been lifted from the eyes of religious people who are said to have discovered a relationship to God or have they failed to see aright perhaps because they are self-deceived? Paraphrased, this question might be put: Even if this model of discovery is thought to apply to those who seem to have discovered a relationship to God, does it in fact apply? The effort here was only to point out a possible application. However, if this possible application has been seen, then the possibility of religious discovery has been seen. And while this is not all, it is something. It is not all, for, if some religious people have in fact made a discovery of their relationship to God according to this model of discovery, one who has not made such a discovery himself could not possibly determine that they have. But it is important, for one who has not made such a discovery can yet understand the possibility that another has. Anyone who has been blind to his relationships to others and has come to realize this can understand his once more being blind to another relationship; although he cannot discover that relationship, or that another has, unless he discovers it.

Notes

[1]John Wisdom, "Gods," *Proceedings of the Aristotelian Society* 45 (1944-45): 185. Reprinted in John Wisdom, *Philosophy and Psychoanalysis* (Oxford: Blackwell, 1964); and in Antony Flew, ed., *Logic and Language* (First Series, Oxford: Blackwell, 1960).

[2]I Kings 18:20–39.

[3]James F. Engel, "Let's Get Serious!" *Student Action,* December 1967, p. 5 (italics in the original). Printed by permission. Copyright © Campus Crusade for Christ Inc., 1967. All rights reserved.

[4]H. H. Price, *Belief* (Muirhead Library of Philosophy. London: George Allen & Unwin, 1969), pp. 481–88. See also H. H. Price, "Faith and Belief," *Faith and the Philosophers,* ed. John Hick (New York: St. Martin's Press; London: Macmillan & Co., 1964).

[5] I shall most often use "nonhypothetical discovery" to refer to the specific sort of discovery just outlined, but sometimes I shall use the term or a cognate in a generic sense. It will be made clear when the term is used generically.

[6] Nonhypothetical discoveries, then, are realizations. The father who discovers that he is jealous of his own son in the above example could idiomatically say either that he has *discovered* or that he now *realizes* that he is jealous of his son: "I have made a terrible discovery! I now realize that...." In what follows when I refer to "religious discoveries" I do not mean to affirm that there are religious discoveries, whether or not there are. Such references should be read as "discoveries or possible discoveries."

[7] *The Varieties of Religious Experience,* Lectures 16 and 17. Actually James is giving a stipulative definition, but he means it to cover all that would normally be counted as religious mystical experience.

[8] *Life,* chap. 32.

[9] I Corinthians 13:3.

[10] Luke 10:27.

[11] *The Future of an Illusion,* chap. 8. See also Alasdair MacIntyre, *Difficulties in Christian Belief* (London: SCM Press Ltd., 1959), pp. 90–97.

[12] James, *The Varieties of Religious Experience,* Lectures 4 and 5.

[13] See Soren Kierkegaard, *Training in Christianity,* trans. Walter Lowrie (Princeton: Princeton University Press, 1944), *passim*; and Soren Kierkegaard, *Attack Upon "Christendom,"* trans. Walter Lowrie (Princeton: Princeton University Press, 1968).

[14] William Hamilton, "The Death of God Theologies Today," *Radical Theology and the Death of God,* by Thomas J. J. Altizer and William Hamilton (Indianapolis: The Bobbs-Merrill Company, 1966), pp. 23–50. Reprinted from *The Christian Scholar* 48 (1965).

[15] Herbert Thurston, S. J. and Donald Attwater, eds., *Butlers Lives of the Saints* (New York: P. J. Kennedy & Sons, 1956 © 1956 by P. J. Kennedy & Sons), I:94.

[16] Thurston and Attwater, *Butlers Lives of the Saints,* p. 315.

[17] See *Butlers Lives of the Saints* for brief sketches of the lives of these and other saints.

[18] I do not mean to imply that those who are truly religious in a religious tradition different from the Judaeo-Christian are, or may be, self-deceived, nor that there are no saints outside the Judaeo-Christian tradition. On the contrary, I believe that it is clear that there are saints outside the Judaeo-Christian tradition. And where their lives are transparently selfless in their case too there would be no room for self-deception. If there is indeed a relationship between men and God, and if these saints do not discover it, even though they are in it and live it, it is not self-deception that causes this but rather their conception of the Numinous, to put it one way.

The point I have made about the possibility of self-deception is meant to apply only within the Judaeo-Christian tradition; when I speak of believers and non-believers I am referring to two groups both within the Judaeo-Christian cultural sphere. And understood thus I believe my point is correct.

Also it might be noted that just possibly this point *could* be extended beyond the Judaeo-Christian tradition. It could be if all religious traditions in which there were saints involved a belief in God so that all saints believed in God, including Hindu and Bhuddist saints. Did they? It is debatable, of course. But the Hindu saints did give a place to Brahman, and the Bhudda does not seem far in conception from the Hindu avatars who were incarnations, in turn close in conception to Christ, an incarnation of God the Father. For there to be a belief in God, it need not be that the Nouminous is called "God," nor need God be conceived of as he is in the Judaeo-Christian tradition. Indeed he is conceived of differently among those *within* the Judaeo-Christian tradition.

If there are men who have lived transparently selfless lives *within* the Judaeo-Christian cultural sphere but who did *not* believe in God, that is another matter. This would mean that, in a sense, there have been secular saints. And it would also mean that there are *both* believers and nonbelievers who have lived lives with no room for self-deception. However, it may be that acknowledging and living wholly according to a recognized relationship to God (or what is regarded as such), as the saints did, *uniquely* requires a giving up of one's life, unlike a secular dedication even of the most demanding sort. Does it? The difficulty of this question is not helped by the fact that if self-deception may prejudice discovering a relationship to God, it may also prejudice ancillary questions. In any case, though, it is surely true that there have been secular saints *in some sense*. Camus perhaps was such a secular saint, but there seems to have been the very real possibility of self-deception in his life. See Conor Cruise O'Brien, *Camus (Modern Masters,* ed. Frank Kermode. London: Wm. Collins Sons & Co., 1970).

3

religious experience, models,

and the

limits of the sayable

3

Closely related to the issue of religious discovery and its possibility is the issue of religious experience and its veridicality. This close relationship is particularly noticeable when one sort of religious experience is focused upon. The term "religious experience" covers, or may be construed to cover, many things. Some are: revelation, as the revelation of the Law in the Bible; mystical experience, ranging from St. Teresa's consciousness affecting ecstasies to what may be called a "sense of awe before God and his creation"; and the detection, or as it is thought to be the detection, of the presence of God in one's life or in the world. This last example is rather different from the other two in that it may involve nothing like the burning bush and its revelation or the ecstasy or expanded consciousness so often associated with mystical experience. And it is this last sort of religious experience that relates closely to religious discovery, or at least the kind of religious discovery we have discussed. We might call it "nonprophetical and nonmystical religious experience," which is not to say that it is necessarily common, but that it may lack the outward or inward spectacle of the other kinds of religious experience and consist entirely of the detection or supposed detection of God's influence. It may strike some people that what this would amount to might more appropriately be called "religious detection" or "religious realization" than "religious experience." Perhaps these terms would be more appropriate, particularly if religious experience has become identified with the experience of the mystics. But, despite this, what has been termed "nonprophetical and nonmystical religious experience" shall be spoken of here as "religious experience" in order to stress 1) that it is not indifferently received (as detecting something may be) and 2) that the philosophical and religious concerns that attach to what falls under the rubric "religious experience" attach to it. William James in his *Varieties of Religious Experience* is typical of many philosophers who write about religious experience in that he is more concerned with the former varieties—particularly mystical experience—than with this kind of religious experience. In any case, the central questions asked of religious experience in general pertain to the nonprophetical and the nonmystical specifically. These questions are: "Is it of God or the Divine, or is it not?" and "If it is, how can we know that it is?"

Most often religious philosophers who investigate religious experience investigate or in some way depend upon a model of religious experience. A model in the context of religious experience takes the form of an extended analogy, which is drawn from the familiar and applied to the religious, such as the sighted man model or the encounter model. Probably if religious experience is to be understood, and the central questions given light, it will be in terms of its relation to the familiar and so such a model will be crucial. However, it is not altogether clear that these two models—the sighted man model and the encounter model—are adequate for this task. At any rate, many philosophers have argued that these models fail to maintain their analogies at critical points. In what follows we shall be concerned with 1) these two models, their adequacies and inadequacies, 2) quite a different model which relates particularly to nonprophetical and nonmystical religious experience, 3) the relationship of this third model to nonhypothetical discovery and 4) implications of this third model for what is sayable in religion.

II

The sighted man model. According to this model the religious person who has religious experience can be compared to a man with sight among the blind or the color-blind, or compared to a man with clear vision among those who have impaired vision. According to the several versions of this model, the religious person who has religious experience sees what his fellow men cannot see and what they cannot even understand perhaps, since they lack the analogue of the visual sense or of color vision or of some other visual capability.

While there exist several versions of this model, each one seems to be misleading in some way. The first version casts the person with religious experience as analogous to a man with sight among those who are totally blind, and the second casts him as analogous to a man with color vision among those who are color-blind. What is misleading about these versions is revealed through noticing unwanted analogies or disanalogies between the model in these versions and religious experience. First, these versions suggest that those who have religious experience have an organ which either is not functioning or is lacking in those who do not have this experience; something analogous to the sighted man's functional eyes and the color-seeing man's functional cones. Clearly, this suggestion runs counter to the intended direction of the model. Second, and more important, these versions of the model suggest that there should be some method independent of religious experience by which any doubter could determine to his satisfaction the veridicality of the experience. A blind person, after all, can verify visual reports. He cannot see the table the sighted person says is in front of him, but he can determine by touch if it is there and thus can confirm the visual report. As C. B. Martin has pointed out,[1] the same holds true for the color-blind version. Naturally one who is blind or color-blind cannot see colors, but he can determine the color of things nevertheless and so verify individual color reports. He could do so with the use of a spectrograph fitted with a tactile register. At this point, then, the model in this version suggests what seems wrongheaded in the extreme: that there should be a similar way for the nonreligious to determine the veridicality of religious experience using special apparatus fitted to compensate for their particular perceptual deficiencies.

In a third version of this model the person with religious experience is assimilated to one who has clear vision—who sees what others are incapable of seeing. More than the other versions, this one invites the following question: Is the person who has religious experience similar to the man with clear vision, or does he resemble the inebriate who hallucinates while those about him have clear vision? This question, of course, is a specific version of one of the central questions regarding all religious experience. What is misleading about this third version of the sighted man model is not that it invites this central question, but that it invites it in these terms. This version of the model suggests that a delusive religious experience is an hallucination, and so accordingly it suggests that a veridical religious experience is the opposite of an hallucination, which in the case of a visual hallucination is seeing an object of some sort. There may be a sense in which it is correct to say that God is an object; namely, the sense in which to say that He is an object (or thing) means that He is not nothing. However, the suggestion of this version of the model is that God is an object in the material sense of the word. Thus we are invited to think of all religious experiences as (alleged) perceptions of material objects. It is not surprising that philosophers developing or examining this version of the model—or the first version—think of the paradigmatic religious experience as that referred to as "seeing God"[2] (as opposed to seeing His purpose or goodness, receiving His grace, etc.). Nor is it surprising that critics of this version of the model think that there should be a way of determining the veridicality of religious experience closely analogous to determining that a visual perception is not hallucinatory.

The encounter model. This model represents religious experience as similar to an encounter with a man: the person who has had religious experience has had a similar encounter with God, and the person who has not had religious experience has not had this encounter with God. This model does not require or suggest that the person with religious experience should have a special sense organ others lack. Nor does it suggest (as the model of the sighted man did) that he perceives something like a material object which others are incapable of perceiving. What this model does require is that there be an awareness of the other who is encountered, even if it be a dim awareness. As Professor H. H. Price, who employs this model, points out, if one encounters another—e.g., a Chief Constable—it must be that he is in some way aware of the Chief Constable.[3] He must dimly see or hear him or at least feel the touch of his hand. Critics of this model consequently urge that this model further requires that there be "criteria . . . to distinguish 'true' experiences of the Divine from 'bogus' ones."[4] It is exactly here, they say, that this model loses its analogy, for while we have criteria to identify him encountered as the Chief Constable, there seems to be none that will identify the encountered as God. What these critics are saying is that this model does not finally resolve the central questions we noted regarding religious experience, and particularly the question: "How can we know that religious experience is of God or the Divine?"

There seems to be something misleading about this model that relates to this question; however, the point about a lack of criteria for identifying the encountered as God does not really bring out this misleading feature, nor does this point about a lack of criteria seem itself to be altogether right or clear. It does not seem clear because when it comes to identifying the Chief Constable there is a sense in which we have criteria and a sense in which we do not. We do in the sense that there are very many considerations that may come into play—sometimes one, sometimes another indicating in a given situation that the man we met was the Chief Constable; and if we think about it we can give examples of these considerations, but we cannot give an exhaustive list. We do not have criteria in the sense that there is no one consideration or set of considerations which is adequate to determine in every situation that the man encountered was the Chief Constable; we do not conduct a simple litmus test as we do to determine the presence of an acid.

We can frequently tell how we recognize someone, but the considerations cited will be various. In a particular situation, one who had met the Chief

Constable might be asked, "Was it the Chief Constable or the Postman?" to which he could reply "It was the Chief Constable; I recognized him by his uniform." In another situation, one who had met the Chief Constable might be asked "Was it the Chief Constable or the Postman in the Chief Constable's uniform?" Here what is cited cannot be the uniform, clearly. Rather the reply would have to cite something independent of the uniform; one might, for instance, reply here that he recognized the Chief Constable by his moustache. In a third situation the question might be "Did you meet the Chief Constable or someone in his uniform disguised to look like him?" Here something else again would have to be cited to explain how the Chief Constable was recognized. One might explain in this situation that he knew it was the Chief Constable because he spoke to him about something only the Chief Constable could know. What figures in these situations is not, of course, one consideration, but neither is it a set of three criteria, each of which or some set of which, is adequate for all situations; rather there are three different considerations, each doing the job in one set of circumstances given the question that arises there. None is adequate for all contexts, nor are all three together adequate for all contexts, for the examples given could be multiplied and, consequently, the considerations multiplied.

Thus, not only is it wrongheaded to demand *one* criterion for veridical religious experience on the basis of the analogy with an encounter with the Chief Constable, but it is equally wrongheaded to ask for criteria where what is wanted is a set of conditions or tests, any one or combination of which would establish the veridicality of religious experience regardless of the situation. But, one might ask, are there any considerations regarding the veridicality of religious experience that are pertinent in any situation? The answer to this question is that there are. One who has had a mystical experience similar to St. Teresa's or who believes that he has detected God's influence in his life or another's might be concerned lest he is deluding himself. Relevant in the context of the question he would put to himself would be these considerations: 1) whether he is proud of the experience, 2) whether he is psychologically and emotionally leaning on it, and 3) whether his life has been morally purified as a result of this experience. This last consideration in particular is one that mystics have pointed out.[5] To be sure, these considerations will not be pertinent in every situation, but criteria in the sense in which we have them for encounter situations are not pertinent in every situation.

What is misleading about the encounter model, then, is not that it suggests that there are criteria for determining the veridicality of religious experience when there are none, for in fact there are such criteria, and they operate just as criteria do in other encounter situations. Before we come to what seems to me to be this model's misleading feature, there is a further critical point that requires our attention regarding these criteria. Certain philosophers are aware that mystics themselves were concerned about the veridicality of their experiences and that they determined tests, employing particularly the criterion of a changed life. These philosophers have propounded what might be called the reduction point: If the criterion for experience of God or the Divine is a morally changed life, then to say that one's life has been influenced by God or that the source of one's experience is God is to say what reduces in factual content to the statement that one's life has been morally changed. These philosophers have said that if this is so, even an atheist might allow that men have veridical religious experience.[6] This reduction point requires closer scrutiny, however. The principle entails that "The source of St. Teresa's experience was God" reduces in factual content to "St. Teresa's life was morally changed." This may be understood in two ways. It may be understood as 1) the latter is evidence for the former or 2) the former means (only) the latter. The first accords with the role given the criterion of a changed life by mystics and, aside from the terminology, is not very different from what religious people have themselves said. The second is another matter. It is in this way, apparently, that the principle is most often understood by the philosophers who articulate it. If the principle were true as understood in this second way, then indeed an atheist could allow that there is religious experience of God and yet remain an atheist. But it appears that the principle understood in this second way is false and would only be true if positivism in one of its extreme forms had succeeded in its program. If positivism in such an extreme form had been successful, then, presumably the statement "There is a magnet" should be reducible in meaning to "There is a piece of metal and around it there is such-and-such a pattern of steel filings" or some similar statement. Clearly, though, the first does not reduce in meaning to the second, for the magnet might not be in proximity to steel filings. And it further appears that no other "observation-statement" or number of them will capture the meaning of the original. The "observation-statement," if it has any chance of equivalence, will require expression as a statement involving a hypothetical; e.g., "There is a piece of metal and if there are filings in close proximity, then there will be such-and-such a pattern." But a categorical like "There is a magnet," by the very fact that it is a categorical (that states that something exists), cannot be equivalent in meaning to a hypothetical (that states that something might exist)[7], for the same reason a categorical cannot be equivalent in meaning to another categorical conjoined to a hypothetical where the second categorical does not assert the existence of what the first does. For another thing (allowing hypotheticals), the statement "There is a piece of metal and if there are filings in close proximity, then there will be such-and-such a pattern" will not do, for there are a plethora of reasons why the magnet might not form such a pattern in the steel filings even when they are nearby. One can attempt to take into account these reasons by specifically enumerating and ruling out countervailing influences in the antecedent of the hypothetical, but whether all were ruled out would be an open question. And this would mean that we would never be sure whether or not we had the meaning of the original statement; an odd development indeed. A. J. Ayer in the introduction to *Language, Truth and Logic* conceded that *no* "finite set of observation-statements" may exhaust the meaning of certain statements;[8] thus in the case of such a statement we could *never* know its meaning. Of course there is one way of dealing with countervailing influences so that the translation statement will be true whenever "There is a magnet" is true. One can make the hypothetical element of the translation statement the following: ". . . if there are filings in close proximity, then there will be such-and-such a pattern, *if* there is nothing that prevents it." In this case the translation statement will be true whenever the original is for the reason that it will be true whenever there is a piece of metal, the hypothetical element having been made tautologous. But the translation statement obviously does not mean what the original does, for the original may be true or false when there is a piece of metal. Thus the translation statement fails. Consequently if the reduction point is to be made at all, it seems that it will have to be understood in the first way, and that way is not at odds with veridical religious experience being experience of God.

However, even though there are criteria for veridical experiences of God, as the encounter model requires, and even though the reduction point can be disarmed, there does appear to be a very misleading suggestion caused by this model of religious experience. If veridical religious experience resembles an encounter with the Chief Constable, then the suggestion is that at least some of the criteria relevant to the religious encounter should be rather like those most often relevant to that encounter. While mystics and others may have formulated criteria for veridical religious experience, these criteria do not appear to be on a logical par with those that most often figure in identifying the man who was introduced as the Chief Constable. As we may want to say, the criteria that figure in religious experience are not as "direct." This model suggests that the more important of these criteria should have to do with the way God Himself looks. In short, whatever other virtues this model may have, it does carry with it the misleading suggestion that we should be able to ask about God's physiognomy and appearance as we can ask about the physiognomy and appearance of the Chief Constable. Or, if these questions are deemed inappropriate, as the surely are, then it seems there should be "direct" criteria of some other sort. So, if this model and its suggestions are taken seriously, we end with some perplexing questions about "direct" criteria for God's presence like and unlike the "direct" criteria for encountering the Chief Constable.

III

Of course, even though the sighted man model and the encounter model carry misleading suggestions, they are not altogether misleading and they do help us understand religious experience (even poor analogies can be helpful at times). But there is a third model that seems to be much more helpful than the other two, at least as it applies to nonprophetical and nonmystical religious experience, and this is the model of seeing another's influence. One can see another's influence in any number of ways and connections; I shall draw upon two examples: seeing the influence of an artist on another artist, and seeing the influence of an uncle on his nephew.

This model is particularly significant because nonprophetical and nonmystical religious experience is not analogous to seeing the influence of another— it actually *is* seeing the influence of another. It is seeing the influence of God in the form of His mercy or support in one's own life or in another's life, or in the form of His goodness in the world (if it is veridical).

Further, it seems that this model escapes the misleading suggestions of the other two. In many situations there is no mystery about two men viewing the same phenomenon and not agreeing about the presence of some influence. For instance, two men might view a painting, and one of them might say that he sees the influence of a master on the artist and the other one might say that he does not; or, two men might observe the actions of a young man whom they know and disagree about whether his uncle has had an influence on him. In such cases the difference between the one who sees the influence in question and the one who does not is not that one has an organ of sight that the other lacks. No organic deficiency needs correction. In such situations one can try to show the other that there is the influence in question, or that there is no influence, by pointing out elements missed by the other, or by bringing into better focus the patterns of elements. The process may be slow and the patterns may need to be traced several times to be clear. Obviously, though, if one sees the influence of, say, Rembrandt on an artist, or of an uncle on his nephew, he does not have to produce Rembrandt or the uncle to bring the other person to see the influence he sees. In fact, it would often be irrelevant to produce Rembrandt or the uncle, if it were possible. If one sees the influence of Rembrandt or the young man's uncle, it does not follow that he has seen Rembrandt or the uncle, and it does not follow that there is a way to see them, for both may no longer be alive. Of course, for one to be able to see and to recognize as such Rembrandt's influence on another artist, he must have some acquaintance with Rembrandt's works and style. And for one to be able to see and to recognize as such the uncle's influence, he must know the character of the uncle, but this does not mean that he personally knows the uncle or even that he has seen him. He may know the uncle's character through reading his diary or through hearing stories about him. Thus this model does not suggest that to see God's influence, or to be sure that one has seen His influence, one must somehow first see God or have "direct" criteria for His presence. If one is to recognize God's influence as such, one must know God's character well enough to detect His influence; this knowledge is provided by the Bible and other scripture. Nor does this model imply that to see God's influence one must already know that there is a God or believe that there is a God. Just as one who is familiar with the uncle's diary and comes to see his influence on his nephew *may* have doubted the existence of the uncle to begin with, so too one who knows the Bible or the Biblical concept of God may come to see God's influence even though at first he claimed that there is no God. For that matter, just as one *could* come to see the uncle's influence before knowing of the uncle or his diary, so too one could come to see God's influence before knowing God or being acquainted with the Bible or the Biblical concept of God; although he would not recognize God's influence *as such,* of course. But later, after becoming acquainted with the Judaeo-Christian concept of God either through the Bible or in some other way, he would recognize God's influence. In these cases one would come to see that there is a God *through* seeing His influence.

One might want to say here that this model *does* suggest or imply that the patterns of God's influence can be traced and that one can bring another to see that influence by tracing these patterns—if the influence exists; and if one cannot bring another to see it, despite diligent effort, then we must conclude that he cannot because the Divine influence is not there to be seen.

This brings us to the most significant aspect of this model. Sometimes when one sees the influence of one artist on another or the influence of one person on another's actions he is not able to bring someone else to see what he sees. He may point out the pertinent elements and patterns and even so fail to bring the other to see the influence he sees. He may succeed, of course, but even when the various elements and the patterns they form have been seen by the other, he still may fail to see the influence seen by the first. This is not to say that he will *never* come to see it. He may, and what may bring him to see what he could not see at first is well worth our noting. It may have one of two natures. First, what may be needed is a continued effort. The one who does not see the influence in question may need to do no more than repeatedly retrace the elements and patterns together to finally perceive that they are signs of the influence he is trying to detect. Here, although he is trying to see, he does not. What brings him to see is reflective scrutiny and a continuation of his sympathetic or at least unprejudiced effort to see. Second, and more important, what may be needed is a change in the viewer. If so, what is needed is not a continued effort to see, but the ability to make a real effort to see. Such cases may not be rare and certainly are not beyond understanding. Significantly, what may sometimes be involved in them is, once again, self-deception. Taking the case of one trying to bring another to see the influence of an uncle on a nephew, if the one who does not see the influence is jealous of the uncle (perhaps without being aware of it) and entertains the notion that the young man looks to *him* for all his guidance, then, even though he can see the elements and patterns in the young man's actions that are pointed out to him, he may be unable to see them as signs of the uncle's influence, for he is unable to admit the possibility of such an influence. Of course he may finally come to see the uncle's influence on his nephew, but not until his self-deception has been overcome and the scales it created have fallen from his eyes.

In conjunction with this last point the model of seeing another's influence as it applies to nonprophetical and nonmystical religious experience suggests the following: 1) regarding those who have not seen God's influence in the world and in the lives of men (and this may include many who are religious), if there is this Divine influence to be seen, what they need is to see the dominance and significance of certain elements and patterns as they emerge in the world and in the lives of men; 2) if there is this Divine influence to be seen, it may be that many who do not see it do not need to investigate the world, to gather evidence, or to trace patterns in the lives of men to come to see it; 3) rather, they may need the ability to see the already familiar elements and patterns in the lives of men in their significance as indications of God's influence; and 4) if so, what is needed is a change in them as perceivers: their blindness to what is before them must be alleviated, a blindness that may be caused by self-deception. In short it may be the nonhypothetical sort of discovery discussed in the last chapter that is involved in coming to see God's influence. It will be if what is needed by those who fail to see God's influence is *not* to gather evidence or to trace patterns, but to change as perceivers so that they might see the evidence and patterns for what they are.

Sometimes, in regard to certain matters, we are capable of overcoming self-deception by vigorous self-examination or with the help of another's sympathetic but pointed questions. However, if self-deception is the source of what prevents many of us from seeing the Divine influence, or even if it is not, it may be that the overcoming of our blindness in this case requires more than our own efforts. It may require grace, as a religious person would say. Ultimately what may be needed is the kind of thing that possibly happened to Ivan Ilych in Tolstoy's story.[9] Whether this is so or not, though, we should note one other facet of the model of seeing another's influence as it applies to seeing God's influence, and this is something that relates back to our earlier concern with the nonhypothetical model of discovery. In the case of seeing God's influence, what is seen, or would be seen, is in effect that one has a relationship to God. If one were to see God's influence in the form of indications of his mercy and support in his own life, he would see that he stands in a relationship of love and concern to God. This, of course, holds equally well for seeing indications in one's own life of another human being's support: In discovering such support one thereby discovers, if he was not aware of it before, the other's concern, which is to say that he stands in a relationship of concern to the other. However, beyond this, in the special case of God's support, even if one were to see indications of God's support only in the lives of others, or in the world at large, he would thereby discover a relationship in which he participates, for he would have discovered a relationship existing between God and man. Consequently the relationship between God and man is one in which all of us (or none of us) may participate, and thus we are all involved in the sense that the question of whether or not one stands in a relation of concern to God applies to each of us individually. To some extent the points noted in this paragraph represent a divergence between seeing God's influence and seeing another human being's influence, but some divergence is to be expected. Seeing God's influence is not seeing another human being's influence.

Professor John Wisdom has reminded us that there are many ways by which questions can be settled.[10] One way is by gathering evidence to determine if an empirical hypothesis is verified. Another way is by redescribing and emphasizing features, as might be done, in combination with rereading, to bring out the excellence of a novel. Still another way is the way legal issues concerning the exercise of "reasonable care" are settled. Wisdom's concern was with the various ways different kinds of questions could be settled and with what counts as rationally proceeding to settle different kinds of questions. He pointed out that there are various ways of settling an issue, not all of which involve an empirical hypothesis and the gathering of data. In a way, then, he has made us see that there are various models of discovery that are not hypothetical (a hypothetical discovery I construe to involve the gathering of data), or, in his terms, that there are various ways of settling questions that are not experimental. However, he did not focus upon the model of discovery I have termed "nonhypothetical." One reason he did not is that he was concerned with situations in which an issue is presented and settled, or at least intellectually pursued. While he was not concerned with investigative situations where data are gathered, he was still concerned with investigative situations of other kinds. Nonhypothetical discoveries are not made in investigative situations, or at least not as the outcome of an investigation. What they require is *not* a gathering of data, an emphasizing of features or patterns, or any intellectual enquiry; they require seeing the gathered evidence in its significance as evidence, or the already traced pattern in its significance as a pattern of excellence in a novel or in its significance as influence of one man on another. That is, they require a change in the perceiver; they do not require his engaging in an investigation. What has been discussed here in connection with discovering another's influence, then, is a way of understanding how men might see God's influence in their lives and the world, not a way of settling the question of whether there is such Divine influence. In fact, it may be regarded as a strength of the influence model of religious experience that, in conjunction with points relating to nonhypothetical discoveries, it provides an understandable explanation of how religious people may have made a discovery of God's influence while yet being unable to bring others to that discovery. Just as one may be unable to bring another to see an uncle's influence on his nephew due to the other's self-deception, so too one may be unable to bring others to see God's influence due to their self-deception or the kind of blindness that is produced by self-deception. There fairly clearly are cases of self-deception regarding our human relationships; why should it be a great surprise that there is or might be the same thing regarding our relation to God? Admittedly, that already noted, perhaps unanswerable question arises here: Has the believer who has seen God's influence, or thinks he has, had the scales lifted from his eyes and seen aright, or has the nonbeliever who has not seen God's influence seen aright? But this same question attaches to nonreligious instances of seeing another's influence where self-deception is or may be involved. It could be asked in the uncle/nephew case if there were reason to think, not only that the one who cannot see the uncle's influence may be deceiving himself, but also that the one who says he does see the uncle's influence may be deceiving himself. Again, the reason that this question asked in a religious situation is so perplexing and perhaps unanswerable is that we are not asking it as uninvolved, neutral observers; we are asking it of ourselves. We are all involved, whether or not we feel involved, in the sense that this question applies to us all.

IV

At the beginning of this chapter we noted two central questions regarding religious experience: "Is it of God or the Divine or is it not?" and "If it is, how can we know that it is?" At this point I think that we have traced the lineaments of a model that makes understandable the viable possibility that nonprophetical and nonmystical religious experience is veridical. This is not much, but it is something, particularly when the epistemological question is considered. The model of seeing another's influence indicates how one can know that religious experience is of the Divine, namely by coming to see God's influence himself; and the model further brings out that what may be involved in coming to see God's influence, and in being blind to God's influence, is involved in common secular situations as well. While religious believers can point to the support in their lives and others' lives that they interpret as indications of God's concern and influence; and while they can sometimes help bring others to see the Divine influence, at a certain point there is nothing more that can be said to point out God's influence. The instances that the religious person sees as instances of the Divine influence have been pointed out and they are either seen as such or they are not seen as such. At a certain point, then, the limits of the sayable have been reached in a sense. But this sense should be familiar, for the same thing may happen in purely secular cases where we may be blind to the influences of other human beings and our consequent relationships to them.

Wittgenstein also apparently thought of religious issues as being beyond the sayable. What he meant by this, however, as it is explained by Stephen Toulmin,[11] is distinct from what I have endeavored to elucidate. What Wittgenstein apparently meant was that religious matters could not literally be "stated" in "representational" language. To try to say something about God was to try to say something that quite literally could not be said; the limits of language prevented it. Toulmin says Wittgenstein speculated that perhaps it is the nature of poetry that poets can "convey insights which could never be literally uttered," and "religious expression" could have "something of the character of poetry." In any case, while Wittgenstein thought of religion as beyond the sayable in this sense, he did not think that it was therefore nonsense. Indeed, he thought that many of the important issues regarding God, freedom, value and immortality were largely in the realm of the unsayable.

What Toulmin understood Wittgenstein to have said about religion and religious matters sounds very much like what many have said of mysticism. But especially when it is said about religion in general it is very misleading. It suggests that when religious people say that they believe in God or that God is concerned for men, they cannot literally mean that they *believe* in God or that God is *concerned* for men. In fact Wittgenstein said something like this regarding belief in God in his lecture on religious belief: One who talks of believing in God, he said, does not use "believe" as one does ordinarily; he does not give it its normal use.[12] Questions that quite naturally arise in the wake of Wittgenstein's comments are: "What is the special religious use of 'believe'?" and "What do religious people mean by 'believe'?"[13] Other questions are suggested as well. Since religious people often express what they call their "belief," e.g., that Jesus is the Son of God, and thereby say what is unsayable, it appears, given what Wittgenstein has said, that religious people in some sense have their own language. So these questions arise: "What is the nature of 'theological language'?" or, "What is the logic of 'religious discourse'?" The idea that there is a unique "religious language" or "religious discourse" is very vague and is probably right in as many senses as it is wrong. But inasmuch as it is right it does not entail that religious belief is not belief (although, of course, it is not just any belief) or that God's concern is not concern (although his concern may be unlike any other in that it is infinite or completely unfaltering[14]).

It is not certain whether Wittgenstein himself thought that religious belief was not belief or God's concern was not concern, but given the way in which he thought that religious matters are unsayable and, it seems, that "religious language" has its own "use," it is not surprising that some should draw this conclusion. There is one well-known example with which Wittgenstein made the point that religious locutions have their own "grammar" or "use." This is the example of the locution "The Eye of God."[15] He asked rhetorically if eyebrows were to be spoken of in connection with the Eye of God.

His implied observation that they would not be is, of course, correct. But does this observation further imply that there is a "religious langauge" with its own "grammar" or "use"? The Eye of God might be spoken of in a religious context to remind us that God sees into our hearts. The locution is rather like "the eyes of the world" in the statement "The eyes of the world are turned toward Berlin." Neither locution, if understood, invites a question concerning eyebrows. Should we say, then, that just as there is a "religious language," so too there is a "world language" or "city language" with its own "grammar"? Or should we say that in both cases if one speaks English and understands what is being said he will know that a question about eyebrows is out of place? It seems to me a tautology that if one were to ask about eyebrows in either case he would not know English or at any rate not the English locutions involved. What this points out is that learning certain religious locutions is not too different from learning certain secular locutions. Consider "seeing" as it is predicated of God when it is said that God sees into our hearts. Clearly, this seeing is not like seeing a mountain ridge against the sky. God's seeing is not an organic seeing; or, as Wittgenstein might have said, the organs of sight— corneas, retinas, etc.—will not be mentioned in connection with God's seeing. But this does not mean that there is a special religious "use" for this term, or that God "sees" in a special religious sense. In Thomas Wolfe's *You Can't Go Home Again,* the blind Judge Rumford Bland sees the grasping character of the civic leaders of Libya and openly accuses them of ruining their town; being blind, of course, he "sees" differently from persons with organic sight. While this kind of seeing does not require organic eyes, and is perhaps most appropriate to a Tiresias figure, it is not limited to the organically blind. The point here is not that God is a Tiresias figure: that does not follow. The point is that we need not go to religion and to God's seeing in order to find a kind of seeing about which questions relating to organic eyes are out of place. To be sure God is very different from man (even though it is said man is in his image). But while there are a lot of questions that can be asked about the man who lives across the street that cannot be asked about God, I should think that anyone who speaks English as a first language or is fluent in English (and consequently knows the word "God" and related locutions) would be aware of this.[16]

What I want to bring out here is this: to say that religious matters are beyond the sayable in the Wittgensteinian sense may leave one with perhaps very misleading questions about the "grammar" of "religious language" and the religious "use" of such words as "believe" and "concerned" as they are predicated of God. These last questions are particularly misleading, it seems to me, if they are equated with questions like: "What do religious people mean by 'believe'?" or "Since what religious people refer to by 'belief' is not belief, what is it?" As a corrective to the Wittgensteinian suggestion, we should remind ourselves that religious people say creeds and describe their relation to God (as they see it) in English or whatever language they happen to speak. Put another way, English is the "religious language" of a religious person whose native language is English.

However, if it is misleading to say that religious matters are beyond the sayable in the way that Wittgenstein said they were, it still may be that religious persons run against the limits of the sayable in the way suggested earlier. If language does not impose limits on what is sayable in religion, it still may be that there are limits imposed by our inability to see the indications of God's influence when they are pointed out to us by the religious. This, at any rate, is the suggestion that I have tried to elaborate. If it is right, then the pertinent difference between the religious and the nonreligious is in their perceptive ability, not in their language. It may be that somehow religious people can see that if a man's life becomes truly saintly, then this is an indication of God's influence. This may be as true to the religious as it is true to the rest of us that if someone is our friend, then he means us no ill. This possibility is brought out most clearly if we think about the inability to see that if someone is our friend, he means us no ill in comparison with the inability to see that if a man has led a saintly life, it is an indication of God's influence.

One might think that the statement "One's friends mean him no ill" is necessarily true. It is true we might say of someone who does not accept this statement that he does not know the meaning of the word "friend." We might say this of someone who said: "I become the friend of those I meet really for but one purpose: to take advantage of them. If they are hurt, so much the worse for them." Similarly we might say of someone who loves selfishly that he does not know the meaning of the word "love." Quite apparently, though, in neither case would we refer the person to a dictionary. The point of saying these things is to give a reprimand or to point out a moral blindness. Consequently, while it may be reprehensible for one to love selfishly or for a friend to intend ill, it is not self-contradictory to say of one that he loves selfishly or of one that he intends ill to someone to whom he is a friend. Yet there is a connection between one being another's friend and his not meaning him ill that is more than an accidental connection. Friends do not just happen to mean no ill. In most situations, if we see that someone is a friend we see thereby that he means us no ill; generally this is the way of the world. It is not nonsense to challenge this connection; although the sense that it makes is a revealing sort. If one wonders why he cannot be a friend to someone and yet take advantage of him, he reveals a kind of moral blindness. And if one wonders if all his friends mean him ill—after he accepts them as his friends— he reveals something like paranoia.

What the morally blind person and this kind of paranoiac needs is not to be shown that they have friends, for they know this; and certainly it is not to learn the meaning of "friend." What they need is a renewed ability to see their friends as friends, to see that kind of relationship for all that it is. The morally blind person needs to see again that a friend is not someone of whom he can take advantage, and the paranoiac needs to see again that his friends do not mean him harm. Particularly in the case of the paranoiac it is clear that what he needs is a change in himself, a renewed ability to see things as they are. This is not to say that there is no evidence for his friends intending him no harm; the evidence may be everywhere, for he may have many friends concerned for him. But if one challenges such indications of concern, as the paranoiac does, then it is useless to point them out to him as evidence that his friends intend him no harm. He does not need to have pointed out to him what he cannot see to be evidence. What he needs are his old eyes—the eyes he had before and has lost.

What the paranoiac needs is beyond the sayable, then, in the sense that there is nothing we can say to point out indications of his friends' concern. That is, it is beyond the sayable in precisely the way that what is needed by the person who does not see God's influence in a saintly life may be beyond the sayable. This does not mean that the nonreligious person, or the religious person who fails to see God's influence, is like the paranoiac. But it does mean that, if there are indications of God's influence to be seen, the kind of blindness that prevents us from seeing them may be similar to the paranoiac's or the morally blind person's.

Notes

[1]C. B. Martin, *Religious Belief* (Ithaca, New York: Cornell University Press, 1959), p. 70. Martin makes the same point in an earlier version of chap. 5 of *Religious Belief* entitled "A Religious Way of Knowing," *Mind* 41 (1952); reprinted in *New Essays in Philosophical Theology,* eds. Antony Flew and Alasdair MacIntyre (New York: The Macmillan Company; London: SCM Press, 1955), p. 83.

[2]Cf. Martin, *Religious Belief.* The title of his chap. 5 is " 'Seeing' God."

[3]H. H. Price, "Faith and Belief," *Faith and the Philosophers,* ed. John Hick (New York: St. Martin's Press; London: Macmillan & Co., 1964), pp. 21–22.

[4]Keith Gunderson, "Are There Criteria for 'Encountering God'?" *Faith and the Philosophers,* p. 58. Cf. R. W. Hepburn, *Christianity and Paradox* (New York: Pegasus; London: Watts, 1958), chaps. 3 and 4.

[5]Cf. William James, *Varieties of Religious Experience,* Lecture 1, particularly his citations of St. Teresa's *Life,* chap. 28, and Jonathan Edwards' *Treatise on Religious Affections.*

[6]Cf. Martin, *Religious Belief,* p. 93. Martin makes the reduction point vis-à-vis the sighted man model.

[7]Cf. Isaiah Berlin, "Empirical Propositions and Hypothetical Statements," *Perceiving, Sensing, and Knowing,* ed. R. J. Swartz (Garden City, New York: Doubleday & Company, 1965), p. 392 and *passim.* Reprinted from *Mind* 59 (1950).

[8]A. J. Ayer, *Language, Truth and Logic,* 2d ed. (New York: Dover Publications; London: Victor Gollancz, 1946), p. 15.

[9]"The Death of Ivan Ilych."

[10]See John Wisdom, "Gods," *Proceedings of the Aristotelian Society* 45 (1944-

45): 185–206. Reprinted in John Wisdom, *Philosophy and Psychoanalysis* (Oxford: Blackwell, 1964) and in Antony Flew, ed., *Logic and Language* (First Series. Oxford: Blackwell, 1960). See also John Wisdom, "The Logic of God," *Paradox and Discovery* (Oxford: Blackwell, 1965); in John Hick, ed., *The Existence of God* (New York: The Macmillan Company, 1964) under the title "The Modes of Thought and the Logic of God." In this later essay, which has yet to receive the attention given to "Gods," it seems that Wisdom brings to light matters more closely related to what I have discussed in this chapter and in other chapters.

[11]Stephen Toulmin, "Ludwig Wittgenstein," *Encounter* 32 (1969): 61–64.

[12]L. Wittgenstein, *Lectures and Conversations on Aesthetics, Psychology and Religious Belief*, ed. C. Barrett (Berkeley and Los Angeles: University of California Press, 1966), pp. 59–60.

[13]Cf. Wittgenstein's own concerns, pp. 53–64. Also cf. Paul L. Holmer, "Wittgenstein and Theology," *New Essays on Religious Language*, ed. D. M. High (New York: Oxford University Press, 1969) pp. 32–34; and W. E. Hudson, "Some Remarks on Wittgenstein's Account of Religious Belief," *Talk of God,* Royal Institute of Philosophy Lectures, vol. 2. (London: Macmillan, 1969), pp. 44–45.

[14]Cf. John King-Farlow, " 'Could God be Temporal?' A Devil's Advocacy," *Southern Journal of Philosophy* 1 (1963): 25.

[15]Wittgenstein, *Lectures*, pp. 71–72. Also cf. Toulmin, "Ludwig Wittgenstein," p. 64.; and G. E. Moore, "Wittgenstein's Lectures in 1930–33," *Philosophical Papers* (New York: Collier Books, 1959), p. 306.

[16]Cf. Hudson, "Some Remarks on Wittgenstein's Account of Religious Belief," p. 40.

4

rationality,

religion,

and fideism

4

I

In his article "Is Understanding Religion Compatible with Believing?" Professor Alasdair MacIntyre says that magic, as practiced by (for example) the Azande, is illogical because magic, or a belief in magic, "fails to come up to our criteria for rationality."[1] His real subject is religious belief. He feels that we today cannot both understand religion and believe, for, in the same way, religion does not come up to our criteria for rationality and intelligibility. Professor Peter Winch, on the other hand, denies that a belief in witches and magic, like the Zande belief, is irrational; and by extension he denies that religion and religious belief are unintelligible.[2] Expressed in this way the opposition between them seems fairly neat and straightforward, but in fact it is more blurred than it seems. For sometimes the issue does not appear to be about either 1) when a belief is intelligible or 2) when a belief is rational, but about 3) when a concept is coherent or makes sense (MacIntyre, pp. 121 and 122) or 4) when a practice is intelligible

(Winch, p. 18); and one might wonder if all these amount to the same issue. However, taking the issue to be that about which MacIntyre and Winch are comparatively neatly at odds, a further difficulty arises. If we look at why Winch disagrees with MacIntyre, two basic reasons emerge. One seems to be confused and inconclusive; the other seems to be forceful and right. In this chapter we shall discuss these two reasons, particularly the second, and also what Professor Kai Nielsen says about the subject of "Wittgensteinian Fideism" in his article of that title.[3]

The first reason that may be drawn from Winch for saying that the Zande belief in magic and witches is rational and, by extension, that religious belief is intelligible, is this: we in our society and culture have our concepts and criteria for intelligibility and/or rationality, and, while the Azande have such concepts and criteria, they are not ours.[4] This reason, it seems to me, is very perplexing. First, it raises these questions: What are our criteria for rationality and intelligibility? And what are the Zande criteria for rationality and intelligibility? One might think that either Winch or MacIntyre would simply state our criteria (since they are in our society and culture) and the Zande criteria (gleaned from anthropology) and then compare them to see if they are the same. But, except for the criterion of consistency, which Winch calls a "formal requirement,"[5] and a brief reference to "effectiveness" by MacIntyre,[6] neither Winch nor MacIntyre says what the various criteria are, and for good reason. I suspect that to specify what figure here as our criteria for rationality would be to state the necessary and sufficient conditions for rationality, or something very close to them, and trying to state such a set of conditions for rationality is probably as misconceived as trying to state such a set for a game. Also, if the Zande concepts of rationality and intelligibility are different from our concepts, whatever this involves, it apparently means that the Azande mean something different by their words, phrases, or gestures that anthropologists or linguists translate as "rational," "intelligible," "He is rational," etc. And if they mean something different from what we mean, then the translations should be different. By extrapolation, terms like "rational" and "intelligible" in a religious context would mean something else also, it seems.[7] Consequently the reason offered by Winch leaves us with some perplexing questions and the implication that when religious belief is said to be intelligible, the word "intelligible" may not mean intelligible at all.

But one may draw a second reason from Winch for saying that the Zande belief in magic and witches is rational and, by extension, that religious belief is intelligible. The second reason is this: we conclude that the Zande belief is irrational only because we impute to the Azande "theoretical interests" appropriate to a scientific endeavor, and these concerns are in fact foreign to their particular involvement with witches and magic.[8] In our culture if a scientist holds theses which together entail a contradiction, he may be criticized for holding an irrational belief. Also, if he holds theses which would in conjunction with certain empirical propositions entail a contradiction, then rational scientific procedure demands that he investigate those empirical propositions to determine their truth or falsity. If he does not, again he might be accused of holding a belief before thoroughly investigating it. But it seems that this is precisely what the Azande do. They apparently believe:

1) if one has "witchcraft-substance" in his intestines (as a post-mortem examination could show), then he is a witch;
2) if one has no "witchcraft-substance" in his intestines (again, which a post-mortem examination could show), then he is not a witch;
3) if one member of a clan (all persons related through the male line) is a witch, all are; and
4) if one member of a clan is not a witch, none is.

It seems, given these beliefs, that if one member of a clan was discovered to have "witchcraft-substance" in his intestines and another member of the same clan was discovered to have none, then it would follow that all the members of the clan are witches and also that none is, which is a contradiction. However, despite the fact that the Azande have the means to check the relevant empirical propositions—they regularly conduct postmortem examinations— still they never do check them to test the consistency of their beliefs with these discoverable empirical propositions. Thus it seems that they persist in their belief in witchcraft irrationally. The problem here is *not* that the Azande persist in holding contradictions to be true. In fact they have ways of dealing with those contradictions that come up, for the Azande sometimes do become involved in contradictions even though they do not test their beliefs regarding witches by checking the implications of these beliefs. For instance, members of a clan may insist that they are not witches even though witchcraft-substance has been discovered in a post-mortem examination of a deceased clan member. When such a contradiction is encountered, the Azande affected offer a resolution. They may say, for instance, that the "witchcraft-substance" discovered was "cool" (inoperative) and so the clan member was not a witch after all.[9] But still it seems they make no effort to check the consistency of their belief in witches with certain discoverable empirical propositions: They do not raise questions about possible contradictions given checkable contingencies. And for *this* reason it seems they hold their belief in witches irrationally.

At this point, though, we may bring to bear the force of the second reason attributable to Winch for saying the Zande belief is rational, namely that in the light of the particular concerns of the Azande and the nature of their position in their situation, their belief is rational.[10] We outside the Zande culture may have a theoretical interest in their belief in witches. As anthropologists, or simply as scientifically-minded cultural observers, we can ask: Is their belief in witches true? As twentieth-century men, we of course have good reason to think it false. Consequently, if we accept this belief as true without tracing through its implications to see if any contradictions are entailed, we would be open to the charge of holding an irrational belief. Further, since what we would be doing is conducting an investigation, not to check the implications of the belief under investigation would be to leave unexamined very pertinent matters, which is a fault in objective investigation.

However, the Azande themselves have very different concerns. Their concern is not investigative: They are not conducting a study of their belief in witches. They have accepted the belief from time immemorial because their fathers have, and—unlike us—they have no initial reason to doubt their belief in witches. Not only would it be impudent for a Zande to doubt the belief of his father, but if he has no reason to doubt it, it would be baseless as well.

Another way of bringing out this point is to note that what is rational for a Zande who has spent his life amid tribal surroundings to believe may be very different from what is rational for a Zande who has spent three years at Oxford to believe. This does not mean that one standard of intelligibility or rationality applies to the one and another standard of intelligibility or rationality applies to the other. It means that in terms of a common notion of rationality—*the* notion of rationality, if you like—if the one has an investigative concern with the belief and yet does not check the implications of his belief in witches, his belief may be irrational; while if the other has very different concerns, his belief in witches may be rational even if he does not check its implications. The belief in witches would be irrational for the Oxford graduate but rational for the other Zande when neither checked its implications given 1) the fact that the Oxford graduate has an initial (anthropologically based) reason for doubting the belief in witches and is investigating the hypothesis that the belief is false, and 2) the other Zande has no initial reason to doubt his belief in witches and is not investigating the hypothesis that the belief is false.

There is one other point that ought to be noted here. Some philosophers take the question "Is the Zande belief in witches a rational belief?" as a straightforward question. Others do not, because they feel that the concept of rationality and/or intelligibility needs to be analyzed or given specific criteria of application.[11] In fact, the question may not be straightforward because, as expressed, it may have several different points. Depending upon its various points it may come to: 1) "Is the Zande belief in witches a belief that can be rationally held; can one (today in our culture) rationally believe as the Azande do?" or 2) "Are the Azande rational in their belief in witches; have they retained reason and not disregarded evidence in holding their belief?" If we separate these two questions, we can see that they might be answered differently. It may be that the Azande have not disregarded evidence against their belief and are cognizant of all that can be expected in a prescientific tradition, but have failed to see the import of what someone scientifically trained might see while pursuing a theoretical interest in a belief in witches.

If so, then 1) would be answered: "No, the Zande belief in witches is not rational, one cannot rationally believe as the Azande do," and 2) would be answered: "Yes, the Azande are rational in their belief, for they have retained reason and have not disregarded evidence." The point of the first question is to find out about the credentials of the belief and whether *we* rationally can or should adopt it; the point of the second is to find out whether we should disparage the Azande as irrational because *they* hold it. If one does not separate these questions, then he might think that if he fails to disparage the Azande as irrational, he will end up allowing that perhaps we ourselves ought to hold a belief in witches. What is required to see that there are two questions here is an appreciation of the fact that, often, looking only at a "form of words" or a sentence—for example, "Is the Zande belief in witches a rational belief?"—will not enable one to understand what is being said or asked. It may be that it is when we have lost sight of the point of the question (and so, in this case, of what the question is asking) that we want to lay down criteria or a test for rationality, in order to make the question understandable to ourselves.

In summing up this section so far, there seem to be two reasons attributable to Winch for saying that the Zande belief in witches is rational. The first seems confused; the second seems right. However, inasmuch as the second is right, it gives us a reason to conclude that the Zande belief in witches is rational in that they have not abandoned reason nor disregarded evidence (the second question); it does not give us a reason to conclude that one (today in our culture) can rationally hold their belief (the first question).

How does all this relate to religious belief, the real issue between MacIntyre and Winch? My suggestion is not that religious belief is rational to the extent that it is like the Zande belief in witches, or to the extent that believers are like the Azande. My suggestion is rather that, as the concerns and the position of the Azande enter into the question of the rationality of their belief, so too religious concerns and the position and situation of religious believers may enter into the question of the rationality of religious belief. What saves the Zande belief from irrationality (in terms of the second question) is the Azande not having a theoretical concern since they are not acquainted with the scientific attitude and anthropological data that raise doubts about the existence of witches. Religious believers similarly have no theoretical concern with their beliefs; they typically do not treat them as hypotheses to be investigated. The reason for their lack of theoretical interest, however, cannot be their lack of acquaintance with the scientific attitude and the data cited against there being a God (e.g., evil). It must lie elsewhere. What is more, if religious belief is significantly rational, then the analogues to both questions 1) and 2) asked of the Zande belief must be answered affirmatively. The two analogous questions would be: 1') "Is the religious belief in God a belief that can be rationally held; can one rationally believe as religious believers do?" and 2') "Are religious believers rational in their belief in God; have they retained reason and not disregarded evidence in holding their belief?" If only the second question were answered affirmatively, then we could consistently go on to say that religious belief is irrational in our culture, and even that it is false, both of which are exactly what we say about the Zande belief in witches.

But 1') will almost certainly be answered affirmatively if 2') is. For most religious believers in the Judaeo-Christian tradition share our culture or the pertinent elements. And 2') will be answered affirmatively if some believers have made a discovery of their relationship to God. The main question here comes down to one about the position of the religious person: Has he or has he not made a discovery?

II

Kai Nielsen in his "Wittgensteinian Fideism" attributes to Winch what I called the first reason for saying that the Zande belief in witches is rational and, by extension, that religious belief is intelligible, namely: We in our society and culture have our concepts and criteria for intelligibility and/or rationality, and, while the Azande have such concepts and criteria, they are not ours. This reason is entailed by the view he calls "Wittgensteinian Fideism," a view he attributes to Winch and others. Nielsen lists eight propositions accepted by Wittgensteinian Fideists. The last two entail Winch's first reason. They are:

7. These general, dispute-engendering concepts, i.e., intelligibility, reality and rationality are systematically ambiguous; their exact meaning can only be determined in the context of a determinate way of life.
8. There is no Archimedean point in terms of which a philosopher (or for that matter anyone else) can relevantly criticize whole modes of discourse or, what comes to the same thing, ways of life, for each mode of discourse has its own specific criteria of rationality/irrationality, intelligibility/unintelligibility, and reality/unreality.[12]

However, by attributing to Winch the first reason, and not the second, it seems to me Nielsen fastens upon the weaker and confused reason and misses what is most penetrating in Winch's treatment.

Nielsen observes the following: Even if Winch is right regarding the Zande culture and ours, and we do have different concepts of reality (intelligibility and rationality)[13] with no grounds for saying that our concept of reality (intelligibility or rationality) is the correct one, still it would not follow that religion and science have different concepts similarly related. For, Nielsen points out, (while the Zande have a language different from ours) there is no "religious language" or "scientific language." Rather, there are English, French, and German among others, and for English speaking people both "religious discourse" and "scientific discourse" would be comprised of English, with all the terms for each being English terms.

So far as this point goes, Nielsen is certainly right; when a scientist refers to one electron and a religious believer refers to one God, both mean the same by "one," namely what the English term means. And when either a scientist or a believer says that a belief is true or rational, both mean what the English "true" or "rational" means. But Nielsen misses Winch's strength by attributing to him the first reason. We should note that the second reason holds regardless of how many languages are involved. Whether or not the Azande have a theoretical concern with their belief in witches, or are in a position where they should have, is independent of what language they speak. So too with religious belief. Whether or not religious believers have concerns distinct from an investigative theoretical concern, and what their position is vis-à-vis their belief, are independent of the language they speak.

It is because Nielsen construes Winch as he does that he goes ahead to argue for a criterion of intelligibility. If he had seen the second reason attributable to Winch, then perhaps he would have understood the relevance of doing more than offering a criterion for intelligibility. Perhaps he would have seen the relevance of looking at the religious contexts in which believers say, for instance, "There is one God, maker of heaven and earth," and the relevance of considering their concerns and the point of their saying such things. But construing Winch as offering the first reason, he sees the issue as: What are the criteria for intelligibility? Accordingly he endeavors to indicate these criteria, or one criterion, namely a criterion for sense or "factual content." Thus, Nielsen's concern, like MacIntyre's, comes down to a concern with what makes sense and what does not. Like both MacIntyre and Winch, Nielsen talks about intelligibility, but what he has in mind is the intelligibility of "God-talk"; that is, the intelligibility (or sense) of statements. And the criterion he has in mind is that of the verificationist, or positivist, which he states thus: "a statement...has factual content only if it is confirmable or disconfirmable in principle. To count as a factual statement, it must assert a certain determinate reality (a pleonasm) ; that is, its descriptive content includes one set of empirically determinable conditions and excludes others."[14] In other words, according to this criterion, a putative statement is a genuine factual statement only if there is evidence or possible evidence for or against it; such evidence is included or excluded by the meaning or "descriptive content" of the statement, and if the statement lacks "descriptive content," it lacks meaning, or at least "factual meaning."

A belief—or a statement, since statements are now the subject—may be unintelligible in at least two ways. A statement may be unintelligible in that the speaker has simply failed to say anything understandable or meaningful, for grammatical reasons perhaps, as when someone barely acquainted with English says something like "He is you go" (instead of "He is going where you go"). Or a statement may be unintelligible in that we cannot understand what the speaker means when he says such a thing because he clearly has no evidence for it and perhaps can have no evidence for it, such as "I believe Thieu is on Hanoi's side," when all of us including the speaker know that there can be no evidence for this. The first is unintelligible in that it lacks sense or meaning; the second is unintelligible in that it does not state a rational belief. It has meaning, but lacks good sense (and more). Saying that a statement is unintelligible in the second way comes to saying that *why* the speaker made the statement cannot be understood, but sometimes this means that *what* he said cannot be understood; although it is not to say it cannot be understood because it lacks meaning, as "He is you go" does. If someone acquainted with Thieu's position in Vietnam seriously said that Thieu was on Hanoi's side, we could say either that we could not understand why he said such a thing or that we could not understand what he meant or that we found what he said unintelligible. (considering the evidence and his acquaintance with it). In each case we would be pointing out that what he said, as it stood, was unintelligible in the sense that it was wholly irrational. Winch is talking about intelligibility in the sense of rationality (in fact, he tends to use the two terms interchangeably), but Nielsen is talking about intelligibility in the sense of meaning. It seems to be a verificationist or positivist tendency to equate intelligibility in the sense of rationality with intelligibility in the sense of meaning, perhaps because they think of meaning as evidence or possible evidence in the way they do.

Nielsen argues for his verificationist criterion in this way: Not only scientists, but religious people too, think of themselves as making factual statements. However, there is a "linguistic convention" governing what is and what is not a factual statement. According to this convention an utterance purporting to be a factual statement must meet the verificationist criterion. Therefore, to be a genuine (meaningful) factual statement a religious utterance must meet this criterion.[15]

In this argument Nielsen cites a "linguistic convention" for what is a factual statement. Perhaps he thinks that this convention holds for all language users, or at least all statement makers, *regardless* of the situation or context and regardless of their concerns and the point of what they are saying. However, while it is open to Nielsen to think this, his saying there is such a ubiquitous linguistic convention is no substitute for his looking to see if this convention holds in all situations. If one does look at different situations in which factual statements are made, then he will find that often, even in secular situations, the verificationist's criterion does not hold. That is, often (to use Nielsen's terms) a statement's "descriptive content" does not "include one set of empirically determinable conditions and exclude others." Or else these conditions must be understood in such a way that "religious utterances" qualify as "genuine factual statements."

Consider the statement "God is lovingly concerned for men." Surely, one might say, religious people can indicate what will show this to be false, or, in Nielsen's language, what the descriptive content excluded is. As the religious might point out, this statement excludes a) constant pointless suffering in the world. But verificationists, I think, would not accept a) as a statement of excluded content in the light of which "God is lovingly concerned for men" would be counted as a meaningful statement about God. If a) is not acceptable as excluded descriptive content, though, then many secular statements similarly do not exclude descriptive content. Perhaps "The cat is on the mat" and "It is raining" do, at least in most contexts, but "John loves Mary," "Pursewarden loves Justine," "Raskolnikov loves Sonia," and "Abraham loves Isaac" do not, at least in some contexts. For example, in recalling the complexities of Alexandria, we may not be able to say what "Pursewarden loves Justine" excludes except a') his making her constantly suffer pointlessly. This, however, is analogous to what we can say vis-à-vis the religious statement. This does not make these statements similar to religious statements about God in all respects, but it does point out the fact that religious statements are only like certain secular statements (in some contexts) in not meeting the requirements of the verificationists.

After a discussion and sorting of the Pursewarden/Justine situation, or after the situation develops, we may come to see what will show us that he loves her and what will show us that he does not. And of course it is also true that if and only if the conditions for the truth of the statement "Pursewarden loves Justine" are met, then he loves her, and if and only if the conditions for the falsity of this statement are met, then he does not love her. But these may not be determinable conditions, for they may not be discernible in advance of discussion and the developing situation. Or, if they are discernible in principle (but no one can discern them beforehand), so too the analogous conditions for the truth or falsity of the religious statement may be discernible in principle. If it is possible in principle, but in fact impossible, to specify beforehand what would show that Pursewarden does not love Justine, so too it may be possible in principle, but in fact impossible, to specify what would fulfill the condition of constant pointless suffering for mankind and show that God is not lovingly concerned for men. In both cases—if the statements are false— what may be needed is sensitivity on our part, and time. Just as 1) if the conditions for the falsity of "Pursewarden loves Justine" are met, then he does not love her, so also 2) if the conditions for the falsity of "God is lovingly concerned for men" are met, then he is not lovingly concerned for men (and there is no Judaeo-Christian God). And just as we cannot now specify in empirical terms what would show that God is not lovingly concerned with men—if we cannot—so, similarly, we cannot specify what would show that Pursewarden does not love Justine.

So while it is tautologically true that if a statement is false, then the conditions for its falsity are met, and if it is true, the conditions for its truth are met, it does not follow, and is not true, that a factual statement must "include one set of empirically determinable conditions and exclude others." Or, if these conditions are understood in such a way that this is so, then religious statements about God qualify. It is this that we discover if we look at the "linguistic convention" suggested by Nielsen.

Perhaps this convention, or some version of the positivist criterion, holds more in the fashion Nielsen supposes for the offering of hypotheses. That is, perhaps some version of the positivist criterion is appropriate as a criterion for tenable or worthwhile hypotheses. It may be a serious fault for a scientist to offer a hypothesis when he is not clear beforehand on what would show it to be false and what would be compatible with its truth; that is, on what "empirically determinable conditions" it includes and excludes. But religious people do not usually offer hypotheses. The point of saying the Nicene Creed is not to offer a hypothesis for investigation. MacInytre apparently thinks that the Azande are irrational for not approaching their belief in witches as neutral anthropological observers investigating the hypothesis that there are witches. Nielsen, who suggests as the standard for a factual statement something more appropriate as a standard for a hypothesis, apparently thinks that religious believers should approach their religions as neutral observers investigating the hypothesis that there is a God. Nielsen goes wrong, it seems to me, in that he requires a factual statement to be a hypothesis. *If* religious people would offer for investigation the hypothesis that there is a God, when there is no clear verification or falsification condition beforehand, then they would have a hopeless task; a hypothesis useless to pursue, or no hypothesis at all. But most of them do not offer such a hopeless hypothesis because they do not offer a hypothesis at all.

Rather, when they state their beliefs, as when they say the Nicene Creed, they are reaffirming their faith. Are these rational beliefs that they affirm? If they are rational beliefs, so that the two questions 1') and 2') in Section I, are answered affirmatively, then it seems that there must be support for these beliefs unlike the support for a hypothesis unearthed by a theoretical concern. We have examined the question of whether there is, or could be, such evidence for religious beliefs in earlier chapters. What I hope was brought out in those earlier discussions is that, while it is a mistake to assimilate religious concerns to the theoretical concern of investigating hypotheses, and while the evidence that primarily relates to religious belief is not the sort that relates to hypotheses, there may yet be evidence that suports and establishes religious beliefs as there may be the discovery, albeit the nonhypothetical discovery, of a relationship to God.

Notes

[1]In *Faith and the Philosophers*, ed. John Hick (New York: St. Martin's Press; London: Macmillan & Co., 1964), *passim* and esp. p. 121.

[2]In "Understanding a Primitive Society," *Religion and Understanding*, ed. D. Z. Phillips (Oxford: Blackwell, 1967), reprinted from *American Philosophical Quarterly* 1 (1964).

[3]*Philosophy*, 42 (1967).

[4]Cf. Winch in Phillips, *Religion and Understanding*, pp. 27–28.

[5]Winch, in Phillips, *Religion and Understanding*, p. 31.

[6]MacIntyre, in Hick, *Faith and the Philosophers*, p. 121.

[7]Cf. W. D. Hudson, "Some Remarks on Wittgenstein's Account of Religious Belief," *Talk of God*, Royal Institute of Philosophy Lectures, vol. 2, 1967-68. (New York: St. Martin's Press; London: Macmillan & Co., 1969), pp. 45–49, where he comments on the view that religion has a "standard of sense and nonsense" different from that "generally accepted in our ... culture" and the implications of this view for the meaning of "petition" in prayer contexts. Hudson does not feel that the program required of this view can be carried through successfully because, if it could be, "petition" in prayer contexts would not mean what it ordinarily means, and in prayer contexts it does mean what it ordinarily means.

[8]Cf. Winch, *op. cit.*, pp. 23–24 and 33 ff. "Theoretical interest" is Winch's term. Theoretical interests or theoretical concerns may be various; but those Winch seems to be referring to, or at any rate those I will refer to, are investigatory concerns with hypotheses.

[9]G. E. Evans-Pritchard, *Witchcraft, Oracles and Magic Among the Azande* (Oxford: Clarendon Press, 1937), p. 25.

[10]This reason may not be precisely as Winch would state it; certainly its development is not pursued by Winch. Nevertheless it seems to me that Winch's comments implicitly contain both.

[11]Cf. I. C. Jarvie and J. Agassi, "The Problem of the Rationality of Magic," *The British Journal of Sociology* 18 (1967).

[12]Kai Nielsen, "Wittgensteinian Fideism," *Philosophy* 42 (1967), p. 193.

[13]Nielsen casts the argument only in terms of the concept of reality.

[14]Nielsen, "Wittgensteinian Fideism," p. 203.

[15]Nielsen, "Wittgensteinian Fideism," p. 203.

5

the ontological principle

and god's existence

5

Central to traditional Judaeo-Christian religion and perhaps to most religions are the existence of God and belief in Him. Often, however, questions regarding the nature and existence of God are a welter for believer and nonbeliever alike. This is not purely a historical comment. Long enduring confusions about God's existence and nature persist and have even deepened recently. Consider the spectrum of things contemporaneously said about God's existence.

(1) God, by his very nature, exists.
(2) Whether there is a God is an open question.
(3) The concept of existence does not apply to God.
(4) God, by his very nature, does not exist.

The first, of course, is the heart of Anselm's ontological argument, while the last is the heart of J. N. Findlay's ontological argument. The second and third, unlike the first and last, are maintained by both believers and nonbelievers. While the four as arranged present a definite spectrum, no two appear to be compatible. Yet each of them is espoused today.

In the following pages, each of these four is discussed.

(1) *God, by his very nature, exists.* This is the ontological principle around which turns Anselm's ontological argument. It has been criticized by Guanilo, Aquinas, Kant, G. E. Moore and generally by philosophers since its inception. The criticism usually voiced can be put in different ways: existence is not a predicate (Kant); "exists" does not stand for an attribute or property (Moore); from one's understanding that the name "God" signifies something than which nothing greater can be conceived, it follows only that it exists mentally, not that it exists actually (Aquinas); the ontological argument at most shows us the hypothetical excellence of a being than which none greater can be conceived, leaving it yet to be proven that such a being exists in reality (Guanilo). According to how this criticism is put, it is stronger or weaker, and each of the above formulations, except perhaps Guanilo's, appears to be unnecessarily weak because each claims too much. For instance, it is not clear why existence in some circumstances cannot be a predicate.[1] One who has discovered unicorns deep in the Himalayas might dub them "unihorses" and in a quasi-scientific fashion define "unihorse" as a "unicorn that exists"; then he could truly say that, given the meaning of "unihorse," those unicorns that are unihorses exist, but those that are not do not exist. The first statement Kant seems to deny,[2] while Moore appears to deny the second.[3] Further, despite Aquinas, there seems to be no good reason why one cannot put "actual existence" as well as "mental existence" into a concept; indeed, it is actual existence that is part of the concept of the "unihorse." Nevertheless the kernel of all these criticisms, when winnowed out, is right and is completely destructive of the ontological argument. Simply put, the kernel is: No concept can carry within itself a guarantee of its application (although it can rule it out, as does the concept of a 400° circle), for the meaning of any term that can apply to something is compatible with that meaning in fact applying to something or to nothing. That this is so becomes perfectly clear when we realize that we can simultaneously 1) understand that unihorses by definition actually exist and 2) intelligibly ask if there are such things.

The ontological principle, then, may in one way be true. It would be true if the concept of God were like the definition of "unihorse." If so, however, it and the ontological argument would be misguided because even if God were a necessarily existing being (actually existed by definition), it would still be an open question whether there were this God we conceive thus. But the ontological principle may be true in another way as well; it may be true not simply as a definitional statement that leaves open the question of the definition's application, but also as an existential statement that answers that question. If the principle is true in this sense we must see that it is true, and in a way quite different from seeing that our definition of "God" includes existence. What may be involved in coming to see that God must exist in this significant way was pointed to by J. J. C. Smart. At the end of an article in which he considered and refuted the main arguments for God's existence, Smart says this:

> ... let us ask 'Why should anything exist at all?' Logic seems to tell us that the only answer which is not absurd is to say, 'Why shouldn't it?' Nevertheless, though I know how any answer on the lines of the cosmological argument can be pulled to pieces by a correct logic, I still feel I want to go on asking the question ... That anything should exist at all does seem to me a matter for the deepest awe.[4]

The religious person confronted by the world in just this way, may ask this question in awe.[5] No such answer as "Because the earth was spun off from the sun" will do, for this question concerns the sun too. The only adequate answer is "Because there is God"; that is, a being unlike all others in that the question *cannot* be asked about Him. And the question cannot be asked about God, for unlike the sun and everything else, God's existence is dependent on nothing else. What the religious person thinks he sees in seeing that this question is answered only by God is this: Given the world, about which this question is asked, there must be a God who by His very nature exists and upon whom the world depends. This is not to say that it follows from God's existence being dependent on nothing else that he exists; it is to say that since only God's existence is dependent on nothing else, only God can answer the religious person's question about the world. In this manner the religious person may come to see that God by his very nature exists. But while what he may come to see is the truth of the ontological principle, he will only come to see it by asking a question about the world. That is, he will realize that there must be a God *given that there is a world;* he will not come to see simply that the concept of God is such that it includes existence. This is the existential discovery that the concept of God applies, not the discovery that the definition of God includes existence. My point is not that religious persons do in fact make this discovery, but that this discovery can be distinguished very clearly from a definitional discovery. Of course to make this discovery, it must be that one asks in awe the question Smart articulated or another near to it, and it must be that he pursues it to its only possible answer. The prerequisite here is overcoming the ambivalence Smart felt about the sense of the question. Perhaps to feel the proper awe and to see the sense of the question one must already believe in God or be on the edge of believing. Perhaps the nonreligious person can only sense the logic but cannot pursue the question to its answer because he cannot countenance the question. (For that matter, this may be so for some religious people as well.) If this is right, then a precondition for seeing that there is a God *in this way* is believing in God, but this should not be too surprising.

Also, if this is right, we have a way of seeing that there is a God distinct from what I have called a nonhypothetical discovery. As I have tried to show, one need not believe beforehand to make a nonhypothetical discovery. One need not believe in evolution to discover evolution, or believe that he is jealous of his son to discover that he is, and one need not believe that there is a God to discover that God exists according to the nonhypothetical model of discovery. To be sure, the evidence that figures in the nonhypothetical sort of discovery is different from the evidence that relates to a hypothetical discovery, as we have discussed. But the difference is not that one must believe beforehand to see the evidence for what it is. Consequently, if one has to believe already to see that there is a God via the question "Why should there be anything?" the discovery he would make would be different from the nonhypothetical sort discussed (although generically nonhypothetical).

None of this counts toward re-establishing the ontological argument. In fact, if anything, it detracts still further from it as an argument. For, if the ontological principle as it is assumed by the argument is definitional, then the argument fails; and if it is existential, indicating that the concept applies, then it must be *seen* to be true, and so the argument is superfluous. (The same points would hold for the cosmological argument, I think.) Also, some questions remain regarding the exact nature of the God whose existence may be seen in this way. His nature must include His being dependent upon nothing else for His existence, or else "Because there is a God" would not finally answer the question "Why should there be anything?" And we can also say that everything—all that would not answer the question—depends upon Him for its existence. These seem to be the only attributes that God's nature must contain. C.B. Martin, commenting on what would answer the question "Why should there be anything?" says that one may indeed end with a being that has the two attributes we have just noted, and a third attribute of having always existed.[6] But, he says, such a being might be a star. One might wonder at this possibility, though, for such a being could be a star only if some stars are not dependent upon anything else for their existence. But stars are by their nature contingent things, one would think. The oddity of Martin's suggestion is brought into relief by considering whether such a being might be a pebble instead of a star. The absurdity of this suggestion is clear because it is clear that pebbles are contingent. Stars are less clearly contingent, perhaps, but still contingent. However, if the being whose existence one may come to see via this question cannot be a star or a pebble, still he is not seen to have all of the nature of the Judaeo-Christian God. For instance, he is not seen to be all-knowing, nor to be the remission of sins.

(2) *Whether there is a God is an open question.* Certainly many have asked the question: Is there this God of the Bible? It will be paradoxical indeed if their question turns out to be meaningless or is asked in every instance by one who does not know what "God" means. What I have pointed

out, though, makes it clear that this question could be meaningfully asked even if the ontological principle were true both definitionally and existentially. If it were true definitionally, this would mean that "God exists" is a necessary truth, true by definition, but the question of whether the concept of God applies would still be open, and hence the question "Is there this God of the Bible?" would make perfectly good sense. If the ontological principle were true existentially, then it would be true, given the world, that God by his very nature exists; that is, that the concept of God applies. One who had seen the truth of the ontological principle in this way would not himself ask if there were a God, but while he would not, the question would still be meaningful to him and could yet be asked by others.

It is only those who think that the ontological argument is valid who would rule out this question as a meaningless, confused question asked by one who does not understand what "God" means. Thus Norman Malcolm, who subscribes to the ontological argument in one form, says that anyone who asks if there is the God of the Bible fails to understand what "God" means[7] (or the concept of God, or the nature of God as the Bible presents it). This seems quite paradoxical, particularly when we bear in mind that Bible scholars can ask this question, and that even those who believe in God may in moments of doubt ask this question. Malcolm must say that even these do not know what "God" means.

The form of the ontological argument Professor Malcolm subscribes to claims that necessary existence, not existence is a requirement of our conception of God. However, even if there is a second form of the ontological argument here, there still seems to be the meaningful and open question "Does this God you speak of and conceive of thus exist?" and this is to say the argument in this form also fails. Whether we say that the concept of God includes existence or necessary existence, what we are saying is that "God exists" is a necessary truth; that is, that the definitional ontological principle is true. But as I have tried to make clear, while this may be so, nevertheless it would be an open question whether this God we speak of exists, whether this concept applies.

Yet at one point in his article on the ontological arguments, Malcolm draws our attention to something that may be very important for an understanding of Anselm's *Proslogion*. He says that if we look at the Ninetieth Psalm we will find there "the idea of the necessary existence and eternity of God."[8] Thus, he suggests, when Anselm drew God's necessary existence out of the concept of God he was working from the concept of God in fact found in the Bible. This may or may not be right: I am not sure that because in the Psalms it says "even from everlasting to everlasting, thou art God" we should say that "God exists" is necessarily true. But if we do, all we are saying is that God exists by definition, that the definitional ontological principle is true. And since the application of the concept of God would still be an open question, it is academic to argue at length about the truth of the ontological principle as a definitional statement. However, if we look again at the Psalms we will find something besides the Biblical concept of God, and it is this other thing that it seems to me important to note. In the Ninetieth Psalm we find:

> Lord thou has been our
>   dwelling place in all generations. . . .
> Thou turnest man back to the dust. . . .
> Thou dost sweep men away; they are like a
>   dream, like grass which is
>   renewed in the morning. . . .

And in the Ninety-third Psalm we find:

> The Lord reigns; he is robed in majesty;
> The Lord is robed, he is girded with
>   strength. Yes, the world is established;
>   it shall never be moved. . . .
> . . . . Mightier than the thunders of many waters,
> mightier than the waves of the sea, the Lord on
> high is mighty.

What we find here is the realization that all things depend upon God—mountains, men, and the turning of the generations; the realization that God establishes the world. Men are like a dream that fades away, while God is God from everlasting to everlasting. Here is the idea of the contingency of all things except God. I suggest that it is not by accident that Malcolm looks to the Psalms for Anselm's inspiration. But what we find there is not a concept of God such that God necessarily exists, or, if that, not that alone; what we find is the setting of awe in which a believer may come to see that, given the world, God necessarily exists. This is not the ontological principle of the ontological argument, but the ontological principle in its existential statement, which makes the argument superfluous.

Let us recall that Anselm in the *Proslogion* is a man of faith addressing God, not a skeptic or agnostic settling a dispute with himself. Further, I suggest, he was a believer in awe who *saw* that God necessarily exists, given the world, and not simply a thinker exploring the definition of "God." He said that unless he believed he should not understand. This could be true if he came to see that there must be a God given the world, for belief may be a precondition here. If so, the fact that he proceeded to formulate the ontological argument indicates that he confused the ontological principle in its definitional and its existential statements, which he may have, for this confusion has no religious bias.

(3) *The concept of existence does not apply to God.* This has been said for several different reasons, some of which are rightheaded and some wrongheaded, it seems to me; in any case, though, I think it is false.

First, one might say that the concept of existence does not apply to God because the question "Does God exist?" is not a proper question.[9] The argument goes this way: The question "Do electrons exist?" is not a proper question because either it would be asked by the uninitiated in Physics, for whom "electron" would have no clear meaning, or by the initiated, for whom the question would not arise. So, too, with "Does God exist?" Just as "electron" gets its meaning from a physical theory in which it plays a part, so too "God" gets its meaning from the part it plays in religious discourse and rites. If one is not a believer he does not know the part it plays, and for him "God" would have no clear meaning, while if one were converted, the question would not arise.

All this, however, seems very questionable. First, religion is made into a kind of theory: God is assimilated to a theoretical entity. Now it may be that scientific theories retain their predictive power whether or not there really are electrons or genes or whatever theoretical entity is involved, and so whether there really are these entities need never be asked. But God hardly has such a role in religion. A religion such as Christianity is not an explanatory theory that would keep its predictive power whether or not there were a God, because it is not a theory in the first place. To assimilate God to a theoretical entity as this argument does is to come very close to talking about what Pascal and Buber call the God of the Philosophers and not the God of Religion. The God of the Philosophers is a postulated entity thought to be needed to explain something (e.g., the *élan vital* or Berkeley's God), and inasmuch as such a God functions as a predictive device perhaps the question of its existence need never arise, any more than the question of an electron's existence. But if God is the God of Religion His existence is most emphatically imperative for believers. They would hardly intelligibly believe in God, or pray to God if they thought that there were no God or, for all they know or cared, there were no God.

Second, while it may be that questions of the existence of theoretical entities need never arise and would never arise within a scientific theory, still it can be intelligibly asked if there are electrons or genes, even by scientists. So such questions are not improper in the requisite sense.

Third, if it were true that the concept of existence does not apply to God, some odd things would follow. Conversion to Christianity is thought of as involving an acceptance of a number of beliefs, the primary one being a belief in God. The first step in conversion is learning what these beliefs are; the second step is accepting them. Often, between these two steps, there is on the part of the convert a struggle to believe, for many of the beliefs he must accept are hard to accept. The hardest to believe, perhaps, is that there is a God. But if "existence" does not apply to God, then there should be nothing for the convert to struggle to believe. There should be no gap between learning what Christians mean by "God" and believing in him. But there is for many converts. Further, if "existence" does not apply to God, it should not be the case that believers are sometimes plagued by doubts about whether there is a God. That they are plagued by doubts, despite the fact that they know the role "God" plays in religious discourse should not be news.

However, if there are wrongheaded reasons for thinking that the concept of existence does not apply to God, there are also rightheaded reasons. The concept of existence does not apply to God, one might say, because the statement "God exists" is a proposition, and religious faith is not belief in the truth of propositions, but belief in and acceptance of a notion of "God." The very last question to ask about God is whether he exists.[10] Either one has faith and accepts the notion of "God" or one does not. Perhaps we would have essentially the same reason if it were said that "existence" does not apply to God because the belief *that* God exists is not a religious belief at all.[11] Both these reasons appear to be essentially rightheaded. What they point out is that religious faith is much more than an acceptance of a proposition. Propositions may be given an indifferent acceptance, but the acceptance of or belief in God cannot be treated indifferently. It is the acceptance of God or belief in God that is at the core of religion, not a propositional belief that God exists. However, even so it does not appear to be true that "existence" does not apply to God. Granted that it is rightheaded to point out that it is not a religious belief "that God exists," it does not follow that belief in God does not logically presuppose a belief that God exists; in actual fact it does. That is, if one believes in God, he must believe that there is the God he believes in.[12] This is not to say that the belief that there is a God precedes belief in God chronologically, but it is to say that the concept of existence applies to God.

(4) *God, by his very nature, does not exist.* This is the conclusion of J. N. Findlay's counterpart to Anselm's ontological argument. Briefly, Professor Findlay's argument is this: If God is to satisfy the religious conception, he must be a being whose existence and excellences we cannot "conceive away" (we should not be able to conceive of God as not existing). But "modern views" make it absurd to speak of such a being and attribute existence to him. Thus it is of the essence of God, as an adequate religious object, that He not exist.[13]

Findlay is looking into the concept of God, as Anselm seemed to be doing, but what he sees is not the necessary existence of God, but His necessary nonexistence. Given that God is conceived of as a necessarily existing being, he cannot exist, because necessary existence is impossible or nonsensical since existence is always contingent. Pivotal to Findlay's argument is the view that the statement "God exists" cannot be necessarily true; however, there

seems to be no reason to think that this is so. As far as the definitional statement of the ontological principle is concerned, it may not be clear that it is
true (as Malcolm maintains), but it could be. Consequently, Findlay cannot
draw his conclusion with these premises. Of course it is yet open to him to
argue that the antithesis of the ontological principle in its existential statement
is true; that is, that God by his very nature cannot exist as something we can
discover extradefinitionally in one way or another. Naturally, any such understanding of God will be at odds with that of believers. If we raise the question
of which understanding is right, Findlay's or the believer's, something interesting emerges. Clearly, if we come to see that God by his nature does exist,
given the world, then he *can* exist because he *does* exist. And, although one
may doubt the truth of the ontological principle in its existential statement,
still something of the way one comes to see its truth can be understood. When
we look for the analogue on Findlay's side, however, there is none. There is
no analogous way in which Findlay could come to see the truth of a non-
existential ontological principle. Believers may come to see that God necessarily exists by seeing that without him there would be no world. This they
may come to see by seeing the relevance of the question "Why should anything
exist at all?" Is there an analogous question that Findlay might ask? It seems
not. The nearest candidate is a question concerning the existence of evil:
"Why is there evil if there is a God of love?" But Findlay is not thinking of
evil and its possible incompatibility with a loving God. Even if he were it
would not have helped, for this question if countenanced can be answered in
a number of ways; one is "Because there is no God," but another is "Because
God has a purpose, one which we can see only darkly." This question, once
countenanced, does not necessarily lead to the answer that there is no God;
on the other hand, the question "Why should anything exist at all?" *once it
is countenanced* does necessarily lead to the answer that there is a God, it
seems. If we look closer to Findlay's concern for what shows him there is no
God, we go further afield. Findlay's concern is with the relation between God
and contingent objects. What question is there here that might lead us to see
that there is no God? There is one question here, of course: "Why are there
contingent objects?" But this question, if it leads anywhere, leads in the
opposite direction.

The indications are, then, that Findlay's antiontological principle is false.
If it is meant definitionally, it is false because contrary to Findlay's argument,
it may be that something—a unihorse or God—necessarily exists by definition.
If it is meant as the antithesis to the ontological principle in its existential
statement, then one wonders how it can be seen to be true. There appears to
be no way to see its truth, in contrast to possibly seeing the truth of the existential ontological principle.

If indeed the ontological principle in its existential statement is true, then
this is something that one must come to see. It is reported that men have in

the past come to this discovery. If they have, they have by asking the question we noted: "Why should anything exist at all?" or one akin to it. But first one must ask the question. And one comes to ask this question, and not merely mouth the words, only when he sees the world as a place of awe.

Notes

[1]See Frank B. Ebersole, "Whether Existence is a Predicate," *The Journal of Philosophy* 60 (1963); reprinted with some revisions in his *Things We Know* (Eugene, Oregon: University of Oregon Books, 1967).

[2]In his criticism of the Cartesian form of the ontological argument in the *Critique of Pure Reason*. The pertinent passage is reprinted in *The Existence of God,* ed. John Hick (New York: The Macmillan Company, 1964), p. 44.

[3]In "Is Existence a Predicate?" *Proceedings of the Aristotelian Society,* supplementary vol. 15, 1936; reprinted in Moore's *Philosophical Papers.* I am indebted to Mr. Dennis Holt for the example of the unihorse.

[4]J. J. C. Smart, "The Existence of God," *New Essays in Philosophical Theology,* eds. Antony Flew and Alasdair MacIntyre (New York: The Macmillan Company; London: SCM Press, 1955), p. 44. Smart's comments are in reference to Aquinas' Third Way.

[5]Cf. H. D. Lewis, *Our Experience of God* (London: George Allen & Unwin, 1959), p. 107 and *passim.*

[6]C. B. Martin, *Religious Belief* (Ithaca, New York: Cornell University Press, 1959), pp. 156–57.

[7]Norman Malcolm, "Anselm's Ontological Arguments," *The Existence of God, Knowledge and Certainty* (Englewood Cliffs, N.J.: Prentice-Hall, 1963), pp. 141 ff. and especially p. 161. Also in *The Existence of God,* ed. John Hick (New York: The Macmillan Company, 1964).

[8]Norman Malcolm, "Anselm's Ontological Arguments," p. 156.

[9]Cf. Smart, "The Existence of God," p. 41. I have drawn the argument that follows from Smart's article. Also cf. Alasdair MacIntyre, "The Logical Status of Religious Belief," *Metaphysical Beliefs,* 2nd ed., ed. Alasdair MacIntyre (London: SCM Press, 1970), p. 193.

[10]Cf. Stephen E. Toulmin, *An Examination of the Place of Reason in Ethics* (Cambridge: University Press, 1961), pp. 212 ff.

[11]Cf. Normal Malcolm, "Is it a Religious Belief that 'God Exists'?" *Faith and the Philosophers,* ed. John Hick (New York: St. Martin's Press; London: Macmillan & Co., 1964), pp. 103 ff.

[12]Cf. Antony Flew, *God and Philosophy* (New York: Harcourt Brace Jovanovich; London: Hutchinson, 1966), secs. 8.33–8.35.

[13]J. N. Findlay, "Can God's Existence Be Disproved?" *New Essays in Philosophical Theology,* eds. Antony Flew and Alasdair MacIntyre (New York: The Macmillan Company; London: SCM Press, 1955), p. 55. Also in J. N. Findlay, *Language, Mind and Value* (New York: Humanities Press; London: George Allen & Unwin, 1963). Reprinted from *Mind* 57 (1948). Findlay's argument is discussed by Malcolm in his "Anselm's Ontological Arguments."

II

religious knowledge

II

6

religious knowledge

and religious belief

6

Perhaps everyone or almost everyone who has ever believed in God has had doubts about his religion at some time in his life. Faith is not an easy thing to maintain; the seeds of doubt lie everywhere, it seems. It is particularly hard for one with a philosophical bent to believe in God. On this point St. Paul and Bertrand Russell are in agreement. There are many reasons why this is true, and some of the important ones have to do with the nature of religious belief, primarily belief in God, and religious knowledge, such as one's knowing that God's goodness is within him. When they look at religious belief and religious knowledge, many with a philosophical bent find themselves perplexed. The root cause of this perplexity is not a lack of clear evidence for what is believed and what is said to be known; although this is an important and related matter. The root lies deeper then that. The root concern is whether belief in God can be belief in the normal sense of "belief," and whether knowledge that one is saved by God's mercy can be knowledge in the normal sense of "knowledge." In fact many have come to suspect that while one who is religious may say that he believes in God, this belief is a peculiar kind of belief, which might come to something like a moral commitment and not be a belief in the normal sense at all. And while one who is religious may say that he knows certain things (e.g., that he is saved) he cannot know them in the full or secular sense. If these suspicions were right, then there would be a good reason for philosophers and for everyone not having faith. For if they were right, then there would be no religious belief or knowledge. Belief in God and knowledge that one is saved would be belief and knowledge in some special sense and not what we mean by "belief" and "knowledge" at all. What we shall do in this chapter is examine this tendency to think of religious belief as belief in a special sense and to think of religious knowledge as knowledge in a special sense or of a special kind. The primary concern at this point is with the tendency as it relates to religious knowledge and we shall begin with it.

II-A

Not only skeptics have followed this tendency. Even philosophers doing religious apologetics have contributed to it; St. Thomas Aquinas is a notable example. In discussing the question of whether the existence of God is self-evident, Aquinas concedes that the knowledge of God's existence is naturally implanted in all of us but says that it only allows us to know that God exists in a "general and confused way."[1] Knowledge in a general and confused way is opposed to knowledge in an absolute sense. Absolute knowledge that God exists would apparently be obtained through a demonstration of God's existence. If so, it would be what he calls elsewhere "scientific knowledge." Aquinas is not talking about knowing God's nature perfectly as opposed to knowing it less than perfectly. He draws or recognizes this distinction, and it is one that is recognizable to us all. But the point that Aquinas is making does not depend upon this distinction. His point is that we will not know *that* God exists in the absolute sense unless we can propound a demonstration. The distinction that he has in mind is one between two senses in which we might know *that* God exists: a confused sense and an absolute sense. Thus if all demonstrations fail, he has provided the philosopher in us with the conclusion we apparently should draw: We can only know that there is a God in a confused way, not in the absolute way in which presumably other things are known.

How does Aquinas explicate the difference between general and confused knowledge and absolute knowledge? He does so by means of a single example. Aquinas says that to know that God exists in a general and confused way is not to know absolutely that God exists, "just as to know that someone is approaching is not the same as to know that Peter is approaching, even though it is Peter who is approaching." We apparently are to understand this example as an example of knowing something in a general and confused way as opposed to knowing it in an absolute way. What, though, is the something that is known in a general and confused way that might be known in an absolute way? On the one hand it is known that someone is approaching, and on the other hand it is known that Peter is approaching. Is the something "that someone is approaching"? It seems not. If it is only known that someone is approaching, however well it is known, it is not known in an absolute or a confused way that Peter is approaching; rather it is not known that Peter is approaching at all, for it is not known who is approaching. Is the something that is known, then, "that Peter is approaching"? Again it seems not. Certainly if it is known that Peter is approaching, it is known that someone is approaching. But they are known equally well. And again knowing that someone is approaching is not a confused version of knowing that Peter is approaching. If one knows that someone is approaching and this is all he knows, he will not know who is approaching. If he finds out that Peter is approaching, then he *knows* that Peter is approaching; he does not simply appreciate that someone is approaching. Aquinas has not given us an example of knowing something in his two senses or ways; he has given us an example in which on the one hand one thing—that someone is approaching—is known and on the other hand something else—that Peter is approaching—is known.

It seems, then, that although Aquinas talks about different senses in which one might know things, he does not make clear these different senses. So far we have not been shown exactly how to think of religious knowledge as knowledge in a different, special sense, nor why we should try.[2]

II-B

Kierkegaard is another writer on Christianity who has suggested that religious knowledge might be knowledge in a special sense. He has not said this in so many words; however, he has laid the groundwork for our reaching this conclusion. Let us look at what Kierkegaard says that might lead us to think this.[3] Kierkegaard was concerned about a pervasive lack of faith among his contemporaries. In his time he saw a plethora of church-attending members of Christendom, but no true Christians. To be a Christian one had to accept Christ on faith, he said, but in his eyes, none of his contemporaries did. Rather they were striving to be "objectively certain" that Christ was the son of God. What Kierkegaard means by this phrase is not too clear, but it is relatively clear that he opposes "objective certainty" to faith, and commitment, and belief. Also he tends to identify it with what one has when he knows something. Kierkegaard is in effect saying that to be a Christian and to have faith that there is a God, one cannot know that there is a God. This *seems* right; knowledge and faith do *seem* to exclude one another. If I have just checked and know that my driver's license has not expired, I do not have faith that it has not expired. If I accept it on faith that the city I live in will become a better place to live, I hope it will but I do not know that it will.

If we have understood Kierkegaard, what would he or we say about Job's cry of faith: "I know my redeemer liveth"? The temptation is strong to distinguish Job's kind of knowledge from the ordinary kind, which we will assume Kierkegaard was talking about, and to allow knowledge in Job's sense to be compatible with faith. Knowledge in the ordinary sense, we will say, which has as its basis evidence or proof, remains incompatible with faith and commitment. It is only Job's kind of knowledge, which is not knowledge in the ordinary sense, that is compatible with faith. But once this step is taken, we have reached the conclusion that knowing as Job knows is *not* knowing that one's redeemer liveth—or, expanding the argument—not knowing that one's sins are forgiven or that one is saved. For when we deny that these are known in the ordinary sense, we are saying that what we ordinarily mean by "knowledge" does not apply.

We find ourselves about to embrace this conclusion because we have distinguished between two senses of knowledge. We have done this because Kierkegaard pressed upon us, or we pressed upon ourselves, the proposition that knowledge and faith are mutually exclusive, which the Job case led us to modify to read that ordinary knowledge and faith are mutually exclusive. So we ended up with ordinary knowledge and the kind of knowledge Job had, which is not knowledge in the ordinary sense. Thus what led us to make this distinction between the two kinds of knowledge was the proposition that knowledge and faith are mutually exclusive. It might behoove us, then, to look at this proposition a bit more closely. Certainly, as we observed, if I know that my driver's license has not expired, I do not have faith that it has not, and if I accept it on faith that the city I live in will become a better place to live, I hope it will, but I do not know that it will. Asked if I know whether my driver's license has expired, I might reply that I do know, that I checked it just this morning and saw that it is valid for another month. There is no room for faith here because no one has any doubts; the driver's license and the expiration date are right there in my pocket. Asked what I think of the city in which I live, I might reply that I look for it to improve immensely in the coming years. I have faith that it will, but of course I do not know that it will. I have not studied the area, nor do I know of any plans by the city fathers. Having nothing to go on, I accept its coming improvement on faith. These two examples support the proposition that faith and knowledge are mutually exclusive.

Now consider a rather different case. A young man's father has been arrested and charged with a serious crime, and the district attorney is confident that he will be convicted. The son, however, says that he knows his father is innocent, because he knows what kind of man he is. He has lived with him all his life and says that his father is incapable of committing the crime with which he is charged. While the son says that he knows his father is innocent, we might say something quite different. If we are acquainted with the strength of the district attorney's case, we might say that the son has a great deal of faith in his father's innocence. Let us say that it turns out that the father is innocent and that, despite the seemingly incontrovertible evidence against him, his innocence is proved. The son said he *knew* his father was innocent, while we who were impressed by the evidence against the father, spoke of the son's faith. In the denouement we come to see that the son *did* know. It is not the case that the son just hoped or suspected that his father was innocent; he *knew* he was. He was sure of his father's innocence, and he had the right to be sure. He was able to tell us how he knew: This man he had lived with so long and knew so intimately was incapable of committing such a crime. *Yet, even though he knew his father was innocent, faith was not excluded.* The son could have thanked God for helping him maintain his faith in the face of the many doubts that the others had. If he had done so, he would not have been thanking God for his knowledge; he would have been thanking God for helping him to maintain what he strove to maintain, his faith; one does not strive to maintain knowledge. Now it may be that knowing something is not compatible with having doubts about it or that thing not being certain, but having faith in these cases does not require that one *have* doubts or that the matter be dubious; it only requires that there be doubts on the part of others (or at least possible doubts) which are resisted. Perhaps faith and knowledge are most often not found together, but they are not mutually exclusive. They can be found together when there are doubts to which one who knows might, but does not, fall prey.[4] In the case of the father and son we can say that we should have listened to the son: *he* knew his father was innocent. Or we can say that the son's faith has been rewarded. We can say either, for both are the case. In this example, unlike in the first two, faith and knowledge coexist. So we reading Kierkegaard need not be concerned that knowing there is a God will preclude faith. Just as the son who knew that his father was innocent might thank God for helping him maintain his faith, so too Job could know there is a God and still thank God for helping him maintain his faith in the adversity he suffered. Of course the point here is not that Job *did* know that there is a God. It might remain in question whether Job knew. The point is that Job's knowing that there is a God, if he knew, would not exclude his having faith for which he might thank God.

Consequently, since faith and knowledge need not exclude one another, the Job case need not tempt us to create two senses of knowledge. *It is not that things are known in different senses, it is rather that things are known in different circumstances.* Sometimes when we know something there is no question about what we know; other times when we know something there is a question—in fact all the evidence might seem to be against what we know and no one else might think what we know is true. At such times, when people strongly doubt what we say, they will speak of our faith, and we might too in the face of their doubts. But in both kinds of cases, regardless of what people think, the facts remain what they are and if we know, we know. The difference between the two kinds of cases is in what other people think and say and in the doubts that they have and that we resist; it is not in our knowledge.

Perhaps it was what differentiates these two kinds of cases of knowing something that Kierkegaard had in the back of his mind when he spoke of *"objective* certainty." If Kierkegaard meant by "objectively certain" something like "broadly accepted, free of any question on the part of anyone and free of the viable possibility of doubt," then he seems to be right in saying that when something is objectively certain there is no room for faith. It is Job's going against the grain of what people think and not falling prey to questions and doubts that allows us to speak of faith in the Job case. In the case of the son who knows his father is innocent, again we may speak of his faith because of the doubts he might have had but resisted. Conversely, it is because there is no possible question about it that there is no room for faith in the case of my knowing that my driver's license has not expired. Also we can see that if Kierkegaard thought of anyone's knowing anything as always being like my knowing my driver's license has not expired, he would conclude that knowledge is not compatible with faith. And it seems that this is what he did. When he thought of someone knowing something, he thought of someone knowing a mathematical proposition.[5] That is, he thought of something about which there could be no questions or doubts on the part of anyone. If Kierkegaard had concentrated on other instances more like the case of the son knowing his father is innocent, then we might not have had urged upon us the proposition that knowledge and faith exclude each other. And that might have meant one less reason for thinking religious knowledge is knowledge in a special sense.[6]

III-A

Whatever Kierkegaard says or does not say about knowledge excluding faith, though, there would remain the most abiding reason for thinking that religious knowledge is not what we ordinarily mean by "knowledge." That reason might be put this way: The basis of religious knowledge is so weak compared to the basis of secular knowledge, that when something is known in the religious sense it is not known in the secular sense at all. In a way this reason was involved in both Aquinas' argument and our construction of Kierkegaard's argument. Aquinas thought that absolute knowledge of God's existence arose from a demonstration, and Kierkegaard, in thinking of knowledge, thought of someone knowing a mathematical proposition. Aquinas goes on to provide us with a contrasting, weaker kind of knowledge—what he calls knowing in a "general and confused way." In regard to Kierkegaard, we must do it ourselves, but he has set the stage. The core idea is that religious knowledge is not knowledge in the full sense because its basis or support is not as strong as that necessary for knowledge in the full sense.

We should look carefully at what this idea presupposes—namely that knowledge is based on a support or grounds. At first glance this idea appears to be largely correct. Certainly if someone were to say he knows that a friend has had an accident, but could give us no reasons to substantiate what he says, we would understandably conclude that he does not know. Perhaps he is anxious about his friend, but he does not know he has had an accident. With no reason to think his friend has had an accident he might *feel* that there has been an accident, but since he has no reason to think so, he cannot know it. This point, however put, does not mean that knowledge must have a support or grounds.

In fact we should say rather that knowledge has no grounds, although this may sound a bit paradoxical. To help dispel this air of paradox let me explain what is not meant. It is not meant that knowing is "just knowing" or "knowing in my heart even though I have no reason." One might "just know" that there has been an accident, or one might "know in his heart" that someone is still alive although he has no reason to think so and every reason to think him dead. I do not mean to equate knowing with either of these, for neither is a case of knowing, as can be made clear. If in the first case he who "just knows" there has been an accident were told that there had been an accident, he could quite correctly refer to his being told as his learning that there had been an accident. Similarly he who knows in his heart that someone is still alive, but has no reason to think this, can learn that the person in question miraculously is still alive. Of course one cannot learn what one already knows.

So what is meant by saying that knowledge has no grounds is not that knowledge is like "just knowing," that is, that one can know something when he has no reason to think it so. What is meant is the following. If someone is asked how he knows something, such as that a friend has had an accident, of course he can reply and tell us how he knows, assuming that he has not forgotten. But in telling us how he knows he does not give us the grounds upon which he knows it. If someone thought, believed, or said that a friend has had an accident, then he might give us his grounds for thinking, believing, or saying this—not so with knowing it. There is no question "On what grounds do you know that?" that corresponds to the question "On what grounds do you think that?" Once we have found out his grounds for thinking that his friend has had an accident, we can evaluate them: There might or might not be some basis for his thinking what he does. But if he knows it, he can hardly know it for bad reasons, or for good reasons. Corresponding to the verdict "You have no reason to think that" there is no verdict "You have no reason to know that," and corresponding to the verdict "You have good reason to think that" there is no verdict "You have good reason to know that." When some-one thinks, believes, or says that a friend has had an accident he might make it clear that his reasons are not conclusive. "I believe that there has been an accident, but what I have to go on is not definite," he might say. If he knows that there has been an accident, he cannot explain that he knows there has been an accident, but what he has to go on is indefinite. It may be that if he thinks there has been an accident, he realizes that he might be wrong, but if he knows there has been an accident, there is no room for such a realization. He cannot tell us, "I know there has been an accident, but I might be wrong." The crucial difference between thinking or believing on the one hand and knowing on the other may be brought out this way: One might think or believe something for good reasons or for bad reasons, but if one attempts to tell us how he knows something and only gives us a bad reason for saying he knows it, then he does not give us his bad reason for knowing it but shows us that he does not know it at all.

None of this, of course, entails that different people cannot come to know something in different ways. One person might find out that the temperature is 70° by looking at the thermometer, and another might find it out by hearing it on the radio. This does not mean that they have different grounds for knowing that the temperature is 70°. It means that they found out from different sources. And *if* each has found out, one's finding out is neither better nor worse than the other's finding out *in the way* that the one's grounds for believing something could be better or worse than the other's grounds.

Yet very good philosophers have thought that knowledge was based on grounds and that there were different senses of knowledge. Norman Malcolm is such a philosopher.[7] We should note one point in particular that he makes. It is a point that he thinks shows that knowledge can be more or less certain, depending upon the strength of its grounds. He observes that if one is asked, for example, "Are you sure that $92 \times 16 = 1472$?" one might reply, "I *know* that it is; I have just now calculated it," but one might also reply, "I know that it is; but I will calculate it again to *make sure*." Granted, if one gives the second reply it may *seem* that he is saying his knowledge is not so certain for his grounds are not as strong as they could be. But what Malcolm fails to note is that in such cases calculating or checking the answer again has the function of reassuring the other person—the one who asked. By checking again I do not improve my grounds for knowing; rather I make it easier for him to believe that I know what I tell him is true. Of course sometimes I check what I know when no one has asked me if I know, and in these cases my checking does not have the function of reassuring another person. But it does not follow that it therefore has the function of reassuring me. As I pre-pare to leave on a trip I may say to myself, "I know I turned off the lights, but I'll just check once more." This may be the fourth time that I have checked. Part of this routine can be put down to my being in a nervous state, which is to say that, after about the third time, I no longer am checking; I am simply yielding to a nervous habit. But there may also be a very good reason for my checking the lights a fourth time—namely that even if I know *now* that the lights are out, later after I am on the trip doubts may plague me; but if I check again I will more likely be able to remember later on that the lights were indeed turned off. Thus even in this kind of case checking again to make sure does not have the function of strengthening one's grounds for knowing; it is more a mnemonic device.

If we are to distinguish between knowledge in the ordinary sense and religious knowledge on the basis of the relative strength of their grounds, we might wonder how to go about it—not because it is so difficult to evaluate the different grounds, but because knowledge does not appear to have grounds at all. While there are grounds for believing, thinking, or saying something that might be better or worse, in the case of knowing something there is nothing corresponding that might be better or worse. Consequently, it appears confused to speak of one man knowing something more strongly, on stronger grounds, and another man knowing it less strongly, on weaker grounds. And for the same reason it appears confused in the same way to speak of different kinds of knowledge, differentiated according to the strength of their grounds.

III-B

We have been examining the idea that knowledge is based on grounds because that idea, if true, would seem to provide a strong reason for thinking that there are senses of knowledge. Knowledge in one sense would have stronger grounds, whereas knowledge in another sense would have weaker grounds. A corollary to the idea that knowledge has grounds is the idea that knowledge and belief are two of several cognitive states that arrange themselves along a scale according to the strength of their support. This idea supports and is supported by the idea that knowledge has grounds. Since it consequently lends indirect support to the idea that there are senses of knowledge, it will be worth our while to examine it too.

If knowledge and belief are both on a scale of cognitive states separated primarily by the degree of support they have, then if one has enough support to know something, he will necessarily have enough to believe it as well. Knowledge then becomes belief plus something, namely more support or better grounds. It might also be thought that certainty is attendant with this extra support; whether this is maintained or not is not important as far as our issue is concerned. The important question is whether knowledge comes to belief plus something, whatever that something may be. If it does not, then of course it cannot come to belief plus extra support. This idea that knowledge is belief plus something is an old one and a tenacious one. Although it dates from the *Theaetetus* it is espoused today, and of course it is not without seeming support. The common phenomenon of one at first being a bit dubious, yet believing something, and then finding out for certain, and so coming to know that it is so, seemingly provides an obvious support. One at first believes and then with added support passes on to knowledge. That something like this happens cannot be contested. What can be contested is whether finding out for sure, and so coming to know, is a matter of acquiring more support so that finally one ends up still believing but on better or more adequate grounds and *this* is knowing. (The oddities of knowing on grounds have already been noted.) The question here is not whether one can half-heartedly believe and then come to know. The question is whether one can half-heartedly believe and then come to know, where knowing is a special kind of believing—believing plus something. In fact, all that this phenomenon we have noted shows is that one can at first half-heartedly believe and then come to know. That this knowing amounts to believing plus something has yet to be supported.

Something else that comes closer to providing a support for this view is the following. If we think that someone knows that a mutual friend is honest, and we ask him to support our contention that he is honest to someone else, and he turns around and says that he does not believe that our friend is honest, then we should no longer think that he knows our friend is honest. Put succinctly it seems that not believing entails not knowing, and this is as it should be, I suppose, if knowing is a special kind of believing.

Also in the way of a support is the following analysis. Sometimes when one is quite certain of something he will insist, "I don't believe it, I know it." However, it would be wrong to take this as a denial that he believes whatever it is of which he is certain. The correct analysis is that he no longer *just* believes it.

These points do seem to lend some support to the notion that knowledge is belief plus something. But if knowledge is belief plus something, then there should be no case in which one knows something but does not believe it. And some such contrary cases do exist. For instance, varying slightly the last case cited, we end up with such a contrary case. If one wants to impress upon us how certain he is of something *and* that the matter is really straightforwardly free from doubt, he might say of it, "It's not a matter of belief at all. It's common knowledge." In effect he is *not* saying "I don't (just) believe it, I know it," but rather, "It is not a matter of belief at all, there is no belief involved; it is something we all know." Here when it is said that something is known, it *is* being denied that it is believed.

Another kind of contrary case is presented by the following. Let us say that someone has learned something to be the case that he would never have suspected; for instance, he has learned that his brother to whom he is very close has betrayed him in some way. He knows this, for the facts are clear, yet he still finds it difficult to accept. "How could he do it? Even with his confession there before me," he says, "I find it difficult to believe that my brother would betray me. I know he did, but I just can't believe it." He knows that his brother has betrayed him, but he cannot bring himself to believe it. What this example points out is an element of difference between knowing and believing totally obscured by the view that knowledge is belief plus something. Sometimes to believe something one must force oneself; even with the facts clear before him he has to bring himself to believe, and he might not be able to do this. There is no bringing oneself to know or forcing oneself to know besides finding out,[8] so when the facts are clear in a case and yet one cannot bring himself to believe what is at stake, it will be known but not believed. It seems we were a bit hasty, then, when we concluded that not believing entails not knowing.

However, lest we be misled about this last case, we should immediately add the following. When one cannot accept the fact that his brother has betrayed him, he can nevertheless in a way answer in the affirmative the question "Do you believe your brother betrayed you?" He can do so when the question comes to "Are you aware that your brother has betrayed you?" or "Do you think it's your brother who betrayed you?" His answer will take the form "Yes, I'm aware that my brother betrayed me" or "Yes, it was my brother." Given that the question has one of these points, then one of these replies answers it. Notably in making neither reply does he say he *believes* that his brother betrayed him. And given another question, "Do you accept the fact that your brother has betrayed you?" his reply will drive the noted wedge between believing and knowing: "Yes, I know he betrayed me. That's clear unfortunately, but I just cannot believe that he would do such a thing."

So at least sometimes, as in the last examples, knowing does not involve believing. The idea that knowledge is belief plus something, then, apparently breaks down—and with it its support for the idea that there are senses of knowledge.

It seems that the tendency to think of religious knowledge as knowledge in a special sense does not have the justification that one might have thought. Of course this does not mean that Job knew that there is a God or that any man knows that God's goodness is with him. It does indicate, though, that a question as to whether a man knows God's goodness is with him is exactly that—a question as to whether he *knows*.

IV

So far in this chapter we have been concerned with the possibility that religious knowledge might be knowledge in a special sense and not knowledge in the ordinary sense at all. The other side of our concern is with religious belief and the possibility that it might be belief only in a special sense. We turn now to that concern. In great part it arises from reflections on the nature of belief that are parallel to earlier noted reflections on the nature of factual statements.

If one believes something, then, it is thought that 1) his belief will be based on grounds or evidence, unless the belief is arbitrary, 2) his belief can be shaken given some conceivable contingency, and 3) he knows what would contradict his belief and show it to be false, this being necessary for him to know what his belief denies and that being necessary for him to know what he believes.[9]

Clearly these conditions are fulfilled in a typical case of someone believing something. If I believe one thing and someone else believes something else regarding, say, the cause of a disease, then presumably 1) we each have our reasons for believing what we do, 2) if new evidence warrants it, each of us will relinquish his belief, and 3) each of us knows what would contradict his belief and show it to be false. Religious belief, on the other hand, does not on the surface appear to fulfill these conditions. 1) It does not appear to have grounds or evidence in the ordinary sense (though it is not to be counted as arbitrary), 2) it seems to be unshakeable (regardless of the contingency, the belief is not relinquished), and 3) it further appears to have no contradiction (it cannot be specified what is being denied, nor, consequently, what is being believed). Because it apparently does not fulfill these conditions it has been suggested that religious belief is not and cannot be what we ordinarily mean by "belief." Rather its expression has some other role, such as that of making an admonition or that of expressing a moral commitment.[10]

Now in fact it is not quite right to say that these conditions are not fulfilled by religious belief. Consider the first—that belief is based on grounds or evidence. One who believes in God might very well be able to tell us why he believes in God. He has at his disposal the Bible, which tells him about God. Also he might see God's goodness all about him and find God's support in his life and in others' lives. Not everyone accepts this as evidence. It is not evidence of the sort that relates to a hypothesis, but it might still be evidence.[11] Often, regarding all sorts of issues, there is no difficulty in gathering evidence, for it may abound; the difficulty is in seeing that it *is* evidence and does count for or against something. We will think that the first condition for belief is not met by religious belief only if we demand the kind of clear evidence one would cite in say, investigating the cause of a disease, that is, hypothetical evidence. It may be, as John Wisdom says, that everything is relevant to the question of whether there is a God—everything from the fall of a sparrow to the fading of a smile.[12] The difficulty is in seeing the relevance.

The second condition is that a belief can be shaken in some contingency. Again it is not quite right to think that a religious belief can never be shaken. One who believes in God may hope and pray that his belief will never be shaken and it may never be. But it may become so difficult for one to believe in God and His goodness that he will lose his belief. Job never ceased to believe in God, though it would have been understandable if he had. In evil times one might succeed in continuing to believe in God, or he might not. Adversity need not affect one directly to challenge his belief; for example, if one is struck by the suffering of the world as Ivan Karamazov was, his faith may be broken by this alone. It is just because one's belief in God may be shaken and broken in different contingencies that there is the prayer for strengthened faith.

The third condition is that he who believes something knows what his belief denies, so that he can know what it does not deny and what it is he believes. What this condition quite rightly points out is that if one knows what he believes, he knows what his belief denies. If one announces to us that he believes there are manticores but upon being questioned admits that he has no idea of what a manticore is, we would be justified (most often) in concluding that he only says he believes in manticores perhaps to impress us, and in any case he quite literally does not know what it is he believes. He could make it clear that he knows what he believes by giving us what might be called a filled out denial or its equivalent. That is, he could prove that he knows what he believes by telling us that his belief denies the nonexistence of creatures with the head of a man, the body of a lion, and the tail of a scorpion. One need not be able to specify in empirical or experimental terms what his belief denies, then. Only a filled out denial is needed; a denial in specific, empirical terms is not. (While there may be an empirical denial for the statement "There are manticores," there is none for the statement "There are succubi" where the filled in denial is that there are no female demons who visit sleeping men, and it is specified that they are undetectable, which rules out an empirical denial.) Now while one who believes in God cannot outline a crucial experiment that, given an adverse outcome, would conclusively show that there is no God (give an empirical denial), he can say what is not compatible with what he believes (give a filled out denial). The God in whom he believes is loving and concerned, not unconcerned and hateful. What is believed necessarily denies that God is either unconcerned or hateful.[13] So it is not quite right that religious belief has no contradiction, and that since what is being denied is unspecified, what is being believed is unspecified. One who believes in God can say what his belief excludes and what it includes. What he cannot do is offer tests which would show experimentally that there is or is not a God.

What does all this mean for our question: Is religious belief belief in a special sense? We have seen that in a way belief in God fulfills the three conditions we considered. But in a way it does not. It does not fulfill the conditions as a tentatively held belief, or hypothesis, does. Such a hypothesis would be held only as long and as firmly as the evidence justified. It would be shaken given any adverse evidence and would be relinquished immediately given strong evidence that it was wrong. Also what it denies is definable in experimental terms. Do these differences between a tentatively held belief and belief in God render belief in God not belief in the ordinary sense? If we are inclined to think so, perhaps we should consider a case of completely unreasonable belief. Here one knows what he is believing—that his wife is still alive after a terrible accident. But he believes it in the teeth of the clear facts, in this case the fact that she is dead. He announces that he does not want to hear what happened at the accident or to talk to witnesses. He is going to believe that she is still alive regardless of what anyone says (like Mitchell's partisan[14]). We can understand this. One can understand someone distraught clutching at imaginary straws. Notice, though, that this completely unreasonable belief, while it does not fulfill the conditions as the hypothesis does, does not fulfill the conditions as the religious belief does either. Here by fiat nothing is allowed to count against the belief, or at least not decisively. It is not that he prays his belief will remain unshaken, it is that he has resolved to believe and not to let anything count (decisively) against it. Should we say that this belief also is not belief in the ordinary sense and not what we mean by "belief"? Is it belief in a third sense then? Rather is it not a belief that is completely unreasonable, flying in the face of the facts as it does, but a belief nevertheless? In fact, if it were not a belief, the advice to "believe as the facts warrant and not as you want to believe" would be pointless. Notoriously this advice is not pointless. It appears then that we can distinguish among kinds of belief, such as, belief tentatively held during an investigation, religious belief which represents a commitment and is not tentatively held, and completely unreasonable belief held in opposition to the clear facts. All are kinds of beliefs. Not all are equally reasonable perhaps, but the differences among them do not arise from one being belief and another not, but from differences in the ways they are held.

It will be surprising to no one that belief in God often is not the most reasonable belief. If there is a discovery of God to be made, and if one has made it, then he knows that there is a God. But if he has not made such a discovery, then his belief is in a God whose influence and nearness are unseen and unknown. And perhaps belief in a God thus unseen must of necessity be at odds to some extent with reason. If so, it should not be surprising that such belief is difficult, and perhaps a gift, and that one might profess his belief and yet ask that his unbelief be helped. It would be surprising, though, if one asked—not that his belief be strengthened—but that he be allowed to believe in a special sense different from the ordinary sense of "believe." One wonders how to understand this request. Would it be a supplication to the God in whom he believes? It could hardly be a supplication if he did not believe in God, and if it is a supplication to the God in whom he believes then of course he believes in God.

Notes

[1]*Summa Theologica,* I, q.2, a.1, *Basic Writings of Saint Thomas Aquinas,* edited and annotated by Anton C. Pegis (New York: Random House, 1945). © 1945 by Random House, Inc.).

[2]Later on, in chap. 10, we shall return to Aquinas' category of "scientific knowledge" and examine its relation to knowledge created by faith (and revelation).

[3]See primarily the *Concluding Unscientific Postscript,* trans. David F. Swenson and Walter Lowrie (Princeton: Princeton University Press, 1941).

[4]Cf. Terence Penelhum, "Is a Religious Epistemology Possible?" *Knowledge and Necessity,* Royal Institute of Philosophy Lectures, vol. 3, 1968-69. (New York: St. Martin's Press; London: Macmillan & Co., 1970), pp. 279–80.

[5]Kierkegaard, *Training in Christianity,* p. 182. Actually Kierkegaard says that in the case of a mathematical proposition "the objectivity is given." That is, it is "objectively certain," and "objective certainty" is knowledge for Kierkegaard.

[6]We shall return to the view that knowledge and faith exclude each other in chap. 10, where it is examined as one of the chief candidates for the relation between knowledge and faith.

[7]See Norman Malcolm, "Knowledge and Belief," *Knowledge and Certainty* (Englewood Cliffs, N.J.: Prentice-Hall, 1963), pp. 62 ff; and in the same volume "A Definition of Factual Memory," pp. 228–29.

[8]Cf. Gilbert Ryle, *The Concept of Mind* (New York: Barnes & Noble, 1949), pp. 133–34.

[9]See the Appendix, Parts A and B, for a discussion of Antony Flew's falsification challenge, which presupposes a stringent version of this last condition as a condition for factual statements. Wittgenstein at one point apparently thought that *something like* these three conditions held for the normal use of "believe." See his *Lectures and Conversations on Aesthetics, Psychology and Religious Belief,* ed. C. Barrett (Berkeley and Los Angeles: University of California Press, 1966), pp. 53 ff.

[10]Cf. R. B. Braithwaite, *An Empiricist's View of the Nature of Religious Belief* (Cambridge: Cambridge University Press, 1955), reprinted in *The Existence of God,* ed. John Hick (New York: The Macmillan Company, 1964).

[11]The distinction between the kind of evidence that relates to hypotheses and the kind that relates to religious belief was developed in chap. 1.

[12]John Wisdom, "The Logic of God," *Paradox and Discovery* (Oxford: Blackwell, 1965), p. 21.

[13]Cf. George I. Mavrodes, "Bliks, Proofs and Prayers," *Pacific Philosophy Forum* 5 (1966): 5 ff.

[14]See chap. 1.

7

on necessary
and sufficient conditions
for knowledge

7

I

In this chapter we are concerned primarily with a secular matter: the necessary and sufficient condition for knowledge, i.e., *knowledge that* something is so. As we shall see, this issue has important implications for religious knowledge. Philosophers since Socrates and the *Theaetetus* have been concerned to find those conditions which are individually necessary and jointly sufficient for knowledge. And, although there has been some disagreement over just which set of conditions will do the job, still there has been a sort of consensus that *some* set must be necessary and sufficient. This, it may be said, is the dominant philosophical model of knowledge, or at least of knowledge that something is so. Recently philosophers have again been concerned with the necessary and sufficient conditions for knowledge. The set of conditions that has been considered a leading candidate is:

　　i) P is the case.
　　ii) S believes that P.
　　iii) S is justified in believing that P.[1]

While an alternative set of conditions is:

　　i) That what one is said to know be true.
　　ii) That one be sure of it.
　　iii) That one have the right to be sure.[2]

　　Though there have been efforts to show that the conditions of neither set are in fact necessary and sufficient for knowledge, these efforts consist primarily in offering counterexamples. Consequently they leave open the possibility that some other set of conditions, if not the set under scrutiny, will suffice.[3] That is, these efforts leave untouched the basically assumed model of knowledge.

　　Here, on the other hand, we shall call into question whether *any* set of conditions can be necessary and sufficient for knowledge. We shall do this by examining the business of *applying* supposedly necessary and sufficient conditions for knowledge, whether the conditions be of either of the above sets or any other set. If there are necessary and sufficient conditions for knowledge, then presumably the way we determine if an alleged instance of knowledge is indeed an instance of knowledge is by applying these conditions to it as a test. What I hope will emerge from this examination of applying what supposedly are such conditions is: 1) Necessary and sufficient conditions for knowledge, even if there were any, would be at least sometimes superfluous when it comes to determining if someone knows what he is said to know, and 2) there can be no such conditions.

II

In considering the business of applying necessary and sufficient conditions for knowledge, i.e., *knowing that,* the first thing that strikes one is that very rarely are such conditions in fact applied to determine if one *knows that* something. Take the second set, for example. Sometimes when we are concerned about whether someone *knows that* something, we ask him if he is sure (apply the second condition) and then go on to ask him why he is so sure (apply the third condition). But other times when we have this concern we ask only if he who says he knows is sure. If he says he is, we may conclude that he knows without asking him further questions. The reason for this, one might say, is that the questioner in such cases infers that the third condition is fulfilled if the second is; that he who says he knows has the right to be sure if he is sure. The same, it can be said, holds for the first condition. Again the questioner infers that if he who says he knows is sure, then what he is sure about is true. Similarly, one might say, when we ask someone if he knows that some P is so by asking simply if he knows that P, we are applying all the conditions implicitly. That is, our question comes to: "Do all the conditions for knowledge hold in your case?" and we take his affirmative reply to mean that all the conditions do hold. So at most all we can say on the basis of such cases as these is that not all the conditions are *explicitly* applied.

There are other kinds of cases, through. Sometimes after an event we want to know if someone knew about the event beforehand. For instance we might ask someone after a dinner party if he knew beforehand that a guest—let us call him G—was coming to dinner. In such cases there may be no question about whether the event took place, in this case about whether G came to dinner, and there may have been no question earlier about whether it would take place, about whether G would come to dinner. As things were, some were aware that G was coming to dinner and some were not. The question we might put to one, then, is whether he happened to know, that is, whether he was aware that G was coming to dinner. In such a case are we applying these conditions for knowledge? Are we explicitly applying one and then inferring that if it is fulfilled the others will be too or applying all of them implicitly? It seems not, for in such a case in asking if someone was aware that G was coming to dinner we are not asking whether *any* of these conditions are fulfilled. We are not asking if it is true that G came to dinner; we know that it is true, for we were there. Nor are we asking the one queried if he was sure that G was coming to dinner in the light of his possible doubts. We know no one had doubts: some because they knew, the rest because they had no inkling of G's coming to dinner. (If there had been doubts about G's coming to dinner, then of course we could go on to ask him if he were sure G was coming, but that would be to go on to ask another question—in another situation.) And a fortiori we are not asking if he had the right to be sure. We are not, then, asking *any* of the questions we would be asking if we were implicitly applying these three conditions. We are rather asking if he happened to learn beforehand that G was coming to dinner. One might say at this point that it is true that G was at the dinner, the one we queried was sure of it beforehand and he had the right to be sure. This may be, but it is beside the point. For even if it is so that the conditions are fulfilled, we do not determine that he who was queried knew G was coming to dinner by seeing that these conditions are fulfilled. Consequently in at least some cases of determining if someone *knows that* something is so an application of at least these conditions will be superfluous. (What is involved in this case is the difference between retrospective concern with an acknowledgement of awareness and a contemporaneous concern with a knowledge claim; there will be more on this in the next chapter.)

Nor is it the case that some other set of necessary and sufficient conditions is always applied to determine if someone *knows that* something is so. Regardless of the set of conditions for *knowledge that*, one condition will always be *that P is the case* or, alternatively put, *that what one is said to know be true*. However, it can be determined that someone *knows that* something is so without it being determined that this condition is fulfilled. The last example does not demonstrate that this is so because, while the question asked—"Were you aware that G was coming to dinner?"—is not a question about the truth of anything, it nevertheless had been determined that it was true that G had come to dinner. What I want to bring out now is that it can be determined that someone *knows that* something although it cannot be determined that this something is true and, hence, since the condition *that what one is said to know be true* will always be one of any set of necessary and sufficient conditions for knowledge, every such set of conditions for knowledge will at least sometimes be superfluous in determining that someone *knows that* something.

Pertinent cases are exemplified by the following. We have been picking wild flowers and searching for a rare species of poppy that grows only in the immediate area. We think that we have found this species, the Chetco Poppy, but we are not sure. For this reason we ask A, who is well known for his ability to identify the plants of the area, if the flower we have picked is in fact a specimen of the Chetco Poppy. After examining the plant he says that he is sure it is not. Our hope, of course, is that the plant *is* a specimen of this rare species and that A is wrong. So we ask someone else—F—if A *knows* that our plant is not a Chetco Poppy. F reasons in this fashion: first he asks us if A was sure the flower was not a Chetco Poppy. We say yes, remembering that A said it surely was not. F then observes to us that A more than anyone is knowledgeable about the plants of the area; if anyone can be sure the flower we picked is not a Chetco Poppy, it is he. So far, then, two of the conditions have been applied. F continues: so, if A says he is sure that it is not a Chetco Poppy, you can be sure it is not. He is never wrong about such things, and he would not say he was sure if he did not know that the flower was not a Chetco Poppy.

Knowing A's ability as he does, and making sure that A was sure, F has determined that A knows that our flower is not a Chetco Poppy. Notably he did not first determine that it is true that our flower is not a Chetco Poppy. In fact he might not be able to make such a determination; he might not have A's ability. We might think that this case is like the cases we noted earlier where a condition is implicitly applied—where one condition is inferred to hold if another does. However, it is different from the earlier cases in a crucial respect. In those cases it must have been that the questioner, the one determining if the other *knew that, inferred* that one condition was fulfilled if another was and so inferred that the other *knew that*. To have made certain that the other *knew that*, a separate application of the three conditions would have been necessary. In the case before us now F cannot tell if our flower is not a Chetco Poppy and so is incapable of applying the first condition. Yet he knows that A knows that it is not. That is, without a consideration of the first condition, he *knows* that A knows that our flower is not a Chetco Poppy; he does not infer it.

So even if in most of the cases that it is determined that someone *knows that* something, all the conditions are applied (only some implicitly) this is not always the case. If it were, we would be in a sorry plight, for we could then at best only infer that people know what they said they knew unless we knew it too by some independent means (which is what being able to apply the first condition would require). This would entail that one could never learn (come to know) something by asking another who knows. For one would not know he knows (that is, not according to any set of necessary and sufficient conditions for knowledge), and consequently would have to consider what he was told as something quite possibly not true. At best one could only learn someone else's opinion which he inferred to be true and something his informant knew. Happily, though, one can learn (come to know) something from another who knows without first coming to know it in some other way. In fact one quite often learns things in the way one could learn from A that a flower was not of a certain species. At such times one learns something from someone who knows and whom he knows to know because of his skill, position, or access.

We may conclude, therefore, that the condition *that what one is said to know be true* is at least sometimes superfluous in determining that someone *knows that* something is so, and, further, since this condition in some form will be one of any set of necessary and sufficient conditions for knowledge, that every such set of conditions for knowledge will at least sometimes be superfluous in determining that someone *knows that* something is so.

III

One might reply at this point: "At most all you have shown is that sometimes in determining if someone *knows that* something not all the necessary and sufficient conditions for knowledge are applied, and you have assumed that a condition of any set will be *that what one is said to know be true*. It may be possible that the necessary and sufficient conditions for knowledge do not include this condition. In any case, there may indeed be such conditions, whether or not they include this condition and whether or not they are always applied in determining that someone *knows that* something is so."

This reply invites two initial comments. First, it is not without reason that the various competing sets of conditions for knowledge contain in some form the condition *that what one is said to know be true*. If they did not, they would exclude the condition that operates whenever it is reasoned that someone does not *know that* something is so but only believes it, because that something is false. Second, while one might distinguish between the necessary and sufficient conditions for knowledge and the considerations we use in determining if someone *knows that* something, doing so puts a new light on the search for the necessary and sufficient conditions for knowledge. No longer will such conditions answer the question "What is knowledge?" No longer will the Socratic wraith be able to rebuke us for saying that something is knowledge when we do not know what knowledge is, for it will have been conceded that we do not need the necessary and sufficient conditions for knowledge to determine if someone *knows that* something.

However, the essential correctness of this reply must be granted. It must be granted that there may yet be necessary and sufficient conditions for knowledge even though they need not be applied to determine if someone *knows that* something. Even so it can be seen through other considerations that there cannot be such conditions for knowledge—considerations which also have to do with applying necessary and sufficient conditions for knowledge. They may be made clear, for example, in terms of one who can predict the weather and two questions that we might ask about him.

1) My friend E, I tell a friend, can usually correctly predict the weather. He has lived in the area many years, I explain, and has developed an ability to predict changes in the weather up to several days in advance. Mildly curious, my acquaintance asks me, "Did he know this storm we now have would blow in?" I reply that he did—that he said there would be a storm two days before it struck. The point of his question "Did he know this storm we now have would blow in?" is to find out if E predicted the storm. Thus I can reply either "He did (know)" or "He said a storm would blow in" or "He predicted this storm." Any of these answers his question. This is not to say that "know" means only "predict" or "say"; it is to say, however, that given this question, in indicating that E predicted the storm I indicate he knew it would blow in. (Similarly, while "promise" does not mean "say," in certain circumstances I can indicate that someone promised to do X by indicating that he said he would do X.)

2) My friend discovers that he has need of an expert weather forecaster and remembering what I told him about E, decides to ask me additional questions about him. His concern in asking these further questions is different from his concern in asking the first question. In asking the first question my friend wanted to know if E had in fact predicted the storm, whatever the nature of his acquired ability to predict the weather. Now he is concerned with the nature of that ability, with its reliability, and with whether it is based on guesswork. So one question he asks is this: "Did E *know* this storm would blow in or was it merely an educated guess on his part?" This question is not the first question, and even though the first question was answered in the affirmative, this one might not be. It will be answered affirmatively if I

know E to have some sort of meteorological expertise; it will not be if his prediction was only generally reliable guesswork.

One thing that should be made clear is that it is *not* the case that the first question is "Did E know the storm would blow in?" while the second question is "Did E *really* know the storm would blow in?" The second question *could be* asked by asking, "Did E *really* know the storm would blow in?" (instead of "Did E *know* this storm would blow in or was it merely an educated guess on his part?"). But the first question could also. If my friend thought that I was being facetious when I said that E knew that there would be a storm, his question "Did E *really* know the storm would blow in?" would come to "Did he really predict this storm, or are you joking?" which is the first question.

The important point, and the consideration crucial for necessary and sufficient conditions for knowledge, is this: if "Did he know?" is the first question, the answer could be affirmative, while if it is the second question the answer could be negative. Regardless of the actual means of determining if one *knows that* something is so, if there are necessary and sufficient conditions for knowledge, every instance that fulfills these conditions (and only such an instance) should be an instance of *knowing that*. It should not be that something is or is not an instance of knowledge according to which question is asked. It cannot be that according to one application something meets the necessary and sufficient conditions for knowledge and according to another it does not.

The argument can be cast in terms of other examples as well. All that is essential is that two questions can be distinguished—two questions that might have different answers regarding one's *knowing that* something is so. We can again bring out two such questions regarding the following case.

1) C lives in a tough neighborhood and one evening surprises some of the roughest fellows of the neighborhood assembled in an alley. They are intently discussing something. At his approach they disperse furtively and rapidly. C tells his wife of the incident and adds, "I know that they're planning something." "I doubt it," she says. That night they break into and rob a store. "I knew it," C says. Later what we shall term the first question arises when C's wife is asked by a friend if anyone knew that the gang was going to rob the store. She answers that C knew that they were planning *something*.

2) The police later ask C the following question: Did he know the gang was planning something, and if he knew why did he not inform them (the police)? C tells the police that he suspected they were planning something, but he had no proof. And when the police put it to him that he did not *know* in that case, he admits that he did not; he was not able to present any evidence to show that the gang was planning something. However, this admission does not impugn his wife's earlier comment; his not *knowing* that they

were planning something does not impugn his knowing that they were planning *something*.

Again, then, the answer to the first question could be affirmative (indicating that C did *know that* something), while the answer to the second question could be negative. And again this could not be so if there were necessary and sufficient conditions for *knowing that*, for it cannot be that one instance both does and does not meet the necessary and sufficient conditions for knowledge.

Perhaps a caveat or two should be offered at this point. If the above reflections are correct, it still may be that there are certain *necessary* conditions for knowledge. That P is true, and that P is certain, for instance, seem to be necessary conditions for someone's knowing that P. Second, there will yet be sufficient conditions for one's knowing that P *in a given context or situation according to a given question*; that is, nothing I have brought out indicates that it is impossible to find out if someone knows that something is so, and this is to say that in a given situation with a given question it is possible to determine if conditions sufficient for knowledge in that situation are met. But neither of these provisos is at odds with the conclusion that there is no set of necessary and sufficient conditions for (all) *knowledge that* something is so.

One who believes that there are necessary and sufficient conditions for knowledge might reply to my last argument in several ways. I would like to note three.

1) It might be said that there are different meanings of "knowledge"; that I have equivocated on several of these and that what is sought are the necessary and sufficient conditions for knowledge in only one sense of "knowledge."

If this reply is made, it must be borne in mind that we have been considering *knowing that* that is explicitly *knowing that*. *Knowing about* and *knowing someone's face,* for instance, have already been excluded. Thus, this first reply says, in effect, that *knowing that* has different meanings.

2) It might be replied that sometimes we conclude that someone *knows that* something when we should not; we reach such mistaken conclusions because we have the wrong or a loose concept of knowledge.

The gist of this reply is that much we call "knowledge" should not be so dignified. The original concern, however, was with what knowledge is, not with what it should be. Socrates asked "What is knowledge?" Ayer thought of his conditions as representing a discovery of what knowledge is. Of course one might want to tighten the concept of knowledge in a quasi-legal fashion. But to do so is, for good or bad reasons, to cease to count as knowledge all that is knowledge—that is, *knowing that*.

3) Finally it might be replied that the necessary and sufficient conditions being sought are for a pure or special notion of knowledge.[4] If nothing qualifies as knowledge in this special sense, then that is to be accepted.

If this reply is made then it is frankly admitted that the concern is no longer with knowledge, but with a special concept of some sort.

In the light of those replies, then, I think we can draw these morals: If what we mean by "knowledge" is knowledge, or even if what we mean by "knowledge" is only *knowing that*, we should think neither that we need necessary and sufficient conditions to determine if someone knows something nor that there are such conditions for knowledge.

This issue of necessary and sufficient conditions for knowledge, i.e., *knowledge that*, has two important implications for religious knowledge. Both have to do with the condition that knowledge have a justification (or adequate grounds), which in some form almost invariably is taken as a necessary condition for knowledge. Both implications turn our eyes from the possibilities of religious knowledge. First, if one thinks that there are necessary and sufficient conditions for knowledge, including the condition that knowledge have a justification, one will fail to appreciate possible instances of knowledge where there is no knowledge claim to be justified, but where there is yet knowledge. Second, one may fail to appreciate a precondition for intelligibly asking "How do you know there is a God?" that apparently entails the possibility of such knowledge. We shall examine these matters in the next two chapters.

Notes

[1] Edmund L. Gettier, "Is Justified True Belief Knowledge?" *Analysis* 23 (1963): 121–23; reprinted in *Knowledge and Belief,* ed. A. Phillips Griffiths (London: Oxford University Press, 1967).

[2] A. J. Ayer, *The Problem of Knowledge* (New York: St. Martin's Press; London: Macmillan & Co., 1956), p. 34. There are other variants as well. See Gettier, "Is Justified True Belief Knowledge?"

[3] Thus this evolution: Gettier in his article presents counterexamples to the set of conditions he considers; but then Michael Clark in "Knowledge and Grounds: A Comment on Mr. Gettier's Paper," *Analysis* 24 (1963): 46–48, augments the conditions of that set so that they exclude Gettier's counterexamples; then John Turk Saunders and Narayan Champawat in "Mr. Clark's Definition of 'Knowledge,'" *Analysis* 25 (1964): 8–9, present counterexamples to even Clark's augmented conditions.

[4] Cf. W. W. Rozenboom, "Why I Know So Much More Than You Do," *American Philosophical Quarterly* 4 (1967): 281–90.

8

religious knowledge:

contemporaneous and

retrospective questions

8

I

In earlier chapters an effort was made to bring out the possibility of religious discovery. This effort consisted primarily in trying to establish the viable possibility of a discovery of God and of a relationship of love to Him. Such a discovery, it was hopefully shown, would or could be made according to the nonhypothetical model of discovery. But, even if there is such a discovery, what of those religious believers who admittedly have not made such a nonhypothetical discovery? What of those who accept the belief of their fathers on the basis of the Bible, who have had no religious experience, and who have not detected God's influence in their lives or in the lives of others? This chapter will explore the possibility that those people have or could have religious knowledge.

For a believer of a certain faith the scripture of that faith is deemed a source of knowledge; the scripture instructs one on how he should live and on the relationship between the believer and God. Believers may even cite scripture as the source of their knowledge that there is a God, and they may do so when they have no justification for their acceptance of their scripture—when they accept it on faith, as they say. An obvious and perplexing question then arises. In the Judaeo-Christian form it is this: How can the Bible be a source of religious knowledge when the believer can offer no justification for accepting the Bible? It is this question with which we shall be concerned. I do not propose to deal with the question: *Can* Jews or Christians offer for their acceptance of the Bible any justification that is not circular or otherwise inadequate? I do not want to argue either that they can or that they cannot. In any case, it is apparent that many believers, both Jews and Christians, who cite the Bible as a source of religious knowledge do so with no justification for their acceptance of the Bible. I want to present a possible way in which we might understand a Jew or Christian knowing that there is a God because the Bible says as much, even though he has no justification for accepting the Bible.

How can it possibly be that such a believer knows that there is a God? Maintaining that he might seems to fly in the face of all that we know about knowledge. When the believer is asked how he knows, he replies he knows because the Bible says as much, and when he is asked why he accepts the Bible, he can offer us no justification. Certainly, we want to say, without any justification of his acceptance of the Bible, his claim to know that there is a God is unjustified, and so we must conclude that he does not know what he claims to know. This presentation of the case seems to be fair and correct. Even so I think that there is a possibility that the believer knows what he says he knows, and a way for us to see that there is this possibility.

As was just noted, given that the believer cannot justify his acceptance of the Bible, we must conclude that his claim to know that there is a God is unjustified, and so we must conclude that he does not know that there is a God. But to say that this reasoning is right is not to say that it is right to reason that justification of a claim to know is a necessary condition for knowledge and so, if this is lacking, there is no possibility of knowledge. If this latter line of reasoning were correct, then there would be no way to understand the believer who cites the Bible in this way knowing that there is a God. But it is not correct inasmuch as a justification of a claim to know is not a necessary condition for one's knowing in the way this reasoning presupposes.

The first task, then, is to make it clear how a lack of justification in the above case allows us to rule out knowledge in that case, but does not rule it out as a necessary condition for knowledge would rule it out. In order to do this we shall consider primarily three cases in which one is said to have knowledge. These are different cases in which a young man says he knows or knew that a certain young woman loves or loved him. These are not cases of religious knowledge, but they preserve the issue, and being secular, they have the merit of being free of any specifically theological problems.

The first case is this: A young man whom we know well announces to us that he intends to ask a young woman, whom we also know, to marry him. Although we know both of them well, this is the first we have heard of anything serious between them. We know him to be rather naive and inexperienced. On the other hand, we know her to be the type who forms liaisons easily and is promiscuous. Consequently, we are surprised and somewhat dubious at this announcement. "Do you know she loves you?" we ask the young man. "Yes," he replies, "she has told me she does." But, we point out, she has said this before to other men. "It was not so then, why do you think it's so now?" we ask him. At this point the young man and a mutual friend supply the justification for accepting what she says: She has changed her ways, they claim, and they tell us things that show she has in fact changed her ways. In this case, then, the young man is justified in accepting what she says and we may conclude that he knows what he says he knows, that is, that she loves him.

The second case is a repetition of the first case up to the point where the needed justification is supplied by the mutual friend and the young man. In the second case this justification is lacking. When we ask "Why do you accept what she says, considering her past?" the young man has no reply, except to say again that he does accept what she says, that is, that she loves him. In this case, since we are given no reason to accept what she says, we conclude that the young man does not and cannot know that she loves him.

II

In the above cases justification for the young man's claim to know that she loves him does seem to operate as a kind of necessary condition for his knowing that she loves him. In the first case this justification allows us to conclude that he knows, while in the second case its apparent absence forces us to conclude that he does not know. But let us note very carefully the role of justification (or lack of it) in these two cases. In both cases we have a question: Why do you accept what she says as the truth? This question is about what the young man cited to tell us how he came to know that she loves him. Consequently this question comes to: Why do you think that what she says is something that brings you to know that she loves you? In the first case the young man adequately justifies to us his claim that he knows she loves him by establishing that what she said is the truth, and so we conclude that he does know. In the second case the young man does not justify to us his claim that he knows she loves him, for he cannot establish that what she said is the truth, and so we conclude that he does not know.

To put the matter another way, we conclude the young man knows she loves him if we are convinced he in fact learned it (was brought to know it by what she said); we conclude he does not know it if we are convinced he in fact did not learn it (was not brought to know it by what she said). The question of justification arises when there is a question about whether what he says he knows was in fact learned (in this case from what the young woman said). If there is such a question and if there is a justification, we conclude that he did learn it and so does know. If there is such a question, but no justification, then we conclude that he did not learn it and so does not know. Lest there be any misunderstanding here, I am not offering an "analysis" of knowledge that something is so in terms of learning that something is so. My effort is not to offer an analysis of knowledge at all, nor, a fortiori, is it to propound necessary and sufficient conditions for knowledge. Rather I want simply to direct our attention to those cases where the question of justification arises and the way in which it arises—namely, where there is a question about whether something someone claims to know or something he believes, was in fact learned.

What these two cases we have considered establish, then, is not what some philosophers have thought. They do not establish 1) that a necessary condition for one's knowing P is his having a justification for his claim to know P or his belief that P. They establish instead 2) that, *if* there is a question about whether one has come to know what he claims to know or believes, *then* a condition necessary for his knowing P is his having a justification for his knowledge claim or belief that P. Strictly, we can conclude only this from such cases.

This is so despite the fact that many philosophers have thought that 1) is a "rule of language" or a "conceptual rule of knowledge"; that is, a necessary condition for all knowledge that something is the case. In fact, whatever cases of knowledge one might cite in support of 1) will support 2) as well. For in each such case there will be a question about whether one really learned what he claims to know or believes. The justification is given in order to answer this question. The question may not be explicit; it may be implicit as when one volunteers the justification for his knowledge claim without being asked. However, if there is the question in each case, such cases support 2) over 1), for if 1) were correct there should be *some* such cases lacking this question.

III

Let us now turn to the third case in which the young man says he knew that the young woman loved him. As in the second case, the young man accepts what the young woman tells him without any justification. In this case, too, *if* he were asked "How do you know she loves you?" he would reply "She told me" and if he were asked "Why do you accept what she says?" he would have no justification to offer us for accepting what she says. But in this case he is not asked either question; he is not even asked "Do you know she loves you?" He is not asked any question in the present tense; rather he is later asked the past tense retrospective "Did you know she loved you?" He is asked this question when, in retrospect, it is clear to all that she did love him, although it was not clear to all before, of course. What this retrospective question comes to is: "Did you know before what we all know now?" or, put another way, "Were you aware then that she loved you?" He replies, "Yes I did know. She told me." If there were a question here about whether he came to know she loved him from what she said, then a request for a justification of his acceptance of what she said would be necessary. But here it seems there need be no such question, for by hypothesis it is clear in retrospect that she was telling the truth. In other words it seems to be clear in retrospect that he *could* have come to know she loved him from what she said, and from that alone, and when he replies as he does he acknowledges that he did come to know she loved him from what she said. Although we had doubts, he did not; although we did not accept what she said, he did, and he accepted it as certain. And he was right, it seems. (This does not mean that all that is true is certain, but it does mean that some of what is certain need not be seen as certain by all.) In this retrospective case, then, where the young woman tells the young man that she loves him, where he accepts it, and it is finally clear to all that she was telling the truth, there appears to be no question about whether he came to know that she loved him from her telling him, and consequently a justification of his acceptance of what she said is not or may not be a necessary condition for his knowing or having known that she loved him.

It is in terms of a similar retrospective viewpoint that we can understand the possibility of a believer knowing that there is a God because the Bible says as much. Let us suppose by analogy with this last case that it will be clear in retrospect that there is a God and that the Bible is his word.¹ The retrospective question here will be: "Did you know that there is a God?" or, alternatively, "Did you know before what we all know now, that there is a God?" The believer's reply who accepted the Bible would be "Yes I did know, for the Bible told me as much." Once again it seems there would be no question about his coming to know from what he cites. By hypothesis there is a God, and the Bible is His word. Thus again it could be clear in retrospect that he came to know from the Bible, that there is a God even though he had no justification for his acceptance of the Bible. We might note that it must be clear in retrospect *both* that there is a God and that the Bible is His word. It would not do for the believer to reply, even in this retrospective case, that he knew that there is a God because the Bible said as much if the Bible were not the word of God. In the same way it would not do for the believer to reply in the case as it is that he knew that there was a God because he saw "There is a God" written on a wall in some major city. This fact does not ruin the analogy with the last case. In the last case two similar things needed to be true, namely that the young woman loved the young man *and* that when she spoke she spoke for herself. However, the latter hardly needed articulation. But just as graffiti could not be cited as the means whereby one learned that there is a God, so too the young woman's reciting of a line in a play ("I love you") could not be cited in the last case. What has been brought out here does not mean that if some-one says he knows something, and later on it turns out by chance to be true, he knows it. There is the crucial element of finding out. To retrospectively acknowledge that one knew there is a God, one must have found out. Being told is one way to find out, and if the Bible is the word of God, it truly tells us that there is a God.

At this point one might raise the following question: What would the young man himself have said in the contemporaneous situation if he had been asked if he thought he knew that the young woman loved him, or what would the believer have said if he had been asked if he thought he knew that there is a God? In the contemporaneous situation, it will be recalled, the young man is asked if he knows the young woman loves him, and when he says he does because she has told him, he is asked what justification he has for accepting what she says. He has none, it seems. So we conclude that he does not know. Now the question is: Does he conclude the same thing? If he does, then we have the curious situation that he knows (as I have suggested he can acknowl-edge retrospectively) even though he concludes contemporaneously that he does not know. If he does not conclude the same thing (that he does not know), then it seems that he is not reasoning as we are—that justification of his claim to know is necessary to conclude that he knows. The resolution of the difficulty is this: The young man with a contemporaneous concern about his own knowledge would reason as we do in that he too would consider justification of his claim to know to be necessary for his knowing. But unlike his hearer, he would take her word to be adequate justification for his knowl-edge claim. And he would be right, I think, if the retrospective case goes the way I have presented it. One thing it makes clear is that her word brought him to know. It also makes clear that although we did not appreciate it at the time, his claim to know was justified. Thus his being told by the young woman that she loves him is crucial to his knowing in that it is the way he finds out she loves him, *and* in that it provides the justification for his con-temporaneous knowledge claim, even though it does not justify his claim to us and even though he has no justification for accepting what she says. The case of the believer is analogous. The Bible is crucial to his knowing that there is a God in that it is the way he finds out there is a God, *and* in that it provides the justification for his contemporaneous knowledge claim even though at the time it does not justify his claim to the rest of us, and even though he has no justification for accepting the Bible.

The point made in terms of the young man's knowing that the young woman loved him, then, is transferable to the case of the believer's knowing that there is a God. Given the retrospective question and viewpoint, it may become clear that one knew what he said he knew, even though when we asked the contemporaneous question we fairly concluded that he did not know. It is thus that we may understand there being a possibility that believers know that there is a God even when they say they know because the Bible says as much, and they have no justification for their acceptance of the Bible.

IV

149995

There is another way to clarify the features of knowledge involved here which make it possible for believers to know that there is a God even though they might not now be able to justify to us their claim to know. The point of what I have called a contemporaneous question "Do you know that . . .?" is often to find out whether one really knows what he claims to know. The point of what I have called a retrospective question "Did you know that . . .?" is often to find out if one was aware beforehand of a certain fact that is now an established fact. That is, the concern behind the contemporaneous question is often with a *claim to know*, while the concern behind the retrospective question is often with an *acknowledgement of awareness*.

Let us recall the principle 1) cited in section II: a necessary condition for one's knowing P is his having a justification for his claim to know P or his belief that P. Now this principle holds for all knowledge *wherever applicable*. Often it is applicable to contemporaneous concerns because the contemporaneous concern is often with a knowledge claim, and a claim is the kind of thing that may or may not be justified. But this principle is not pertinent to acknowledgements of awareness. Acknowledgements are not the kind of thing that may or may not be justified, at least not in the requisite sense.[2] One may be asked "Do you *know* today is Sunday?" or "Do you *know* you are trespassing?" and when he replies in the affirmative he may be further asked how he knows—what is his justification for his claim to know. Also, though, one may be asked "Are you aware today is Sunday?" and "Are you aware you are trespassing?" In this case his affirmative reply acknowledges his awareness of what is an established fact. Given that his reply is an acknowledgement and not a claim, there is no further question as to his justification, although there may be a further question as to how he found out. This question is answered by his indicating how he found out, which is not a justification of anything. Acknowledgements are unlike claims in the following way. If a knowledge claim is adequately supported, it is justified; if not, it is unjustified, but still is a claim; and it remains a knowledge claim whether or not the one making it knows what he claims he knows. If, in such cases as the above, one who has indicated that he was aware of a fact is asked how he found out and cannot reply because he in fact never did find it out, he should not have said in the first place that he was aware of the fact.

This, however, does not mean that he made an unjustified acknowledgement; it means he did not in fact make an acknowledgement of his awareness at all for he had no awareness to acknowledge (similarly, one who is not guilty but says he is does not acknowledge his guilt). If acknowledgements did take justification, there would be unjustified acknowledgements analogous to the unjustified knowledge claim one makes when he does not know and lacks justification for his claim to know, but when one says he was aware when he was not, he has not made an unjustified acknowledgement; he has not made an acknowledgement at all. And this, again, is a mark of the fact that acknowledgements do not take justification. The principle 1) that a necessary condition for one's knowing P is his having a justification for his claim to know P or his belief that P, then, will not hold in cases where one acknowledges that he knows or knew something that is an established fact. This means that this principle will often not be pertinent to what I have called a retrospective question, for the retrospective concern frequently is not with a knowledge claim, but with an acknowledgement of prior awareness of what is (later) seen by us all to be an established fact. In the case of the religious retrospective question "Did you know before what we all know now, that there is a God?" one would be asked if he were aware before of the (later) established fact that there is a God. If his reply were affirmative, he would indicate that he was aware that there is a God. Further, if he were asked, he could tell us how he found out: from the Bible. Therefore, even though it may be true that a religious believer now has no justification for his acceptance of the Bible, the believer *may* even now know that there is a God. He would, if he could (one day), give a true affirmative answer to the religious retrospective question, as he could if he were now in truth aware that there is a God—and would he not be aware that there is a God if he were truly told there is a God and accepted it?

V

H. H. Price tells us in one of his articles:

> There is a story about a celebrated philosopher who was the guest of honour at a dinner of a society of agnostics. One of them asked him, "What would you say if God Himself suddenly appeared among us in this room?" The philosopher replied: "God," I should say, "why did you make the evidence for your existence so inadequate?"[3]

There is a point about contemporaneous and retrospective questions that this celebrated philosopher might be anxious to make. It is this: The young man or the believer may be asked retrospectively "Did you know . . . ?" and he may reply "Yes, I did know, she (or the Bible) told me." But one can go on to ask: "Why did you accept what she said (or what the Bible said) back then?" This point, of course, is right; one can persist with concern with justification even in asking the retrospective question. It is one thing, however, that this question can be asked in retrospect and another that it must be answered before we can truly say that the young man knew that the young woman loved him or that the believer knew that there was a God.

A further question that Professor Price's philosopher might want to ask is "*Did* he know back then?" This question would be similar to the second question asked of the friend in the last chapter: "Did he know this storm would blow in?" That question came to "Did he know or did he make an educated guess?" Price's philosopher's question would come to something like "Did he know back then, or was what he had to go on insufficient to answer all rational doubts?" This question can be asked, and given its burden, the answer will be that he did not know, for clearly what he had to go on (the Bible in his case) does not speak to the doubts of many rational doubters. However, this does not mean that the answer to the retrospective question we have been considering is not affirmative, nor does it mean that there is an other than affirmative answer to the question "Was his contemporaneous knowledge claim justified?"

If we want to ask "Did he really know?" then the answer is "Yes, he really knew"—given the questions put to the believer; the questions analogous to those put to the young man. Will this satisfy Price's philosopher? I suppose not. We will only think that it should if we think his question is the only one, and we will think his question is the only one if we think that there are necessary and sufficient conditions for knowledge *and* his question amounts to asking if they are met.

No doubt many like Price's philosopher—will still want to argue that in *no* case can one know that there is a God because the Bible says as much when he has no justification for his acceptance of the Bible. And they will say that if finding out is coming to know (as it is) then finding out through the Bible necessarily requires justification for accepting the Bible. My purpose in this chapter was not to show conclusively that those who argue in this way are wrong, but to raise a possibility of knowledge by reminding ourselves of certain examples of knowing; examples where an acknowledgement is made that one was aware of something, as opposed to a knowledge claim. One such example is the case where the young man acknowledges retrospectively that he knew that a young woman loved him. If these examples are right, then one *could* know that there is a God because the Bible says as much even though he has no justification for accepting the Bible. He could know because in making an acknowledgement of his knowledge, while he must have *found out*, he need have no justification of anything—since he is not making a claim or advancing a belief—and a fortiori no justification for accepting the Bible.

Of course one may insist that a necessary condition for *all* knowledge is that there be justification for a knowledge claim or for a belief and, further, when someone accepts a source (such as another person's word or the Bible), there must be justification for his accepting it in order for *it* to provide adequate justification. That is, one may insist that only those cases that meet his predetermined conditions, as he understands them, can ever be cases of knowledge. This comes to insisting upon applying these predetermined conditions for knowledge to every example before it is admitted to be an example of knowledge. One who reasons this way need never worry about counterexamples to his analysis, since he will not recognize anything as a counterexample. But by the same token, he may never see the inadequacy of his analysis; for his analysis, after all, is supposed to apply to all that is knowledge, or at least to all that is *knowledge that*. Applying the conditions of the analysis to proposed examples *before* they are admitted to be examples begs the question of the adequacy of the analysis. In the face of the tendency in ourselves to reason in this way one can only say with Wittgenstein: don't think but look.

Notes

[1]How one comes to see these things and what looking back in retrospect in this case requires are admittedly difficult matters involving many questions. These questions cannot be treated here, and I think that they need not be as long as the point is understood to be about knowledge, which in this case happens to be the knowledge that there is a God. That is, these questions need not be treated as long as the conclusion is in terms of religious knowledge inasmuch as it is like, e.g., the young man's knowing that the young woman loved him.

[2]An acknowledgement of one's awareness of a fact might be justified or unjustified morally; although, strictly, what is morally justified or unjustified may be one's *making* an acknowledgement.

[3]H. H. Price, "Faith and Belief," *Faith and the Philosophers,* ed. John Hick (New York: St. Martin's Press; London: Macmillan & Co., 1964), pp. 19–20.

9

an aspect of

the logic of knowing

that there is a god

9

I

In an article on religious belief Professor Norman Malcolm gives us the following account of an encounter between two philosophers:

> A good many years ago I was told about a public discussion in which one philosopher repeatedly threw at another philosopher the question, 'But how do you *know* that God exists?' At last the latter replied, 'Because my father told me so!' It was a long time before I saw what was impressive in this reply. My first reaction was to think it was absurd; it did not offer anything which could be considered a *good reason*. But do we know what a good reason would look like? I do not believe so.[1]

Malcolm's point here has to do with the belief that God exists. However, he has obliquely pointed out something very significant for the logic of knowing that there is a God, and that is this: sometimes when the believer is asked

"How do you know that there is a God?" neither the believer nor the questioner knows what an adequate answer would be. In what follows we shall discuss a confusion that surrounds this question as it is often asked of the believer, an indication of which is that neither the believer nor the questioner knows what an adequate answer would be. We shall also discuss an implication for religious knowledge of the removal of that confusion.

The confusion often found surrounding the question "How do you know that there is a God?" and the reason for that confusion I shall try to bring out by contrasting it with another question. To introduce the contrasting question it will be necessary to set the stage. Let us imagine that I am a member of a family that finds itself in a certain crisis. It is a very serious affair and threatens to ruin the family. Scandal and legal action seem imminent, and many members of the family have resigned themselves to the worst. It is my hope, however, that my granduncle will somehow save the situation, although I have never met him. He is something of a myth in our family—someone from the East who is very influential and who looks after the entire family. Although the family has not heard from him in years, according to stories cherished by the family, he has saved such a critical situation before on darker days, suddenly appearing from nowhere to help. I believe in my granduncle and that he will save us.

A doubter in the family asks me: "How can you believe he'll help us? Those stories about him are all myths. You say that he'll help us, but how do you know that you even have a granduncle?" It is this question "How do you know that you have a granduncle?" that I want to contrast with our question "How do you know that there is a God?" I understand this question because I know what I could point to to show the doubter that my granduncle does exist: letters from him, his aid arriving in the form of money, he himself appearing, or letters from others in the family telling us that they had heard from him. Any of these would be proof. At this point, one concerned with belief in God and knowledge that there is a God might say: "This is precisely where the difference lies between knowing that your granduncle exists and knowing that God exists. In the one case we know what to point to; in the other case we do not." However, this point cuts two ways. I know what will indicate to the doubter that my granduncle exists because I understand his specific doubts and what will remove them. He thinks that perhaps my granduncle is a myth. His question is not asked in a vacuum with no definite doubts behind it; if it were, then I would not know how to answer it, just as the religious believer (often) does not know how to answer the question put to him.

Let us observe in some detail what would happen if the question about my granduncle were asked in a vacuum where it is not clear what doubts lie behind it. I understood the question asked before because the source of the doubt was clear—namely the possibility that all the stories about my granduncle were myths. This time, though, the source of doubt is not clear. Again I am challenged and asked how I know that I have a granduncle, but this time I have no idea what doubts I should try to allay. Should I reply that I have a granduncle because just this morning the family received a letter from him? This fact would still the doubter if he thought that possibly the stories were myths, but it would not if he thought that the idea of a benevolent granduncle was perpetrated by a conspiracy. In that case the letter would prove nothing; it could have been sent by the conspiracy. Similarly, if I were to reply that I knew I had a granduncle because some trusted friends in the East had finally located him and sent word, this would still my questioner's doubts if he thought that there might be a conspiracy perpetrating the idea of a granduncle, but it would not if he thought that there was such a man but he was only a clever impersonator. In that case finding such a man would prove nothing. It has to be understood what the doubts of the questioner are before his "How do you know?" question can be answered. If I did not understand my questioner's doubts, I would not know how to assure him that I know my granduncle exists. The confusion surrounding the philosophical and religious question "How do you know that there is a God?" is that it *is* often asked in a vacuum with no reason, explicit or implicit, for doubt. Thus even if a believer did not know that there is a God, he would not know what to point to show that he knows.

Moreover, it should be clear it is not the case that this question "How do you know that there is a God?" with no definite doubts behind it can be answered, but it must be answered randomly, one hoping to hit the answer. If it has no doubts behind it, it cannot be answered. Consider what would happen if an attempt were made to answer it with no doubts behind it. If one were to reply to it "I know because I see God's support in my life," there is no reason not to challenge God's support. If one were to reply to it "I know because the Bible tells us of God and his relation to me," there is no reason not to challenge the Bible. Regardless of what answer is given it can be challenged. This might seem like a careful and rigorous skepticism. This state of affairs, however, arises from our treating the philosophical and religious question "How do you know that there is a God?" as the question "How does *one* know there is a God!" "What, though, is faulty with this treatment?" one might ask. Does it not make it clear that one cannot know that there is a God, for whatever he cites can be challenged?

What is wrong with this treatment, and what is confused about asking the general question "How does one know that there is a God?" can be clarified by looking again at knowing that one has a granduncle. What happens if we ask the analogous general question "How does one know that he has a granduncle?" What happens is that, again, whatever is cited to explain how one knows can be challenged; that is, there is no reason not to challenge it. If one replies that he knows he has a granduncle because he received a letter from him, the authenticity of the letter can be challenged. If one replies that he knows he has a granduncle because trusted friends have located him, the identity of the man located can be challenged. If one replies that the granduncle himself has appeared, it can be challenged whether he is the granduncle. And so on without end. It seems, then, that if one cannot know that there is a God, so too he cannot know that he has a granduncle. Perhaps this conclusion will be welcomed by extreme skeptics, but if it is right, our inability to know that there is a God is only one instance of a general inability to know anything. In fact my argument was intended as a reductio ad absurdum, and so it will be for anyone who fancies that he upon occasion knows what he says he knows.[2]

We ended up with the implication that one cannot know that there is a God or that he has a granduncle only because there were no doubts behind the "How do you know?" questions. Since there were no doubts there was no reason to challenge or not to challenge any answer that might be given. Thus every possible answer could be challenged, or at least we could mechanically ask about the validity of each. We felt that because there conceivably could be doubts about something, there were doubts about it, and because we could imagine someone having doubts about something, it had to be dubious.

If, in contrast to its being asked with no doubt behind it, the question "How do you know that there is a God?" is asked with some understood doubt, then it can be understood and—perhaps—it can be answered. One taking instruction in Christianity might find himself plagued by certain doubts. He might even doubt that there is a God, for he might ask himself who has ever seen God or felt his presence? After some hesitation he might express his doubts to his instructor. "How do you know that there is a God? Have you ever seen him or his influence?" he might ask the instructor. The instructor might answer, "I know that there is a God, for I receive His support and goodness daily." This reply answers the question as asked and speaks to the doubt expressed. This is not to say, however, that it speaks to every doubt that might be expressed in a range of such questions. Part of what I have been trying to suggest is that there is something odd and confused in expecting an answer to do this. It is comparatively easy to find the doubt that is not allayed by the above answer given to the above question. If the expressed doubt had been concerned with whether what is pointed to as God's support and God's goodness really came from God, then the answer given would not have spoken to the doubt. Perhaps the religious instructor could speak to this doubt as well. But in no case could he reply to "How do you know that there is a God? How do you know that what you point to as His goodness and support really come from Him?" by saying only "I know that there is a God, for I receive his support and goodness daily." But this fact does not mean that one can never answer the question "How do you know that there is a God?" Given the doubt he expressed, his reply does answer the catechumen's question "How do you know that there is a God?"

We might note here one reason why many philosophers have thought that a "How do you know?" question could be asked without specific doubts, that is, in a vacuum. As we have seen, philosophers have tended to think of knowledge as analyzable into three necessary and sufficient conditions, such as:

i) P is the case.
ii) S believes that P.
iii) S is justified in believing that P.

The way in which these three conditions are stated might vary slightly, but there is usually some condition similar to the third. If it is not "S is justified in believing that P", it is "S has adequate evidence for P", or "S has sufficient grounds for P", or "One has the right to be sure." The net suggestion of this condition, however formulated, is that when one knows that such-and-such, his knowledge rests on a body of evidence, or on a number of grounds, or on a specific justification. And naturally if one thinks this, he will also think that this evidence or these grounds can be produced, like a package or a license, upon demand—regardless of what doubts the questioner may or may not have. That these three conditions are the necessary and sufficient conditions for knowledge has hopefully been challenged; indeed it has hopefully been brought into question whether there are any necessary and sufficient conditions for knowledge at all. But for our purposes in this chapter we need only recognize the misleading suggestion of the third condition.

Given what has emerged, then, it does appear that unless there is an understood doubt of some sort there can be no understandable question "How do you know such-and-such?" Of course this does not mean that the one asking the question must have beforehand a clear idea of what specifically will answer his doubt. If he doubts that there is a granduncle because he thinks that the stories about him are myths, his doubt might be answered by his being told that letters have been received from him, even though the possibility of such letters had not occurred to him. Nor does the doubt have to be simple or single. It might be that one doubts that there is a granduncle in the family because he thinks he might be a myth *or* a perpetration of a conspiracy. If, thinking this, he asks me how I know I have a granduncle, and I reply that I know because a letter was received from him this morning, the doubter will go on to ask how I know that the letter is from my granduncle and not from a conspiracy. This last question I may or may not be able to answer. His doubts might be so deep-seated that I might have to spell out in detail how I know that there is no conspiracy. When I tell him that trusted friends have located my granduncle in the East and have confirmed that there is no conspiracy, he may ask me how I know I can trust these friends. And this question, when answered "Because I've known them for years," might give way to another question, "How do you know it was they who contacted you and not a conspiracy impersonating them?" Finally, though, all the "How do you know?" questions generated by his doubts will be asked, and when they are, if he has articulated all his doubts and if I have adequately answered all of them, I will finally have answered his original question and perhaps will have shown him that I do know that there is a granduncle in the family. So, whether the doubts lying behind the question "How do you know that you have a granduncle?" are simple or many-faceted, it is because I can speak to these doubts that I can answer the question, and it is because these doubts are understood that this question and the "How do you know?" questions to which it gives way are understandable. Sometimes, however, when we ask how someone knows something our doubts are vague and hardly recognized; we have them, but we are not quite sure what they are or what would answer them. But there are doubts and they can be answered. If it is not clear at all what doubts underlie the challenge "How do you know?" then, as we have seen, there is no way to understand and answer the question —and on such occasions such questions must necessarily go unanswered.

However, we should not say that the philosophical and religious question we want to ask in a vacuum is not understandable. Rather, if it is indeed asked in a vacuum, it is not understandable in the way the question "How do you know that you have a granduncle?" is. It may be understandable in a different way. Sometimes when there is no doubt about something we can be asked an understandable "How do you know?" question—for instance in circumstances where the question is asked by a paranoiac and we know he has paranoia. If a paranoiac were to first ask if someone who was a friend meant him harm and then, when we say that he certainly does not, ask us how we know he does not, we would understand his question because we understand the nature of his disturbance. We do not understand his question because it is a good question or because we know how to answer it; in fact we do not know how to answer it. We cannot allay his doubts, for there are no sane doubts to allay. But we do understand him asking his question given his paranoia, and so we might try to reassure him by expressing our concern and support.[3] It is in something like the way that we understand the paranoiac's question that we can understand our philosophical question. That is, *if* we cannot understand it in terms of the doubts that lie behind it, we can understand it *or one's asking it* in terms of the philosophical and religious concern that precipitates it.

Another instance in which we can understand a "How do you know?" question with no doubts lying behind it is when such a question is not a challenge. If a friend of mine invariably knows where another friend of mine is, I might ask him how he always knows. In doing so I would not be challenging him; I have no doubt about his knowing where my other friend is. My question is rather one expressing an interest in finding out his means of knowing what he knows. In such a case the interest is not in what one would cite as justification for a knowledge claim or to convince someone else that he knows—it is clear that he knows. The interest is in how he found out what it is clear that he knows. But we are not really concerned with this kind of question. We are concerned with "How do you know?" questions that are challenges, for the philosophical and religious question "How do you know that there is a God?" is certainly a challenge if it is anything. And so far as "How do you know?" questions that are challenges are concerned, the necessity of understood doubts for an understandable question holds. Also we can sometimes ask "How do you know?" questions that are challenges with no *real* doubts behind them. This is the case when one wishing to test another's knowledge asks a "How do you know?" question. Clearly in such a case the tester might himself have no doubts about the matter. The sole point of his question might be to find out if the one queried does indeed know whatever is being asked about. However, it should be clear at this point that the tester's question will be understandable because the presumed doubts underlying his question are understood.

None of what has been said shows that anyone does in fact know that there is a God. The concern has been to bring out a confusion detected behind the question "How do you know that there is a God?" as it is often asked. That confusion, I think, has now been delineated. It should now be clear that there must be some understood doubt behind the question "How do you know that there is a God?" before it will be understandable and answerable. As was noted, this does not mean that the doubt has to be completely clear. But the more vague the doubt is, the more difficult it is to understand the challenge. There is nothing in the gist of what has been said so far, then, to prevent someone from saying that there are doubts behind *his* question "How do you know that there is a God?" and that *these* doubts make his question unanswerable. At least some doubts that might lie behind this question can be answered. The case of the catechumen's question and his doubts would be a case in point. Are there other doubts, then, that have no possible answer?

II

Would a doubt concerning the authority and authenticity of the Bible be an unanswerable doubt which would make the question "How do you know that there is a God?" unanswerable? In the last chapter the concern was to bring out the possibility that, even though a believer might have no justification for accepting the Bible, still he might know that there is a God because the Bible says as much. Here the concern is with whether the question "How do you know that there is a God?" asked by one who doubts the Bible, can be given an answer that is not ruled out by his doubt. Such an answer would have to cite either something independent of the Bible that justifies accepting the Bible or some source of knowledge that there is a God independent of the Bible. Now of course much of what a believer might cite to show that he knows there is a God would ultimately depend on the Bible. For instance a citation of St. Paul's conversion would depend on the Bible, as would a citation of the authority of St. Augustine when it itself is grounded in the authority of the Bible. And in these cases the questioner's doubt about the Bible would not be stilled by what is cited. However, it does not seem that the Bible is the source of everything one might cite to tell another how he knows there is a God. In the above case of the catechumen, the citation of support in his own life by the catechumen's instructor does not depend upon the Bible and its authority.

So far as knowledge that there is a God is concerned, there are other *possible* sources besides the Bible or other scriptures, such as a nonhypothetical religious discovery. The case may be different with regard to knowing that Jesus is the Son of God. It may be that the only possible way of knowing this is through the Bible. One might say at this point that the question as to how one knows there is a God also would allow no reply if the doubt involved were not only about the Bible, but about miracles, mystical experiences, God's influence on our lives, the possibility of there being a God of love when the world is a place of suffering, and virtually everything taken to be of God. It seems right that one can doubt everything that another would cite to explain how he knows there is a God, just as one can doubt everything that another would cite to explain how he knows that he has a granduncle. However, we should be clear on the implications of this point. We have seen that if an understandable question is to be asked in the form of the questions "How do you know there is a God?" or "How do you know that you have a Granduncle?" there must be doubts behind these questions. It cannot be that they are general questions of the form "How does *one* know such-and-such?" which have no doubts behind them. If they were, then it would not be surprising that they could not be finally answered. Nor of course can the questioner have simply *resolved* not to accept any answer, whatever it may be. If so, it would not be surprising that his "How do you know?" question could not be answered. To some extent the onus is on the questioner to make his question understandable by making clear his doubts. If he makes them clear, then inasmuch as he does so he begins to make it clear what would answer them. In this sense his question, if it is understandable and answerable, must have a *possible* answer—namely that which speaks to his doubts. If what is asked about is known, then the questioner's doubts will perhaps be answered. But whether it is known or not, there is the possible reply. If it is given (and appreciated) it answers the questioner's doubts. Its not being given confirms his doubts. Consequently, while it might be that everything that *would be* replied by someone would leave the questioner's doubts unanswered, this cannot be the case for every possible reply. This is just as true in the case of asking how someone knows that Jesus is the Son of God. It is only *as things are* that there is no possible reply to a doubt concerning the authenticity of the Bible. If Jesus or the prophets were among us today, we could reply to doubts about the authenticity of the Bible without circularity. It is precisely because this reply is impossible (as things are) that these doubts about the Bible are so final. So even if the doubts behind the question "How do you know that there is a God?" concern the Bible, mystical experience, God's influence on our lives, and virtually everything taken to be of God, we should not conclude that there can be no reply which would answer these doubts. We should not even conclude that there is no reply as things are, for even if the authority and authenticity of the Bible may be justified only with circularity as things are, the ways of answering doubts about God's influence on our lives do not ask us to presuppose God's influence on our lives. Characteristically such replies ask one to look at the lives of certain men in the hope that he will see God's influence. Such a reply with its citation of the lives of religious men might or might not dispell his doubt. Similarly when it is doubted that I have a granduncle because it is thought that no one has ever been helped by him, and I reply that I know that I have a granduncle because people *have* been helped by him, and I recount such cases, even though my reply speaks to the other's doubt, it might or might not dispel it.

To summarize:

1) "How do you know?" questions that are challenges need understood doubts behind them to be both understandable and answerable.

2) Many times the question "How do you know that there is a God?" can be answered because the doubts behind it are answerable.

3) Even if it cannot be answered because the doubts behind it cannot be answered by him who was asked, we should not conclude that there is no possible answer; in fact, we should conclude just the opposite.

4) While it may be true that *as things are* there in fact is no possible answer to the question "How do you know that Jesus is the Son of God?" when the Bible is doubted, it is not true that as things are there is no possible answer to the question "How do you know that there is a God?" when the Bible, mystical experience, God's influence on our lives, and virtually everything taken to be of God are doubted.

It is open to the religious skeptic to reply that his question "How do you know that there is a God?" is not a "How do you know?" question at all, but rather an effort to get the believer to state which of the traditional grounds for theism he subscribes to, so that they may be criticized. And, too, the religious skeptic may want to say that no one can know that there is a God because it is not an assertion and so not the kind of thing that one can know.[4] This would be the verificationist or positivist skeptic's reply. Of course this reply rules out the other and, if correct, makes it unintelligible.

And it is open to the religious skeptic to reply that he is asking a "How do you know?" question with the logic of a "How do you know?" question, his doubts being about the Bible, mystical and religious experience, miracles, God's influence on the lives of men, and virtually everything taken to be of God. If this is how the religious skeptic's question is to be understood, it may well be that it cannot be answered by anyone, but, again, this cannot mean that there is no possible answer, or that there is nothing that would answer his doubts. Indeed, it must mean just the opposite.

Notes

[1]Norman Malcolm, "Is it a Religious Belief that 'God Exists'?" *Faith and the Philosophers,* ed. John Hick (New York: St. Martin's Press; London: Macmillan & Co., 1964), p. 108 (italics in the original).

[2]Tautologies aside of course.

[3]Cf. Stephen Toulmin on "limiting questions," *An Examination of the Place of Reason in Ethics* (Cambridge: The Cambridge University Press, 1961), pp. 201 ff., esp. pp. 210–11.

[4]On this see sec. II of chap. 4 and the Appendix, Parts A and B.

10

faith and knowledge

10

I

We know what it is for a man to have faith in another man, and we know what it is to have faith that someone will do what he promised. Perhaps we cannot say what faith is in a way that would have satisfied Socrates if he had asked "What is faith?" But still we have all had faith in another and told him of our faith, praised or ridiculed others for their faith, hoped for faith, been surprised at the faith of others and perhaps at our own and said so, and in short, generally demonstrated that "faith" is one of the words we do not need to learn. Similarly we know what it is for a man to know that something is true, say, that another needs help or that another will help him. Although, again, we may not be able to answer the Socratic request for the nature of knowledge—a request that, apparently mistakenly, sets us looking for the necessary and sufficient conditions for knowledge, and a request that we need not answer to have the word "knowledge" and its cognates in our vocabulary. In the clear sense that we do not have to learn either the word "faith" or the word "know," we know what it is to have faith and to know that something is true.

But what is the relationship between having faith that a man will keep his promise and knowing that he will? And generally what is the relationship between faith and knowledge? Is faith the path to religious understanding and knowledge? Or is faith a condition necessarily characterized by a leap of uncertainty and at the far extreme from knowledge and its certainty?

We will be concerned in this chapter with these questions and the general issue of the relation between faith and knowledge. I shall endeavor to present points and the general discussion in terms of secular faith and knowledge as well as in terms of religious faith and knowledge. I of course do not mean by "religious faith" and "religious knowledge" faith and knowledge in a special sense or of a special kind, but rather faith in and knowledge of religious matters; that is, God-related matters. In regard to the secular, our concern with faith will cover, for example, faith in one's father, faith that a man is innocent of a crime with which he is charged, belief in someone, faith in a doctor's ability, faith that someone will keep a promise, and faith that one's wife is concerned for one; and our concern with knowledge will cover, for example, knowing that one's father is innocent, knowing that someone will help one, knowing that someone will keep his promise, and knowing that one's wife is concerned for one. In regard to the religious, our concern with faith will cover faith in God and faith that God will help one, and our concern with knowledge will cover knowing that there is a God and knowing that He is concerned for men. At this point the concern is not with whether there is any religious knowledge; it is rather with the relation to faith of such knowledge, if there be any.

The relation between faith and knowledge (particularly between religious faith and religious knowledge) has been thought of in various ways by religious thinkers. At least four basic ways can be distinguished.

   I Faith excludes knowledge, and knowledge excludes faith.
  II Faith is a special source or condition for some knowledge.
 III Faith is a kind of knowledge more certain (or less certain) than knowledge derived from reason.
 VI Faith is knowledge.

We shall first develop and examine these four ways, being sure to note the difficulties that attach to each, and then, in section VI, we shall try to winnow out what is right and wrong about each. In doing so we shall have an opportunity to relate the present concern with faith and knowledge to the earlier concern with religious discovery.

II-A

We turn then to the first view of the relation between faith and knowledge, which is:

I *Faith excludes knowledge, and knowledge excludes faith.*

Kierkegaard apparently accepted this; in fact it may be said that he insisted upon the antithesis of knowledge and faith as a crucial truth about the nature of religion and faith. To some extent we have already discussed Kierkegaard's view in discussing whether religious knowledge is knowledge in a special sense (chapter 6). Now, however, we shall have to go into the matter in more detail bringing out, for instance, how Aquinas subscribed to this view, with some qualifications. Kierkegaard tells us that faith is holding fast "an objective uncertainty" with "the infinite passion of the individual's awareness."[1] What he seems to have in mind here is an act of commitment, which he regards as distinct from and antithetical to knowledge. If we look in the *Concluding Unscientific Postscript,* we find there an implicit argument for the mutual exclusion of faith and knowledge. Drawing it out, I think that we may formulate it as follows:

1 —Faith requires risk.
2 —Risk requires a lack of certainty.
3 —Knowledge requires certainty.
∴. Faith and knowledge exclude each other.

We can spell out the argument a bit in terms of the following example: We know that $2 + 2 = 4$; no one who understands the terms of this proposition can doubt its truth. (It is "objectively certain," Kierkegaard would say.) Precisely for this reason there is no risk in accepting this proposition, and because this is true it is ruled out that one can have faith that $2 + 2 = 4$. Conceptually it is impossible to have faith in what is certain; although Kierkegaard did not put it this way. (Fairly clearly, it is part of Kierkegaard's thinking that faith is passionate, but knowledge is indifferent. When one has faith, he commits himself and does so with "passionate inwardness," to use Kierkegaard's language. But when one knows something, Kierkegaard tends to think of it as an "indifferent truth." The proposition "$2 + 2 = 4$" is perhaps his paradigm of knowledge.)

Specifically regarding the existence of God, Kierkegaard implies that one can have faith or believe that there is a God only as long as it is not known or is not certain that there is a God. This means that for there to be faith there must be no proof of God's existence. Thus, faith or belief that there is a God is incompatible with a demonstration and knowledge (and so certainty) that there is a God. By extrapolation there are also implications for faith *in* God.

One might think that even if Kierkegaard's view (I) is right, still a demonstration of God's existence would not rule out faith *in* God. This is perhaps true where the demonstration proves the existence of an unmoved mover, for in this case nothing about the concern or other attributes of God has been demonstrated. But if the existence of God in the Biblical concept is demonstrated, then the matter is different. For in that case the existence of a Being with absolute concern, mercy, power, and wisdom has been demonstrated and is certain. That is, the existence of an absolutely trustworthy Being has been demonstrated. Since God's concern, power, and mercy are certain, one *knows* that God will be merciful and concerned toward men, and it seems we must conclude there no longer is the necessity for, or even the possibility of, faith *in* God. Thus, if (I) is correct, religious faith in God, as well as faith that there is a God, would be ruled out by extensive knowledge.

But surely, one might say, faith is compatible with certainty, for it is common for those who do not know, but only have faith that so-and-so is the case, to say "I'm sure that so-and-so" or "I'm certain that so-and-so." When one makes such an avowal he is expressing his certainty. Kierkegaard seems to have been aware of expressions of certainty of the faithful; he implicitly drew a distinction between "subjective certainty" and "objective certainty" and allowed that those with faith express "subjective certainty."[2] Other philosophers have said similar things in reference to such avowals of certainty. They have said that they express *commitment to action*[3] or else the *conviction* or *certitude* of the speaker, but not that the matter at hand is *certain*. In the *Critique of Pure Reason* Kant says this:

> *Opining* is such holding of a judgment as is consciously insufficient, not only objectively, but also subjectively. If our holding of the judgment be only subjectively sufficient, and is at the same time taken as being objectively insufficient, we have what is termed *believing*. Lastly, when the holding of a thing to be true is sufficient both subjectively and objectively, it is *knowledge*. The subjective sufficiency is termed *conviction* (for myself), the objective sufficiency is termed *certainty* (for everyone).[4]

What Kant means by "conviction" has been called "certitude" and stands opposed to "objective certainty" in Kierkegaard's terms and presumably to the certainty involved when one says, e.g., "Although I was at first as sure as I could be (had certitude), I found out that the matter was doubtful (and not certain)." There is an element of confusion concerning these categories and we shall have to return to them later and also to a consideration of the argument that was drawn from the *Concluding Unscientific Postscript*.

Aquinas in a way agrees with Kierkegaard in (I). In fact, John Hick sees (I) as an essential part of the Thomistic view of faith.[5] (As we shall see, Aquinas' conception of the relationship between knowledge and faith is complex enough for him to also hold some of the other views about the relationship; however, this need not concern us here.) As far as (I) is concerned,

Aquinas maintains that faith is incompatible with "scientific knowledge." What this means for Aquinas is that while some religious matters can either be (scientifically) known *or* be an object of faith, they cannot be both for the same person at the same time.[6] Such matters can be (scientifically) known because they can be "demonstrated" or "seen" and are called "preambles to the articles of [faith]."[7] They contrast with the articles of faith themselves, such as that the Godhead is a unity,[8] which are "of faith absolutely"[9] and can only be objects of faith.

One noteworthy thing is that while Kierkegaard and Aquinas agree on (I), they do not agree on the place of knowledge (or "scientific knowledge") in religion. Aquinas feels that if one has the intelligence and can master a demonstration of a preamble to an article of faith, this will not harm his piety or religious character, although it will rule out his holding that matter on faith. Aquinas even suggests that we may one day *see* the truth of the articles of faith themselves, which would mean that then they too would no longer be objects of faith; and he makes this suggestion with no lamentations about a loss of believers' piety or religion. Kierkegaard, on the other hand, sees knowledge as inimical to religion. He reasons that faith is the essence of religion, and that knowledge, which rules out faith, thus rules out religion.

Kierkegaard apparently would say that regardless of *how* one comes to know, knowledge once attained excludes faith. Aquinas, however, might not concur. Indeed, at times he suggests that faith, far from excluding knowledge, is a source of knowledge. (Here he holds a variant of (II).) However, the knowledge gained from faith, for Aquinas, is not "scientific knowledge." In any case, Kierkegaard and Aquinas agree that knowledge gained through a demonstration that something is so, for example, that there is a God, excludes faith that there is a God.

What of the truth of (I)? It certainly seems that a number of ordinary cases of faith and knowledge support it.

Kierkegaard's own example of a mathematical proposition (e.g., $2 + 2 = 4$) is apposite. Just as Kierkegaard suggests, it is certainly not the case that we who understand the proposition's terms have *faith* that $2 + 2 = 4$; we know this to be true. As there is no possible doubt about the matter, faith is ruled out.

Another case: Before my friend demonstrates his ability to solve a complex mathematical problem I have faith that he can. After he demonstrates his ability I know that he can, I no longer have faith that he can. These cases can be multiplied, and while they are not conclusive, each is a case where faith and knowledge do not reside together.

II-B

The burden of this Kierkegaardian view of faith and knowledge strikes one as basically right: where there is faith that something is so there cannot be knowledge that it is so, and where there is knowledge that it is so there cannot be faith. To many, the implications of this view have seemed to be insights in their own right. One implication is that if faith is essential to religion, knowledge and the pursuit of knowledge are foreign to religion. Thus, the arguments for God's existence would be not irrelevant, but antithetical to religion. For they would not increase faith, but by rendering matters of faith matters of knowledge, they would actually make faith impossible.

However, there are some problems with the Kierkegaardian suggestion—problems that arise within the religious perspective. For one thing it must be recalled that not only skeptics have been concerned with arguments for the existence of God, but Saint Anselm and Saint Thomas Aquinas were concerned as well. Should we say that they were blind to the implications of finding what they sought and felt they had found? And what should be said of those who look upon the Bible as a source of knowledge of God and His ways toward men?

The most penetrating problem arises over Job, the Biblical man of faith. We are already familiar with this problem.[10] The Kierkegaardian view of the relation of faith and knowledge is meant to bring us back to a realization of what religious faith is and what it is not, and what it demands of one. As an example of the demands of religious faith, Kierkegaard uses the story of Abraham and Isaac to good effect.[11] As one reads Kierkegaard's version of Abraham's trial of faith, one feels that Kierkegaard has indeed captured the living experience at the center of religion. It comes as a surprise, then, to find that the Kierkegaardian view of the mutual exclusivity of faith and knowledge is at odds with the Biblical account of Job, and the traditional religious understanding of him and what he said and did. Job, of course, is the paragon of faith—the paradigmatic man of faith. But recall Job's cry of faith: "I know my Redeemer liveth." It is not "I believe" or "I have faith that," but "I *know* my Redeemer liveth." It will be odd indeed if the exemplar of faith could only have made a cry of faith if what he cried was false, as it would be if he did not know. Yet if Kierkegaard is right, Job could not have known—not if he had faith. Skeptics could say that this is precisely the case: Job was wrong; he did not know that there is a God to redeem him. But the problem is more abiding for a religious person. Either Job did not know and could not possibly have known, or he did not mean by "know" what is normally meant,[12] or something about the Kierkegaardian view of faith and knowledge is not quite right. There is indeed something about the Kierkegaardian view that is not quite right, as I tried to bring out in chapter 6. Later we shall return to a more detailed discussion of just where this view goes wrong.

III-A

The second view of the relation between faith and knowledge is this:
   II *Faith is a special source or condition for some knowledge.*

There are several ways in which we can understand the view that faith is a *source* of knowledge. One way is according to Hebrews 11.1, where it is said that "faith is the substance of things to be hoped for, the evidence of things that appear not." Of course this passage may not contain at all the notion that faith is a source of *knowledge,* but instead, the view that faith provides some support for *belief* or, perhaps, provides conviction. From another perspective, however, this passage presents us with a model for the view before us, namely, that faith is a source of knowledge. Understanding the view according to this model involves assimilating faith to empirical data. The suggestion is that, just as empirical data are a source of information on things seen, so too faith is a source of information on things not seen. Or, if we think of our physical senses as sources of knowledge, this view might be understood as assimilating faith to our senses. Faith, then, would be a source of knowledge in the way our seeing something is, where faith itself is thought of as a kind of seeing or special perception.

Differing slightly from the last two is another version of the view that faith is a source of knowledge. According to this version, *faith along with revelation* or *revelation-assented-to-by-faith* is a source of knowledge. At times Locke, Aquinas, and Calvin seem to articulate this as the relation between faith and knowledge. Locke says that there are some things we know, for instance "that the dead shall rise, and live again,"[13] that we could not have learned using only our "natural faculties." We have discovered these things through revelation and faith—that is, by the "testimony . . . of God himself"[14] who can neither "deceive nor be deceived" and whose testimony is "evidence beyond exception," which is accepted on faith, which in turn is "a settled and sure principle of assent and assurance."

Aquinas also seems to have held this view. In one place he says "in order that men may arrive more quickly at divine truth" and "in order that the knowledge of God may be more widespread" and men may have "certitude" in things concerning God, "it was necessary for divine truths to be delivered to them by way of faith, being told to them, as it were, by God Himself who cannot lie."[15] Thus, for Aquinas even if one could not master the discipline of science and demonstrate God's existence, he could arrive at this knowledge through faith; although, of course, it would not be "scientific knowledge." While Aquinas does not mention revelation as such, presumably when he speaks of "divine truths" being "delivered to men by way of faith," he has in mind what Locke explicitly called revelation.

Calvin also apparently holds this view as indicated in the *Institutes.* He says:

> Profane men think that religion rests only on opinion, and, therefore, that they may not believe foolishly, or on slight grounds desire and insist to have it proved by reason that Moses and the prophets were divinely inspired. But I answer, that the testimony of the Spirit is superior to reason.[16]

Later on he adds:

> Such, then, is a conviction which asks not for reasons; such, a knowledge which
> accords with the highest reason, namely, knowledge in which the mind rests
> more firmly and securely than in any reasons; such, in fine, the conviction which
> revelation from heaven alone can produce.[17]

Calvin would hold the view that *faith along with revelation* is a source of
knowledge if he agreed with Aquinas that "divine truths are delivered...
by way of faith."

Instead of casting faith as a source of knowledge, (II) may be understood
as asserting that faith is a condition for knowledge. This version of (II) is
outlined by Jerry H. Gill in an essay on Kierkegaard, in which he says:
"[according to Kierkegaard] unless someone (God Himself) supplies him with
the condition (faith) whereby he can receive the truth, the learner will always
remain without knowledge."[18]

To clarify the view before us—that faith is a *condition* for some knowledge—
let us note what is not meant. This view does not mean that faith is a condition for knowledge as it is when a scientist has faith in an investigative effort
and then proceeds to investigate and discovers what he thought he would.
In this case, faith does lead to knowledge; and, in a sense, it is a condition
for the knowledge the scientist gains. But the burden of (II) is that faith is a
condition for knowledge in quite a different and much more embracing sense.
Two elements seem to be important for the burden of (II) in this version:
first, that faith is a contributing and prior necessary condition for some knowledge and second, that faith persists after the knowledge is attained (as the
condition of one's mind remaining open could persist after he had made a
discovery). Neither element seems to belong to the case of the scientist's
discovery. While the scientist's faith may have been helpful, the discovery
could easily have been made without it; all that was required for the discovery
was the investigation. Once the discovery is made, the scientist's faith in his
investigation disappears. As Gill puts it, (II) in this version says that faith is a
condition whereby one can receive the truth, or come to know, and is a condition granted by God himself. And what Kierkegaard meant, if Gill is correct
in his view, was that first, one can only come to a knowledge of God through
faith and, second, faith continues after knowledge is attained.

III-B

This second view of faith, like the first, does seem to capture something important about religious faith. Certainly many religious thinkers have cast faith
as a path to a knowledge of God, either as a source or condition of such
knowledge.

However, there are problems attaching to this view. The first arises from
the strong suggestion that the knowledge obtained through faith (and revela-

tion) is a special kind of knowledge in its nature, as well as in its source and subject. In Aquinas' terms this knowledge is different from "scientific knowledge," and both Locke and Aquinas agree that it is "above reason." Now inasmuch as the kind of knowledge derived from faith (and revelation) is different in its nature from what we ordinarily mean by "knowledge," several questions arise. 1) What is the relation between what we ordinarily mean by "knowledge" and this special kind of knowledge? 2) If this special sort of "knowledge" is not what we ordinarily mean by "knowledge," then why should we think that it is knowledge at all? Thus here we are confronted with the same problems that arose when we thought of religious knowledge as knowledge in a special sense.

The second problem that attaches to (II) has to do with the difference between conviction and knowledge. Let us concede that faith is a source or a condition leading to conviction. Now even if faith (and revelation) can produce conviction that something is so, what is it that indicates that it (or they) can yield knowledge that something is so, as opposed to just conviction? Each of the three religious thinkers mentioned above—Locke, Aquinas, and Calvin—invites this problem. Locke implies that faith and revelation are a source of discovery and knowledge beyond our "natural faculties," but also speaks as though what they yield may be only "assurance," to use his term.[19] In Aquinas we find a similar tension between knowledge and "certitude," and in Calvin between knowledge and "conviction." But while it may be that knowledge entails conviction on the part of the knower, conviction does not entail knowledge. That is, perhaps to know that so-and-so one must be sure that so-and-so, but, upon reflection, often one is sure that so-and-so and yet does not know that so-and-so. This is the case whenever one is sure and yet is mistaken. And, too, one can irrationally be sure and have an irrational conviction with no support whatsoever, as when the mother who receives an official telegram from the government telling her that her son is dead refuses to believe it and continues to insist that he is alive. In such a case, again, there would be conviction, or could be, but not knowledge (even if the son is still alive, the mother did not *know* that he was).

Part of the reason for the problem here is a confusion between one's feeling certain and the matter itself being certain. Sometimes Locke and Calvin speak as though one's feeling certain (having certitude) were the *same thing* as the matter's being certain, or as though the first entails the second. This clearly is not the case (one can feel sure, perhaps due to his ignorance, about a matter that is dubious).[20] It may be that this confusion arises for the following reasons: When one expresses the certainty that he feels (his certitude) he cannot go on to say that the matter itself is not certain. He cannot seriously say with good sense "I'm sure that so-and-so, but the matter is doubtful." He *can* say that *he* is sure and that *someone else* is not, but he cannot express his certainty and then say that the matter is not certain. He cannot do this, because in saying that the matter is not certain he thereby expresses his *lack* of certitude.[21] Now perhaps religious thinkers such as Locke and others were vaguely aware of this fact and erroneously concluded from it that the certainty one feels (certitude) comes to the certainty of the matter involved, or that the two are more intimately linked than they really are. If one were to draw such a conclusion, he could well think that having certitude was sufficient for knowledge. That the two are not, or need not be intimately linked at all, becomes forcefully clear when we remind ourselves of what can be meaningfully and sometimes truly said about *other's* certainty ("He is certain that so-and-so; but he shouldn't be, for the matter is highly doubtful.") and about one's own *past* certainty ("At first I was certain that so-and-so; but later I saw that the matter was doubtful.").

If Locke, Aquinas, and Calvin have only made a case for faith (or faith along with revelation) being a source of feeling certain or conviction, then they have not thereby made a case for its being a source of knowledge. Even an atheist might allow that they have made a case for faith causing or producing conviction (the atheist of course will not give any role to revelation). The atheist's granting that faith produces conviction—which he could say is an irrational conviction with no evidential support whatsoever—is perfectly consistent with his denying that faith is a source of knowledge and that any religious beliefs are true. Thus the view advanced here by Locke, Aquinas, and Calvin, or any version of (II), must be that knowledge, and not just conviction, is obtained through faith and revelation. The core of the problem is that knowledge (e.g., that there is a God) requires support or evidence when there is a knowledge claim, and when there is no knowledge claim it requires at least a possible answer in some situations to the questions "How do you know?" or "How did you find out?" And these questions are not answered by "By faith" or "By belief." We, including the atheist, can understand one's faith or one's belief (or wanting to believe or jealousy or love) causing conviction, but knowledge, unlike conviction, cannot be created by such nonevidential causes. Knowledge (e.g., that there is a God) requires a finding out, to put it one way. And while we can be caused to believe something with conviction by wanting to believe or by some other nonevidential cause, what we come to believe in this way has not been found out and so is not known. Somehow, if (II) is right, faith has to supply a finding out.

Yet as we shall see, while there is much in this second view of the relation between faith and knowledge that is confused and misleading, there is an insightful element at its center.

IV-A

We come now to the third view of the relation between faith and knowledge:

III *Faith is a kind of knowledge more certain (or less certain) than knowledge derived from reason.*

(III) involves two views. One is that faith is a kind of knowledge more certain than knowledge derived from reason, and the other is that faith is a kind of knowledge less certain than that derived from reason. Although both views are part of (III), they are odd companions and, construed generally, they are incompatible. This third view in one or the other of its forms seems discernible in the writings of both Locke and Aquinas.

The passages in the *Essay Concerning Human Understanding* that we have noted so far suggest that, if Locke held a version of (III) at all, he thought of faith as a kind of knowledge at least as certain as knowledge derived from reason. Other passages from the *Essay*, however, suggest that faith might be a kind of knowledge less certain than knowledge derived from reason. In discussing the provinces of faith and reason Locke says that:

> Whatsoever truth we come to the clear discovery of, from the knowledge and contemplation of our own ideas, will always be certainer to us than those which are conveyed to us by *traditional revelation*. For the knowledge we have that this revelation came at first from God, can never be so sure as the knowledge we have from the clear and distinct perception of the agreement or disagreement of our own ideas...[22]

By "traditional revelation" Locke means an "original revelation" conveyed to others in words—as for instance in the Bible. Fairly clearly, in this passage Locke is saying that although revelation discovers truths to us, they are not as certain as truths discovered by reason. They are discovered and known truths but are still to some extent dubious, he seems to be saying. In the last sentence of the passage just quoted Locke tells us why truths discovered by reason are more certain than truths discovered by revelation, and also makes it perfectly clear that he sanctions the notions of more sure and less sure knowledge. His reasoning seems to be that since the knowledge we have *that* a revelation of some truth came at first from God can never be as certain as our knowledge *of* this truth derived from reason, we ought to conclude that while we have knowledge *of* this truth derived from revelation, it is less certain than our knowledge of it derived from reason.

Aquinas, too, at times seems to suggest that (III) captures the relationship between knowledge and faith. At one point in the Second Part of the Second Part of the *Summa Theologica*, Aquinas, in discussing the interior act of faith, says that "its knowledge [i.e., the knowledge of belief or faith] does not attain the perfection of clear vision" and so "agrees with doubt, suspicion and opinion."[23] This suggests that Aquinas thinks that while faith is a kind of knowledge, it is less certain than the kind he refers to as "scientific knowledge."

Elsewhere Aquinas seems to suggest the other version of (III), namely that faith is a kind of knowledge more certain than knowledge derived from reason. In discussing "Whether faith is more certain than science and the other intellectual virtues?" he says that faith is more "certain absolutely" and that science is more "certain relatively, i.e., for us."[24] This distinction apparently comes down to one between certainty and certitude, or between the certainty of the matter and the certainty one feels. If so, what Aquinas is saying is that regarding the intellectual virtues—one of which is "science" or, presumably, "scientific knowledge"—we may feel more certitude, but regarding faith there is more certainty so far as the matter is concerned. And this, given that Aquinas thinks of faith as a kind of knowledge, comes to saying that the kind of knowledge faith is is more certain than the kind called "scientific knowledge."

Let us at this point try to reconstruct the reasoning that apparently leads to (III). There are two or three courses of reasoning to be noted. The first might be given this form:

1. First we note that something (e.g., the Bible or the encyclopedia) can make us feel certain that so-and-so is true.
2. Then we identify this conviction or certitude with knowledge or with the certainty of the matter.
3. Now we note that our conviction can vary: we are more certain of some things than others; and, further, the certainty of the matter can vary: some things are more certain than others (which re-enforces the notion that certitude and the certainty of the matter are identical).
4. So we conclude that some knowledge is more certain than other knowledge.
5. Finally, we identify faith with either the more certain or the less certain sort of knowledge.

The second line of reasoning that could be marshalled here is this:

1. First we allow that some sources of knowledge (e.g., the Bible and the encyclopedia) are more certain than others.
2. Then we conclude that knowledge obtained from the more certain sources is more certain and knowledge obtained from the less certain sources is less certain.
3. And then, again, we identify faith with either the more certain or the less certain sort of knowledge.

The key step in any reasoning that leads to (III) is the step that establishes that there is more certain and less certain knowledge. And any considerations pertinent to the validity of this step are thereby pertinent to the truth of (III). Norman Malcolm, who does not maintain (III), does maintain that there is more certain and less certain knowledge. He distinguishes between knowledge in the more certain strong sense and knowledge in the less certain weak sense and draws this distinction in terms of the strength of the grounds for knowing. If one knows in the strong sense, one's grounds are such that he does not allow that there is anything that he would count as evidence against what he knows. If one knows in the weak sense, one's grounds are such that he allows that there might be evidence against what he knows.[25] Even though Malcolm himself might not be inclined to argue for (III), nevertheless the distinction he develops gives rise to the following third line of reasoning:

1. First we allow that knowledge is based on grounds.
2. Then we observe that the strength of these grounds can vary.
3. Then we distinguish between more certain knowledge based on stronger grounds and less certain knowledge based on weaker grounds.
4. And finally, we identify faith with either the more certain or the less certain sort of knowledge.

IV-B

The third view of the relation between faith and knowledge has a number of problems with which we must contend. First there are difficulties that attach to each of the three lines of reasoning that lead to (III), and second there are problems that attach to the view itself. Let us look first at the difficulties with the three lines of reasoning.

The first line of reasoning suffers from the already noted confusion between certitude and the certainty of the matter. We discussed this confusion in reference to (II).

The second line of reasoning seems to be more forceful. It is free of any confusion between certitude and the certainty of the matter, but there are difficulties. The first step is to allow that some sources of knowledge are more certain than others. Now what does this mean? All it can mean is that some sources are more *dependable* than others; that is, some sources give us truths more often than others. This does not mean that they, as opposed to other sources, give us a more certain knowledge, as the second line of reasoning would have it; it means that they, as opposed to other sources, more often give us pure and simple knowledge if undependable sources *ever* give us knowledge.

One might still think that a source of knowledge can be more certain in *this* sense—in the sense that it is more dependable—and so the knowledge it yields would be more certain; but this is not quite right. It is true that if I look in a dependable reference book and find there that so-and-so is said to be the case, I will be certain that so-and-so is the case; and further I have found that it is certain that so-and-so—that is, that the matter is certain. And if I look in a reference book I know is not dependable and find there that so-and-so is said to be the case, I will be less certain that it is; and also it will be less certain that so-and-so. But what is not certain, or not so certain, when the source is not dependable is *that so-and-so is the case*. It is not my *knowledge* that so-and-so which is not so certain. Just as my certitude that so-and-so is different from the certainty of the matter, so too the certainty of the matter is different from my knowledge that so-and-so. Thus, while the certainty of the matter can vary, it does not follow that the certainty of knowledge can vary. Indeed, one way for me to concede that I do *not* know (at all) that so-and-so is to concede either that it is not certain or that it is not so certain that so-and-so. Think of the oddity of one saying, "It is not so certain that this is the case, but I know that it is." (It is hardly less odd if he says, "... but I uncertainly know that it is.") To concede that something found in a reference book is not so certain is to indicate that in order to know, we must look further.

The third line of reasoning hinges on the view that knowledge is based on grounds, a view we examined earlier and found wanting.[26] If this view were correct and if there were different kinds of knowledge based on stronger or weaker grounds, then we should be able to make sense of someone assuring us that he knows his friend is telling the truth but adding that his grounds for knowing it are not as good as they might be. But this can only be a curious way of admitting that one does not know, after all, that his friend is telling the truth.

There are also difficulties that attach to (III) itself. Inherent in the view is the proposition that knowledge can be more certain or less certain. We have just seen that what might be thought to provide support for this proposition really does not. Let us now ask if this proposition can possibly be right. Can we understand one kind of knowledge being more (or less) certain than another kind? Certainly the proclivity to talk about more or less certain knowledge has persisted among thinkers and philosophers for some time; however we should not think that this fact in itself validates the proclivity. In fact, if this third view of the relation between faith and knowledge is right, and knowledge can be more certain or less certain, then a number of rather odd things should make sense. In the first place, one should be able to say meaningfully what in fact one cannot say with good sense, namely, "It is not so certain that this [something that is in question] is the case, but I (uncertainly) know that it is." Also when someone tells us that he knows his friend is telling the truth, we should be able to ask him in what sense he knows—more certainly or less certainly. That is, we should be able to ask him this where the question would not come to the question "*Do* you know?" which impugns his knowing at all. We should be able to ask this question and get the reply, "I know, but only in the weak sense, I'm afraid." Further, if one knows in the weak, less certain sense, then he should be able to say quite correctly, "I know it, but of course I just might be mistaken." But this last statement is what a comic character might appropriately say in a farce—not realizing that in admitting he might be wrong he is admitting that he does not know at all.

V-A

The fourth view of the relation between faith and knowledge is simply stated but not simply established. It is:

IV *Faith is knowledge.*

(IV) is obviously at the far horizon from (I), yet they are alike in having an apologetic thrust. (IV) is also akin to the apologetic view that both science and Christianity operate with beliefs accepted on faith without evidence, a view used to defend religion on the grounds that it, after all, is no worse off than science.[27] And (IV) is also close to, yet different from, the view that faith underlies knowledge.[28] What is distinctive about (IV) is that it asserts an identity: faith *is* knowledge.

According to passages from the *Institutes*, Calvin seems to have held this view. For instance he defines faith as:

> . . . a firm and certain knowledge of God's benevolence towards us, founded upon the truth of the freely given promise in Christ, both revealed to our minds [in the Bible] and sealed upon our hearts through the Holy Spirit.[29]

To the extent that he thought of faith as knowledge that was *more* certain than other knowledge he would have held the third view, but in this passage Calvin may be thought of as simply identifying faith with knowledge. John Hick also holds the view that faith is knowledge—a view he develops in his book *Faith and Knowledge*. However, Professor Hick does not rush to embrace Calvin as an ally because Calvin tends toward the "intellectualist" notion that faith means "primarily and centrally the holding of unevidenced beliefs."[30] And Hick wants to say, following Luther, that "faith is not belief *that,* but belief *in.*"[31] As we have seen, though, while it is true that religious belief is primarily belief *in* God, and not a belief *that* there is a God, this does not rule out belief that there is a God; rather it necessitates it;[32] and certainly it leaves the way open to belief *that* God is concerned for men and that he created the world. Hick is aware of this, as his discussion of faith and knowledge makes relatively clear. Further, since his view is that faith is knowledge, and he has in mind primarily knowledge *that,* he has to allow some place for faith *that.* The reason Hick does not fully accept Calvin as an ally, then, is not that Calvin allows faith to include faith that a proposition is true and Hick wants to categorically deny this. Rather the reason is that Calvin identifies faith with "firm and certain knowledge," as he puts it. And while Hick identifies faith with knowledge, he wants to say that knowledge is a fallible "mode of cognition."[33] In short, while both Calvin and Hick say that faith is knowledge, Calvin tends to make faith into knowledge, and Hick tends to make knowledge into faith. Calvin's view is charged with a confusion between conviction on the one hand and knowledge and the matter being certain on the other. It is Hick's view and argument that we shall examine.

In *Faith and Knowledge* Hick offers several considerations directed toward the conclusion that faith is knowledge. The overall argument they comprise is not formulated in any one place, but I think that it can be drawn out. It seems to be this:

1. There are "certain knowledge" in "the strict rationalist sense" and a contrasting sort of knowledge.
2. There can be certain knowledge only of tautologies.
3. The contrasting sort of knowledge is the kind we have most often, relating to most if not all "matters of fact"; it is a fallible mode of cognition.
4. As a fallible mode of cognition, it is to be equated with a (subjective) interpretive element within religious (and all) experience.
5. This interpretive element is faith.
6. Therefore, knowledge is faith.[34]

We shall soon have to examine this argument and in so doing we will make an effort to fill in its background, as well as weigh its merits. But first let us note a secondary argument found in Hick's book that supports the reasoning of the first as it relates to religious knowledge.

1. If it is evident that there is a God, then we are not "cognitively free" to recognize God; that is, we are forced to recognize his presence and do not do so freely.
2. Unless we freely recognize God's presence, there can be no *personal* relation to him.
3. Thus a personal relation to God requires that it not be evident that there is a God.[35]

At this point Hick can argue that our knowledge of God, and that there is a God, is achieved by us "as a voluntary act of interpretation," that is, as an act of faith. And a good thing it is too, he can say, for if it were known that there is a God because it is evident, knowing that there is a God would rule out having a personal relation to God.

V-B

To assert that faith *is* knowledge is to assert a view whose very statement is burdened with paradox. However, more serious than this air of paradox are the several difficulties that attach to the fourth view. I shall try to bring out the nature of these difficulties by examining the two arguments given in the last section, beginning with the second argument.

The first premise of the second argument maintains that there is a connection between God's presence being evident and one's freedom to be aware of God's presence. Several philosophers have questioned the sense of saying that awareness or knowledge is either free or compelled.[36] And, upon reflection, it does seem odd to speak of someone being forced to know something, to be aware of something, or to recognize something; and it seems equally odd to say of someone that he knows something, is aware of it, or recognizes it voluntarily or of his own free will. It is more understandable to speak of someone being forced to *conclude* something (this is the position the prosecuting attorney says the jury is in); and we also speak of being forced by the evidence to *believe* things we do not want to believe. Hick does not ask whether it is good sense to say that someone was forced to know or to be aware of something. He seems to assume that this is as sensible as saying that one was forced to conclude something. Given Hick's categories, it is not surprising that he would make this assumption. Recall that Hick thinks of knowledge as faith and thinks of faith as interpreting. In regard to the second argument, he also thinks of recognizing and being aware as interpreting. Does interpreting resemble knowing or does it resemble concluding and believing, regarding the good sense of saying that one was forced to do it? Clearly it is similar to concluding and believing; it is sensible for me to say that although I do not want to, I am forced to interpret what someone said as an insult. Thus, by thinking of knowing, recognizing, and being aware as interpreting, Hick understandably but wrongly ends up thinking that it is sensible to say that one can be forced to recognize or to know.

The greater difficulty with this second argument, however, relates to the second premise and the conclusion. The conclusion affirms that a personal relation to God requires that it not be evident that there is a God. Presumably, if this conclusion is right, a matter's being evident or certain would rule out personal relationships among human beings as well. But is this conclusion right? If I finally discover that my love is requited—if I am certain of it and it is certain—*must* a personal relationship at that moment become impossible? True, just when I discover that my love is requited I might lose interest: some hearts are fickle. But must I lose interest? Does the certainty of requited love make a personal relationship between human beings impossible? Let us hope not. The problem here, of course, is that while Hick has rightly seen that *force* applied in a relation with God or in a human relation makes a *personal* relation impossible, he has gone astray in thinking that if one perceives a matter to be certain, that this certainty constitutes such force. (As though, if it were certain that someone else would keep his part of an agreement, I could not freely enter into the agreement at that point!) In section VI we shall return to Hick's concern with this matter and to Kierkegaard's similar concern with the implications of the certainty of knowledge.

Hick's main argument is the first argument. The first premise of that argument is that there are "certain knowledge" and a contrasting sort of knowledge. The first premise, in other words, affirms the presupposition of (III), namely, that there are more certain and less certain sorts of knowledge. The correctness of this notion was questioned in the last section.

In the third premise we are told, in Hick's words, that knowledge, or knowledge of the most common sort, is a "fallible mode of cognition." When Hick says that knowledge is fallible he does not mean that someone can know something is so and yet be mistaken; he means that whenever one says that he knows something that is a matter of fact, he might be mistaken. Hick's point is sometimes advanced by skeptics. And, given his view of faith as nearly ubiquitous interpretation, it is understandable that he would accept and even insist upon the skeptical point that we might always be mistaken. We interpret what is before us when it is not altogether clear and when there is a possibility of more than one interpretation. If what is before us is straightforwardly a man, say, then no interpretation is called for. But now let us say that nothing is ever straightforwardly before us, that what presents itself is always ambiguous and unclear. If this were so, then interpretation would always be called for, and there would always be the possibility that the interpretation was mistaken. Hick wants to say that interpretation *is* always required, for what confronts us in the world *is* always ambiguous. He accepts the implication that all our interpretations might be mistaken, but since he identifies faith with interpretation and knowledge with faith he ends up by saying that knowledge is fallible; that is, whenever one says that he knows something is so, he might be wrong.

However, a central problem seems to arise at this point. One way to put it is this: Since Hick accepts the skeptic's point that whenever one says he knows that something is so he might be wrong, why does Hick not also accept the skeptic's conclusion, namely, that whenever one says he knows, he really does not. The skeptic reasons quite correctly that if I might be wrong when I say that I know that so-and-so, then I do not really know. One cannot say consistently "I know that he is coming, but I might be wrong" or "He knows that it is raining, but he might be mistaken." The admission of a possibility of being mistaken about so-and-so is tantamount to an admission that one does not know that so-and-so. The skeptic is correct about this at least. Of course Hick does not want to accept the skeptic's conclusion; if he did he could not say that faith is knowledge since he would have just concluded that there is no knowledge, unless he wants to say also that there is no faith. Hick clearly wants to say that there are many instances of faith and knowledge. But how can he escape the skeptic's conclusion? That is the problem. To put it another way: Why does Hick conclude that faith, which he construes to be of the ambiguous and questionable, is knowledge? Why does he not conclude instead that there is faith relating to these matters, but no knowledge?

Hick has this problem because he accepts the skeptic's premise, but he does not want to accept his conclusion. He could, of course, reject the skeptic's premise, as he would if he said that sometimes when we say we know that so-and-so, the matter is in fact certain and there is no chance that we are mistaken. This after all is not so extravagant: I do know in this way that my driver's license is valid and that my eyes are blue. Rejecting this skeptical point would also make knowledge possible without the necessity of characterizing it as uncertain or less than certain. But, on the other hand, if Hick were to reject the skeptic's point, it would undercut or perhaps rule out his thesis that we have to interpret all that presents itself in the world. This would mean he could not argue that religious faith is another instance of the faith we exercise (the interpreting that we do) every day in confronting the world.

There are related problems attaching to Hick's argument and to his view. One has to do with the nature of matters of fact as opposed to tautologies. Hick apparently allows that there can be "certain knowledge" of tautologies, but not of matters of fact. A matter of fact can never be certain, he thinks.[37] In subscribing to this view Hick follows a strong tradition in British Empericism and philosophy generally. Roughly, this tradition has it that matter of fact statements (or factual or synthetic statements) as opposed to tautologies (or relations of ideas or analytic statements) are hypotheses or are basically like hypotheses in that they are always open to disproof and thus should only be tentatively held. This view involves two alternatives: whenever one makes a factual statement *either* 1) he puts forward a hypothesis *or* 2) he puts forward what has the *status* of a hypothesis even if it was not meant as one.

(Before turning to these alternatives, though, let us parenthetically note and remind ourselves of why it is so misleading to think of *religious* statements as hypotheses. There are two major reasons for not thinking of religious statements as hypotheses. First, some things that religious people do when they make religious statements, such as expressing their faith, are not compatible with putting forward a tentative view for investigation, that is, a hypothesis; if one says tentatively, putting forward a hypothesis, "I *think* there is a God," he hardly expresses his *faith*, or at any rate the faith he expresses is weak and lacking in commitment, while if one says "I believe in God," expressing his faith and commitment, he cannot be tentative without undermining the very faith he means to express.[38] Second, it may be that religious statements, e.g., "There is a God," can be discovered to be true, but if so they will be discovered according to a nonhypothetical model of discovery.[39] To the extent that Hick tends to think of all factual statements, including religious statements, as hypotheses, or as having the status of hypotheses, he would tend toward thinking of a religious discovery as discovering that a hypothesis is confirmed, and would tend toward accepting and trying to answer what is called the falsification challenge.[40])

Both alternatives seem open to question. Sometimes when one makes a factual statement, he is putting forward a hypothesis, but it hardly seems that this is always the case. Sometimes one is pointing out what is obvious once it is pointed out, as with: "You have forgotten your hat." Other times one is underscoring a fact that is known but not adequately appreciated: "Hurry up, I'm waiting for you." And other times one is dramatically proclaiming what is clear to all: "We are even now engaged in a war in Southeast Asia." Each of these is a factual statement; yet no one in any of these instances is offering a hypothesis. This seems to refute the first alternative. Further, although each is a factual statement, none is worthy of only tentative acceptance, as a hypothesis is. And this seems to refute the second alternative.

Now Hick or a skeptic might say here that these points indicate only that religious statements and factual statements sometimes are not *meant* as hypotheses (the first alternative). But, he could maintain, they do not indicate that religious statements and factual statements generally do not have the *status* of hypotheses in being worthy only of tentative acceptance, whether or not the speaker is tentative (the second alternative). This kind of reply is open to Hick, but at a cost that involves the final problem, or problems, I wish to point out. If Hick were to make this reply, and I think his argument dictates it, he would in effect reject at least one of the above points, namely the point that we do occasionally use a factual statement to call attention to what is obviously true. How, though, could Hick reject this point? He says that what presents itself to us is ambiguous and calls for interpretation. But what is ambiguous about something that appears clear and obvious at its root (e.g., that I have blue eyes)?

At this point let me quote from Descartes' *Meditations,* for Descartes seems to supply Hick's answer, or at least begins to.

> Now I am truly astonished when I consider how weak my mind is and how apt I am to fall into error. For even though I consider all this in my mind without speaking, still words impede me, and I am nearly deceived by the terms of ordinary language. For we say that we see the same wax if it is present, and not that we judge that it is the same from the fact that it has the same color or shape. Thus I might be tempted to conclude that one knows the wax by means of eyesight, and not uniquely by the perception of the mind. So I may by chance look out of a window and notice some men passing in the street, at the sight of whom I do not fail to say that I see men, just as I say that I see wax; and nevertheless what do I see from this window except hats and cloaks which might cover ghosts, or automata which move only by springs? But I judge that they are men, and thus I comprehend, solely by the faculty of judgment which resides in my mind, that which I believed I saw with my eyes.[41]

Note the similarity in tone between this quotation and Hick's argument. Descartes talks about "judgment" and a "perception of the mind"; Hick talks about "interpretation" of "significance."[42] But Descartes might just as well have used Hick's word and said that we *interpret* hats and cloaks to cover men and not automata. At this point, then, Descartes has in a way explained how it is that the factual statement "There are men in the street" is not obvious and clearly true and thus calls for interpretation. And we might even think that he has done this for the statement regardless of its setting, and regardless of the speaker or the window from which he peers. There is a flaw, though; so far Descartes' answer is not complete. For, what about the factual statement "There are cloaks and hats there in the street"? What makes this factual statement unclear, and where does interpretation come into it? Here we must extend Descartes some, but little pressure is required: We say that there are cloaks and hats in the street because this is the way we interpret the patches of color and texture that we see (or their "significance" as Hick would have it). Now either the story stops at these patches of color and texture (or their significance) or it goes on. If it stops, then there are some factual statements that do not require interpretation after all. If it goes on, it ends with sense-data. Sense-data statements are not supposed to be statements about the world, they are statements about one's private sense experience; although they are supposed to provide the bases of our factual statements about the world. Here, then, is an answer to the question that faces Hick. Perhaps it is not the answer Hick would give, but it is the kind of answer he needs to supply. And so we come to the final problem that is posed for Hick: How would he make it clear that factual matters are at their root ambiguous? Would he rely upon a sense-data theory? Sometimes he suggests this, as when he talks about our "phenomenal experience" and our interpreting "a presented field of data."[43] How then would he solve the nest of problems that surround the notion of sense-data?[44] We find in the train of this fourth view of the relation between faith and knowledge something that we perhaps did not suspect—the sense-data theory and its attendant problems—or else a rather large gap.

Despite all this, (IV) carries at its center an insight about faith and knowledge worth putting into perspective. We turn to it now and to a re-examination of all four views.

VI-A

It is time to go back over the four basic relationships between faith and knowledge (I-IV) and to try to say what is right and what is wrong about each. I shall draw upon two human situations, one secular and one religious, which will hopefully serve as an illustration and a ground for the points to be made. Both situations are, or at least may be, discovery situations. First let me sketch in the two situations.

The Secular: In this situation a man comes to see that another is concerned for him. He is a man who has long believed that his wife has only feelings of indifference or veiled animosity toward him, but then he comes to see her attitude toward him in a different light—in its true light, as he later says. Why he had failed before to see her concern for what it was need not greatly occupy us. It may be that sometimes when we cannot see that someone is concerned for us it is because we cannot bring ourselves to admit that that person may be concerned; somehow for some reason we may need to believe that that person is unconcerned. Recall Claggart's apparent inability to recognize Billy Budd's concern for what it was and how that inability fed Claggart's purpose. In such cases self-deception and the need for self-deception may play a central role, a possibility we have discussed. But whether self-deception plays a role in the case before us, where the husband fails to see his wife's concern, need not be decided. For whatever reason, he fails at first to see her concern and then his eyes are opened and he comes to see what he could not before. I do not mean that he discovers her concern through some dramatic proof, such as her risking her life for him or his finding moving confessions of concern in her diary. I mean instead that, while their lives continue on as they had before, he sees many of the things she says and does as expressions of her concern, and seeing them as such he sees them for what they really are, as he did not before. In short he makes what I have called a nonhypothetical discovery.

I want to note three variations of this first situation, which shall be important for our discussion later on.

1. In the first variation the husband discovers his wife's concern in the way described, but he cannot bring others to see it. Although he now sees all or most of the things she says and does as indications of her concern, others see these same things as he saw them before, that is, as indications of indifference or even animosity. He speaks of her thoughtfulness and warmth; they speak of her selfish calculations and her keeping up appearances. He at first tries to get them to see his wife's concern for what it is but finally gives up. He concludes that they are too enamoured of the idea that his wife is not worthy of him, an idea he knows they have, for he once shared it with them.

2. In the second variation, the husband discovers his wife's concern in the same way, but in this case he does not need to convince others of her concern. They see it too, and, what is more have seen it all along. In this variation the husband in discovering his wife's concern discovers what he was blind to, but what others saw clearly.

3. In the third variation the husband does not quite discover his wife's concern. Again, he believes that she is not concerned for him at all. Then he begins to see to some extent what his wife says and does in a new light. He comes to see *some* signs of her concern, but not enough to completely convince him that he was wrong before. In this case he does not see all or most of what his wife says and does in a new light, as indications of her concern; but he does see some things anew. He does not discover her concern, then, as he does in the other variations, but he does see enough to rather shakily believe and hope that she may be concerned for him.

The Religious Situation: Here again a man comes to see that another is concerned for him, or so he says. But here the "other" is God. To begin with the man does not believe in God's concern and love; in fact he believes that there is no God. Then something happens to him and to his life. Nothing dramatic happens like a voice telling him to stop just as he is about to walk over a precipice at night. But he comes to see much about him in a new light; he comes to see on every side signs of a concern to which he was before strangely blind, as he now feels. That is, he now sees much for which to thank God, as he puts it; and he sees everything for which he thanks God as an indication of God's concern and love. In short, in the religious situation, as in the secular, a relationship to another is discovered, i.e., a relationship of concern, and the discovery is again according to the nonhypothetical model.

Here too there are three variations to be noted. In the first the man who becomes religious discovers what he cannot bring others to see. In the second variation he discovers what those about him have seen all along. And in the third he does not discover God's love and concern, but only comes to see enough to believe and to hope for that love. If indeed there is a religious discovery to be made, it will be made in the first or third variation of the religious discovery situation; although, strictly, in the third God's concern is not discovered, but believed in and hoped for. The second is ruled out by the fact that there are many nonbelievers today.

VI-B

In the situations just outlined an individual comes to see what he could not before. Something happens to the husband and to the religious man: their eyes are opened. Or at least this is what happens if they have made real discoveries. Let us consider (I) in its relation to these discovery situations, particularly in their first variations, where others do not see what the husband and religious man comes to see. Here the friends of the husband will speak of his *faith* in his wife's concern, and the husband may too given the doubts of others, *even though he has discovered and so knows that she is concerned. He has faith:* He could speak of a trial of his faith, given the assault of others' doubts, and it would not be out of place for him to pray for sustained faith, if he were religious. In such a case we can speak of faith because there is risk— risk in the face of *others' doubts*—which faith must stand against.[45] Often when one prays for supported faith he himself has doubts. In these cases one's faith is threatened not by the doubts of others, or not only by the doubts of others, but by one's *own* doubts, which one has because he realizes that what he believes is dubious, or at least thinks it is. Such a prayer for supported faith asks that one continue to believe. But one can also pray that others' doubts not become one's own, and this prayer too is a prayer that one's faith be supported. One need not have doubts to realize that others' doubts might become his own, particularly if one recalls the time when he did not believe and was blind to what he now sees, or thinks he sees. *But though the husband has faith, he also has knowledge.* It does seem to be as Kierkegaard says: faith requires risk. It is a strength of the Kierkegaardian view (I) that it brings this out. But his view is also misleading in that it suggests that the risk of faith is essentially the risk of being wrong about what is believed. It can as well be the risk of not maintaining the relationship one commits oneself to when one says "I believe" or "I know" as it is said by the husband and religious man. Construing the risk of faith as he does, Kierkegaard suggests that it requires a lack of certitude on the part of the one with faith (which would rule out knowing), or else that it requires a lack of certainty of the matter (which would also rule out knowing). Kierkegaard only has to say one or the other, and the latter is the one he would take, I suppose, given the choice. But both are wrong, I believe. In the case of the husband his eyes have been opened and he has seen what is there to see: his wife's concern. He has discovered his wife's concern: he has come to know that his wife is concerned for him. He is now certain that she is concerned for him, and it is certain that she is. That is, it is certain *if* he has really discovered her concern, and it is part of the example that he has. Yet there is a risk because *others* have doubts, and these doubts must be resisted. If he does not resist the doubts of others but rather lets them become his doubts, then he loses his certainty and no longer sees the matter as certain. He would thus cease to know. His coming to know does not guarantee that he will always know, and his ceasing to know—his allowing the doubts of others to become his doubts—is at least a partial failure of faith. If he begins to have doubts, his faith relationship is lost or at least is weakened. It is this risk which makes his relationship one of faith.

In this kind of case, then, there are *both* knowledge and faith, for there are both certainty and risk. If knowledge requires certitude and that the matter be certain, it does not require that the certainty of the matter be clear to everyone. And the doubts of others could necessitate faith on the part of the husband or the religious man. As I suggested earlier (in Chapter 6), perhaps what Kierkegaard has in mind as "objective certainty" could be defined like this: something would be objectively certain when the certainty of the matter is clear to almost everyone and there is no viable possibility of doubt. If so, it may be that faith does require a lack of objective certainty, for faith requires risk, and risk may require at least a possibility of doubt. But this is not to say that faith or risk requires the matter to be uncertain. Similarly knowledge may require that the matter be certain, but it does not require that the matter be objectively certain in the sense just noted. Thus while faith perhaps requires that the matter not be objectively certain, it does not require that the matter be uncertain; and while knowledge may require that the matter be certain, it does not require that it be objectively certain.

If I am right that knowledge and faith are compatible, that does not mean that all instances of faith are instances of knowledge or that all instances of knowledge are instances of faith. Most often when one has faith, I suppose, it will be when the matter is not certain, and in these cases one does not know. If I am correct, though, if the matter were certain, one could know that it is and in some circumstances still be correctly said to have faith. This would make understandable Job's cry of faith "I know my Redeemer liveth." And this would make understandable the man of faith saying "I am certain that my father is innocent; nothing will shake my faith." Otherwise we must understand what he is saying as "I am certain (have certitude) that my father is innocent, but the matter is doubtful; although I continue to have faith." That is, we must understand the man of faith as saying something that concedes that he does not even have certitude, for in conceding that the matter is not certain he concedes that he is not certain of it. (As we saw, this entailment accounts for the easy confusion between certitude and certainty of the matter.[46]) The alternative way to understand the man of faith's cry, "I am certain my father is innocent, nothing will shake my faith," is to say that it is utterly confused; the speaker expressed his faith and also his certitude, not realizing that in expressing his faith he indicates the matter is *not* certain and in expressing his certitude he indicates the matter *is* certain. However, this alternative is barely logical, involving the extraordinary notion that English paradigms are inherently confused. It should also be borne in mind that the man of faith could as well have said, "It's certain that my father is innocent. Nothing will shake my faith." And here the certainty of the matter is explicitly stated and conjoined to an expression of faith.

At this point we should remind ourselves of the analysis of knowledge (i.e., *knowledge that*), viewed earlier,[47] that makes belief a necessary condition or a part of knowledge. What is wrong with this analysis is not that belief is never part of, or accompanies, knowledge, but that sometimes it does not. Sometimes what is known is perfectly clear and not a matter of belief at all; other times, though, what is known is a matter of belief, which accounts for the tenacity of this analysis. As we have seen, Aquinas and Kierkegaard both speak of belief as faith. Of course not every instance of belief is faith: tentative belief is not faith, or at least not a very strong faith. But then tentative belief is not part of knowledge either, not if one must be sure to know that something is so. Also not every instance of faith is an instance of the belief that is said to be part of knowledge; faith can be ill-founded and such a belief, being ill-founded, would not be part of knowledge. But faith can also be well-founded; it is not self-contradictory to say that someone's faith is rationally based or justified. In this case faith would have the same character as the belief said to be part of knowledge, namely, justified belief of which one is sure. This is not to say that every instance of *knowledge that* which involves belief thereby involves faith. It is to remind ourselves that it has long been recognized that one can know and believe at the same time, and to note that this belief at least sometimes could have the character of faith.

Kant, as we saw earlier, distinguished between "conviction (for myself)" and "certainty (for everyone)" and said that knowledge requires both. Philosophers as distant from Kant as A. J. Ayer would agree that knowledge requires what Kant calls "conviction (for myself)"[48]; even Kierkegaard could accept this. Believing (or faith), Kant said, requires "conviction (for myself)" and a *lack* of "certainty (for everyone)." Kierkegaard might well accept this too. But here a problem arises about what Kant means by "certain (for everyone)." It is ambiguous. He might mean "objectively certain," i.e., that there are no doubts on the part of anyone and no possible doubts; if this is what he means, then perhaps faith requires its lack, but knowledge does not require it. Or he might mean that the matter is certain. If he means this then indeed this certainty will be for everyone in the sense that it does not depend upon anyone's feeling of certitude—but still not everyone may accept the matter as certain; if Kant means this, then knowledge requires it, but faith does not require its lack.

Let us return for a moment to an argument cited earlier.

1 —Faith requires risk.
2 —Risk requires a lack of certainty.
3 —Knowledge requires certainty.
∴. Faith and knowledge exclude each other.

At this point we should ask: What kind of certainty is meant here?

It could be that what Kant calls "conviction (for myself)," i.e., conviction or certitude or being sure. If so, while perhaps knowledge requires it, risk and faith do not require its lack. Thus, if this is what "certainty" means in the argument, while premise 3 might be true, premise 2 would be false.

Or it might be that "certainty" means "objective certainty." If so, and if we have understood this Kierkegaardian notion, then risk and faith require its lack, but knowledge does not require it. Thus premise 2 would be true, but 3 would be false.

Or it might be that the certainty referred to in the argument is the certainty of the matter at hand. If so, knowledge requires it all right, but risk and faith do not require its lack. Thus premise 3 would be true, but 2 would be false.

If what I have been trying to bring out is correct, then one can have faith even when he knows; one can have faith when the doubts and questions of others assail him, even though he at present has no doubts, and the matter is certain, as it would be if he has made a true discovery. All this is the case when the husband discovers his wife's concern but everyone else thinks that she is not concerned and ridicules his discovery. And similarly in the case of Job it may have been that he indeed knew that his Redeemer liveth and yet made the cry of faith "I know my Redeemer liveth." His cry, then, need not have been false to have been a cry of faith.

What would be the case, though, if the discovery situation were of the second variation, that is, where the husband discovers his wife's concern and in doing so comes to see what has been obvious to everyone except him all along? In such a case he comes to know that she is concerned, but there seems to be no room for faith. There are no doubts on the part of anyone, nor a viable possibility of doubt, to supply the risk that faith requires. As pointed out earlier in the religious situation, if there is a real discovery to be made, it seems that this second variation of the discovery situation is ruled out, for clearly there are many nonbelievers with doubts to provide the condition of risk. But let us suppose that all men at once made the discovery of God's presence and concern, and too that there no longer was the viable possibility of doubt. In such a case would the relationship of faith between believer and God be lost? It would, but in a way it would not.

Aquinas as well as Kierkegaard, accepts it that knowledge and faith are incompatible (although Aquinas means what he calls "scientific knowledge"). To a great extent on this matter at least, the insights of these two rather divergent religious thinkers coincide, although their attitudes toward religious knowledge do not coincide. Kierkegaard takes religious knowledge to be anathema, but Aquinas (even when it is "scientific knowledge") does not. The reason Aquinas does not is worth our noting, I think. The reason is that even if faith is ruled out by knowledge a man may still have a will ready to believe, and it is this will that maintains the relationship to God. Aquinas says, ". . . when a man has the will to believe what is of faith . . . although he may have reasons in demonstration of some of them . . . the merit of his faith is not, for that reason, lost or diminished."[49] And I think that Aquinas would say the same thing if we had (scientific) knowledge of *all* the articles of faith, as he believes we some day shall, when we no longer see through a glass darkly, but face to face. In such an event Aquinas would say that faith is completely ruled out: yet the will to believe, the readiness to accept, could remain; and if it did the heart of the faith relationship would remain.

Let me bring out in a different way the importance of Aquinas' insight. Aquinas thinks that knowledge rules out faith, I think this is wrong. But it may be right that everyone knowing because it is perfectly clear, with no viable possibility of doubt, rules out faith. Even so, though, a will ready to believe would not be ruled out, and in this way not faith, but the readiness to accept on faith, would remain unaffected by knowledge. Thus while knowledge rules out faith under certain conditions, namely those present in the second variation of the discovery situation, still the attitude of the believer that in other circumstances would be faith would remain. If there is the scent of paradox here, bear in mind that what makes faith impossible in such situations is *not* one's making a discovery and so coming to know. It is, rather, the attitudes of *others* changing; faith becomes impossible when others cease to doubt. Thus when faith is excluded in this way there is no real change in the religious man at all. It is not as though he lost his faith; it is only that the exterior conditions that made his attitude one of faith, namely the doubts of others, have ceased to exist.[50] To give an analogy: Say that a man and his only son are stranded on an island where they perforce remain and make do with what they find about them. They are there for years and grow close to one another in mutual dependence and affection—these elements are at the heart of their relationship. Now say that six months after their accident the man's wife gives birth to a second son. In this case the first son is not his father's only son; thus his relationship to his father has changed, through a change in external conditions. But in a clear sense their relationship on the island remains just as it was. Analogously, if others cease to have doubts about God and his love, this change in external conditions will change the believer's faith relationship; yet in a clear sense the relationship remains the same, for the readiness to believe which is at the heart of the faith relationship remains as it was.

Perhaps what Aquinas has in mind as a will ready to believe correlates with what Kierkegaard reminds us: that faith carries commitment. If the husband says of his wife, "I *think* that she is concerned for me" or "I *hope* that she is concerned for me, but I can't be sure," he hardly expresses his faith in her and her concern. If he says the first, he indicates that he has a suspicion or a hypothesis that she is concerned for him. And if he says the second, he indicates his hope that she is concerned for him. In neither case does he indicate his faith because he shows that he lacks commitment; he only tentatively accepts it that she is concerned because he lacks a will ready to believe in her concern.

Kierkegaard in the *Concluding Unscientific Postscript* reminds us of the commitment of faith, but he goes astray in suggesting that if one knows something, then that knowledge by its very nature must make him indifferent toward that something. What he suggests, then, is that if the husband knows his wife is concerned for him, he will be indifferent toward her concern. This is related to but different from Hick's suggestion that God's existence being certain or evident would make a *personal* relationship to him impossible. Hick seems to reason that certainty *compels* knowledge and this makes a free personal relationship impossible. According to Hick, it is not knowledge that rules out the relationship to God, but "certain knowledge." Thus by broadening the scope of knowledge to include the uncertain, Hick allows knowledge to co-exist with a personal relationship to God. In doing so he differs from Kierkegaard, but the nub of his concern remains the same—namely, that if God's existence were certain, it would undermine the relationship to God by making it a matter of indifference, as Kierkegaard suggests, or by making it less than a personal relationship, as Hick puts it.

To see that this concern is misdirected let us look at Kierkegaard's suggestion which has it that knowledge, being of a matter that is certain, will involve indifference. I suppose that we are indifferent towards all sorts of things we know, such as those commonplace facts of the day that have no obvious bearing on our lives. But this does not mean that knowledge by its nature involves indifference. If the husband hopes for his wife's concern and then discovers that she is indeed concerned for him, he need not at that point become indifferent toward her concern. It may be true that faith requires commitment, as Kierkegaard helps us see. Certainly this is so if commitment is a will ready to believe—a readiness to believe in the face of odds, to cast oneself upon "the seventy thousand fathoms of water." And indifference may make commitment impossible. But knowledge does not entail indifference: the man who discovers that his wife is concerned may rejoice at his discovery.

Kierkegaard's concern should not have been with knowledge, but with investigation. If the man does not know whether his wife is concerned for him, but wants to know and so begins to investigate to see if she is, reserving judgment until he finds out, *then* his attitude is hardly that of commitment. His attitude is that of the investigator of a hypothesis, and comes to tentative acceptance if it involves acceptance at all. But what rules out commitment here is not knowledge or certainty—it is one's tentative attitude. What is antithetical to the commitment of faith is seeking to confirm a tentatively held hypothesis, not discovering and coming to know that something is true.

Coleridge says, "He prayeth best who loveth best/All things both great and small." We need not think that he who knoweth not loveth best. Knowing the nature of him who is loved need not rule out the commitment of love. So too the husband's knowing that his wife is concerned for him does not rule out the commitment of faith (the readiness to believe) in that concern. Everyone knowing because it is perfectly clear might rule out faith, yet even here the heart of the faith relationship remains, for the will to believe remains—that is, the commitment at the heart of faith remains. Aquinas and Kierkegaard seem unclear on a number of these points, but both, once winnowed, could essentially agree on the centrality of commitment to faith and the compatibility of that commitment with knowledge.

If Kierkegaard unwinnowed obscures this point, he still helps us see other related things integral to the nature of faith. First, Kierkegaard helps us see that to have the relationship to God of faith or commitment it is not necessary to have knowledge of God's exact nature. At one point in the *Concluding Unscientific Postscript* he contrasts the idol worshipper who prays with a true spirit to the man who has the true conception of God but who prays with a false spirit:

> If one who lives in the midst of Christianity goes up to the house of God, the house of the true God, with the true conception of God in his knowledge, and prays, but prays in a false spirit; and one who lives in an idolatrous community prays with the entire passion of the infinite, although his eyes rest upon the image of an idol: where is there most truth? The one prays in truth to God though he worships an idol; the other prays falsely to the true God, and hence worships in fact an idol.[51]

Perhaps Kierkegaard's question "Where is there most truth?" is not altogether happy. But his point is clear, I think. Philosophers have recently said that belief *in* God, or faith in God, presupposes belief *that* there is a God. This seems to be right, for it does appear to be nonsense to say "I believe in God but I do not believe that there is this God in whom I believe." However, this being right, it is not right either that he who believes in God must *know* that there is a God or that he must know the nature of God. It is the latter that Kierkegaard helps us see in this passage. Granted, at this point a question arises: To what extent can one be wrong about the nature of God and still truly be said to believe in God? The answer, I think, depends upon the attitude of the believer. In Kierkegaard's example the true believer prayed before an idol, but he *did* pray. In our age and society it is hard to understand someone believing that God is a spatially located statue made of stone or brass. What would make this understandable is the believer showing his commitment and his readiness to believe in what he sees as God, as he could by prayer and worship. It is hard to understand someone in our society worshipping an idol in a true spirit; but *if* a believer were to do this, he would show his relationship of commitment to and trust in God, regardless of how he thought of Him. There is, though, a *logical* or psychological limitation here, it seems. One can believe in God however he thinks of God except where thinking of Him in a certain way excludes faith in Him or, rather, does so in the thinking of the believer. Are there any notions or conceptions of God that exclude faith in God? I think that the conception of God as the perfect embodiment of evil may do just that. Certainly it does if trust and worship of God are bound up with faith in God. The suggestion here is not that if a man primarily fears God rather than trusts in Him, he does not believe in God. Rather it is that if the operating conception of God for a man is such that trust and worship are ruled out so that the man cannot worship, and cannot trust in God, and cannot pray reverentially—as in Devil "worship" —then it is not that God is thought of in a different way, but that what is thought of is not God.[52] Even given this limitation, though, what Kierkegaard helps us see remains: that the relationship of commitment, of faith and trust in God, does not presuppose that God be thought of as he is in every respect.

Second, Kierkegaard, although he did not put it this way, reminds us that while those who seek to prove *that* there is a God may or may not succeed, there can be no proof for belief *in* God. One can prove that a proposition is true; so one can logically prove, or try to prove, that "God exists" is true. And if a proof is found, then all rational men who understand the proof will accept this proposition. But faith *in* God involves more than the acceptance of a proposition; it involves commitment and trust in God. And these things are not similarly created by the conclusion of an argument—not even for rational men. Norman Malcolm, who holds that the ontological argument in one form is sound, says something very close to this when he discusses the significance of the argument:

> What is the relation of Anselm's ontological argument to religious belief? This is a difficult question. I can imagine an atheist going through the argument, becoming convinced of its validity, acutely defending it against objections, yet remaining an atheist. The only effect it could have on the fool of the Psalm would be that he stopped saying in his heart "There is no God," because he would now realize that this is something he cannot meaningfully say or think. It is hardly to be expected that a demonstrative argument should, in addition, produce in him a living faith. Surely there is a level at which one can view the argument as a piece of logic, following the deductive moves but not being touched religiously? I think so.[53]

The lineaments of faith that Malcolm and Kierkegaard bring into relief, and those traced earlier, together expose this about faith: Let us suppose that there is a sound argument that establishes that there is the God of the Bible (not just an unmoved mover, for instance). If so, then all rational men acquainted with the proof will know that God exists; although they will not by this alone have faith *in* God. But further, if there were such a proof, both faith that there is a God and faith in God may be rendered impossible. If they are rendered impossible, it is not simply because there is this proof. Rather it is because this proof would make it clear to everyone that there is a perfectly good and merciful Supreme Being, and hence there would be no doubts and no viable possibility of doubt to provide the risk faith requires. This would be true for both faith that there is a God and faith in God, given that the God *of the Bible* were proven to exist. At the same time the heart of the faith relationship—commitment, the readiness to believe that there is a God and in God—would not be ruled out, even though faith was. Nor would it be created. If a proof that is clear to everyone cannot rule out commitment, neither can it create it.

VI-C

As the first Kierkegaardian view about the relation between faith and knowledge (I) helps us see into the nature of faith, so too does the view that faith is a source or a condition for some knowledge (II). This view, however, is also misleading.

In the discovery situations sketched above, where the husband discovers his wife's concern and where the believer discovers God's love and concern, what happens if real discoveries are made is that there are changes in the husband and in the believer: their eyes are opened to what surrounds them. In the case of the husband who discovers his wife's concern, it may be that he and his friends will say of him that his eyes have been opened. Or perhaps only the husband will say this, and his friends, failing to see what he sees, will regard him as blind or deluded. In either case a conversion or something resembling it takes place. Somehow the husband comes to see his wife's concern for the first time. He may even speak of a revelation. And particularly if his friends do not see what he sees, they will speak of his faith in her concern—his blind faith, they may say. And here we have the seedbed for thinking that faith is a source of knowledge—in this case the husband's knowledge of his wife's concern, which appears to be yielded by his faith when he is converted.

Now it is true that if the husband discovers his wife's concern, he comes to know that she is concerned for him. It is also true that nevertheless he may still have faith that she is concerned for him. But these two facts are not tantamount to the husband's faith being a source or a condition of his knowledge. What yields the husband knowledge of his wife's concern is what he comes to see—namely, signs of her concern all about him. Less esoterically put, the husband comes to know his wife is concerned for him because he comes to see signs of her concern in all or most of what she does. In short, what he discerns is the source of his knowledge, not his faith. Nor can we say that faith is a prior or necessary condition of his knowledge, for he may have vehemently denied his wife's concern and then, his eyes being opened, come to see what was obvious to everyone but him. In such a case faith could not be a source or condition for his knowledge, for since he denied her concern, he of course had no faith to begin with. To be sure, faith may *accompany* knowledge in the circumstances that prevail in the first version of the discovery situation. But even in this kind of case it should be clear that faith is not a source or a vital condition for knowledge. For if the discovery remains just as it is, but the exterior circumstances (the doubts of others) change so that the situation is transmuted to the second version of the discovery situation, there no longer is room for faith; yet the husband who makes the discovery still comes to know.[54]

It should be particularly clear, I think, that faith is not a *source* of knowledge. If the husband who has newly discovered his wife's concern is asked by a doubter how he knows that she is concerned for him, he can indicate how he knows, namely by the signs of her concern which he has now come to see. What he indicates may not convince the doubter, for the doubter may not see these signs of concern for what they are. In this case the husband's effort to answer the doubter fails. But the husband cannot try to answer the doubter's question, or indicate how he knows, by replying that he knows "on faith." In fact "I know on faith" as opposed to "I accept it on faith" makes dubious sense. If the citation of faith serves a function here, it is not to indicate how anyone knows anything. Its function is quite different. Consider the following short dialogue:

The doubter: How do you know that your wife is concerned for you?

The husband: I see signs of her concern in what she does; for instance in the way she smiles at me and asks about my day.

The doubter: How do you know that these are real signs of concern and not pretended?

At this point the husband could reply by indicating how he knows she is not pretending. But he could also reply, "I just know" or "That's not possible" or "I accept that on faith." These replies do not answer the doubter; they do not indicate how the husband knows anything. Rather they reject the doubter's question and indicate that no reply will be forthcoming. In fact I think that this reply—"I accept that on faith"—with this function is made rather often by believers in answer to religious doubters, particularly in regard to acceptance of the Bible. We should not conclude that if this reply is given, the husband or the religious man does not know what is in question. But similarly we should not conclude that faith is being cited as how one knows—an equally misguided conclusion; rather we should note what in fact is the function of the reply.

Despite all this, there is something important and right about the nature of faith that (II) brings out. What this view of faith helps us see is that there is an element in many important instances of coming to have faith that leads to knowledge. I have referred to that element as "having one's eyes opened." It is what happens to the husband when he comes to see the signs of his wife's concern for what they are. This element is not in itself faith; however, it leads to faith when there are doubts on the part of others, or a viable possibility of doubt, to provide the risk of faith. In itself this element is more revelation than faith. (The husband's eyes are opened to the signs of his wife's concern: her concern is revealed to him for what it is.) What this perhaps suggests is a version of (II) we found in Locke: revelation-assented-to-by-faith is a source of knowledge.

This view remains misleading in several respects, however. For one thing, it still suggests that one's faith somehow is part of how he knows or finds out. It may be that in the face of others' doubts without faith in his wife's concern the husband would not have conviction, not be sure, and so not *know* that his wife is concerned for him. But this does not make the assent of faith part of the source of the husband's knowledge, or even a prior or a necessary condition. It does, however, in an important way make it a *kind* of condition for his knowledge, but again only sometimes. If the husband whose eyes are opened and who discovers his wife's concern is surrounded by doubters, he is said to have faith, and does. What is more, assuming he must be sure to know, if he ceases to have faith in his wife's concern and begins to doubt it, he ceases to know also. Other times, though, when the discovery situation is in its second variation and the husband's eyes have been opened to what is "objectively certain," to which only he was blind, there is a discovery and the husband comes to know; but there is no assent of faith, for the discovery is of the obvious.

What (II) points out then, is that something often associated with faith is a source of knowledge. This is revelation, or rather what is revealed when our eyes are opened. In a secular setting it may be signs of a wife's concern (to which a husband was blind); in a religious setting it may be signs of God's love and concern (to which many of us may be blind). And further, sometimes it is just when there is a failure of faith and others' doubts become our own that we cease to know, despite our earlier discovery. In this way, if there is indeed a discovery in the world as it is, where the doubts of others surround us, sustained faith may be a condition for continued knowledge for the husband and for the religious man.

VI-D

It remains to bring out one or two things about (III) and (IV)—the views regarding faith and knowledge that stood on the verge of skepticism. (IV) in a dramatic way alerts us to the close connection between knowledge and faith, but it is misleading when it identifies one with the other. In that version of the discovery situation where the husband comes to see signs of his wife's concern for what they are, but no one else sees them for what they are, he discovers his wife's concern and therefore comes to know that she is concerned. But he also has faith in her concern. He cannot point out to the others the signs of her concern, for they cannot or will not see them for what they are. They say that he has faith (a silly faith) in his wife's concern. And he, in the face of their doubts, thanks God that their doubts are not his and that his faith remains whole. In such a case, then, the husband knows that his wife is concerned for him *and* has faith in her concern. And (IV) alerts us to this initially unsuspected possibility. Where it goes wrong is in suggesting that the husband's or the religious man's faith *is* his knowledge. This suggestion is misleading because it either implies 1) that since faith is knowledge, what is known is open to interpretation and question and is dubious (and so is not really known at all, but is at best firmly believed); or it implies 2) that since faith is knowledge, what is accepted on faith is for that reason certain (and so faith carries with it certainty of the matter and is *never* of anything that is doubtful). Hick's equation of faith and knowledge makes knowledge into faith and carries with it the first implication. Calvin's equation makes faith into knowledge and carries with it the second implication. Both are superfluous, it seems to me; neither is an implication of what is right about (IV).

One version of (III) is that faith is a kind of knowledge less certain than knowledge derived from reason. To see how one might come to think that

(III) in this version is true, let us recall several features of the discovery situations we have before us, particularly the secular and particularly in two of its variations. As we have seen, in the second variation the husband may both know that his wife is concerned and have faith in her concern. The husband may have both knowledge and faith together because his discovering his wife's concern, and his coming to know that she is concerned, does not rule out the doubts of others, which provide the risk that makes possible, and necessitates, his faith. Let us say, though, that the husband's eyes were opened to a lesser extent, so that he does not discover signs of his wife's concern in all or much of what she does; instead he discovers a few signs of her concern, only enough to awaken in him the belief and hope that she may be concerned for him. In this case the husband would have faith in his wife's concern, but would not yet have discovered her concern. True, he would have discovered for the first time *some* signs of her concern, enough for his hope and his belief, but he would not yet have discovered that she was definitely and truly concerned for him, which is to say that he would not have come to know that she is concerned for him. Now observe what happens if we conflate this last situation, which is the discovery situation in its third variation, with the former, which is the discovery situation in its first variation. Such a conflation could lead one to say correctly that 1) given the first variation of the discovery situation the husband, or the religious man, has faith but also comes to know and 2) given the third variation the husband, or the religious man, has faith; and then go on to say incorrectly that 3) given the third variation the husband, or the religious man, comes to know in a weak sense of "know," which allows dubiety. It also furthers the tendency on the part of some religious thinkers and apologists to think that every instance of knowledge, or at least knowledge of "matters of fact," is at bottom dubious and not certain, thus opening the way to the idea that all knowledge is really faith, a view that creates a place for religious knowledge only by denying most if not all knowledge and creates a place for religious faith only by finding faith everywhere.

Notes

[1]Soren Kierkegaard, *Concluding Unscientific Postscript*, trans. David F. Swenson and Walter Lowrie (Princeton: Princeton University Press, 1941), p. 182. I shall refer to (I) as the Kierkegaardian view; Kierkegaard did, I think, implicitly hold this view, but our main concern will be with the burden of (I) and not with whether Kierkegaard held it.

[2]Kierkegaard insists that those with faith lack "objective certainty," although they embrace what is "objectively uncertain" with "subjectivity" or "the most passionate inwardness." Kierkegaard was aware, then, that the man of faith would not be tentative, but would be definite and sure. But he must lack "objective certainty." This leaves what by implication stands opposed to "objective certainty": "subjective certainty."

[3]Cf. Raziel Abelson, "The Logic of Faith and Belief," *Religious Experience and Truth*, ed. Sidney Hook (New York: New York University Press, 1961), p. 122.

[4]Immanuel Kant, *Critique of Pure Reason,* trans. Norman Kemp Smith (New York: St. Martin's Press; London: Macmillan & Co., 1961), p. 646.

[5]John Hick, *Faith and Knowledge,* 2d ed. (Ithaca, N.Y.: Cornell University Press, 1966), pp. 14–15, 23.

[6]*Summa Theologica,* II-II, q.1, a.5, and q.2, a.5., *Basic Writings of Saint Thomas Aquinas,* edited and annotated by Anton C. Pegis (New York: Random House, 1945). © 1945 by Random House, Inc.

[7]*Summa Theologica,* I, q.2, a.2.

[8]*Summa Theologica,* II-II, q.1, a.8.

[9]*Summa Theologica,* II-II, q.1, a.5.

[10]In chap. 6.

[11]Soren Kierkegaard, *Fear and Trembling,* trans. Walter Lowrie (Princeton: Princeton University Press, 1941), pp. 9–30.

[12]See chap. 6 for a discussion of this possibility.

[13]John Locke, *An Essay Concerning Human Understanding,* bk. 4, chap. 18, sec. 7.

[14]Locke, *An Essay Concerning Human Understanding,* bk. 4, chap. 16, sec. 14. Elsewhere Locke stresses the role of "reason" as the arbiter of whether or not a proposition is divinely revealed or gotten from "enthusiasm." See bk. 4, chap. 18, sec. 8, and chap. 19.

[15]*Summa Theologica,* II-II, q.2, a.4.

[16]John Calvin, *Institutes of The Christian Religion,* bk. 1, chap. 7, sec. 4.

[17]Calvin, *Institutes of The Christian Religion,* bk. 1, chap. 7, sec. 5.

[18]Jerry H. Gill, "Kant, Kierkegaard and Religious Knowledge," *Essays On Kierkegaard,* ed. Jerry H. Gill (Minneapolis: Burgess Publishing Company, 1969), p. 66.

[19]Elsewhere in the *Essay,* though, Locke is quite clear that "firmness of persuasion" does not amount to knowledge. See bk. 4, chap. 19, sec. 12.

[20]However, cf. H. A. Prichard, *Knowledge and Perception* (Oxford: Clarendon Press, 1950), pp. 85–91 and 96–97.

[21]"I am certain, although I shouldn't be" is interesting in that it seems to but does not indicate certitude along with an awareness that the matter is not certain. If the one who said this were asked whether he feels certain about the thing in question, he could hardly reply "Yes, I do" as he could if he had certitude. Perhaps he would reply, "I don't know what I feel," or, more likely, "I don't know what to think," as he apparently does not, which clearly is *not* feeling certain or having certitude.

[22]Locke, *An Essay Concerning Human Understanding,* bk. 4, chap. 18, sec. 4.

[23]*Summa Theologica,* II-II, q.2, a.1.

[24]*Summa Theologica,* II-II, q.4, a.8.

[25]Norman Malcolm, "Knowledge and Belief," *Knowledge and Certainty* (Englewood Cliffs, N.J.: Prentice-Hall, 1963), pp. 62–63; and, in the same volume "A Definition of Factual Memory," pp. 228–29. Also see chap. 6.

[26]In chap. 6.

[27]See Raphael Demos, "Religious Faith and Scientific Faith," *Religious Experience and Truth,* ed. Sidney Hook (New York: New York University Press, 1961), pp. 130–36.

[28]Gordon D. Kaufman, *Relativism, Knowledge and Faith* (Chicago: The University of Chicago Press, 1960), p. 111.

[29]*Institutes,* bk. 3, chap. 2, sec. 7; quoted by Hick.

[30]John Hick, *Faith and Knowledge,* 1st ed. © 1957, 2d ed. copyright © 1966 by Cornell University Press (New York: Cornell University Press, 1966), pp. 30–31.

[31]Hick, *Faith and Knowledge,* p. 30.

[32]See chap. 5.

[33]Hick, *Faith and Knowledge,* pp. 205 ff.

[34]Paraphrased from John Hick, *Faith and Knowledge,* first edition © 1957, second edition copyright © 1966 by Cornell University Press. Used by permission of Cornell University Press. For premise 1 see pp. 78 ff; for premise 2 see pp. 85–86; for premise 3 pp. 85 ff. and 205 ff; for premise 4 pp. 96–97, 120–22 and 200; and for premise 5 p. 200.

[35]Paraphrased from Hick, *Faith and Knowledge,* pp. 120 ff. Used by permission of Cornell University Press.

[36]See for instance: D. F. Henze, "Faith, Evidence and Coercion," *Philosophy* 42, (1967); John King-Farlow, "Cogency, Conviction and Coercion," *International Philosophical Quarterly* 8 (1968); and D. R. Duff-Forbes, "Faith, Evidence, Coercion," *Australasian Journal of Philosophy* 47 (1969).

[37]Hick, *Faith and Knowledge,* pp. 85, 97, 205–9.

[38]For a discussion of this point see sec. 5 of "The Falsification Challenge" in the Appendix, Part A.

[39]See chap. 2.

[40]As he does; although he seeks to show that religious statements are real statements because they can be verified, not because they can be falsified. See his "Theology and Verification," *Theology Today* 17 (1960); Chap. 8 of *Faith and Knowledge* is a revised form of this article. For a discussion of the falsification challenge see the Appendix, Parts A and B.

[41]Rene Descartes, *Meditations on First Philosophy,* Second Meditation, trans. L. J. Lafleur, 2d ed. (Indianapolis: The Bobbs-Merrill Company, 1960), p. 31.

[42]Hick, *Faith and Knowledge,* pp. 95 ff.

[43]Hick, *Faith and Knowledge,* pp. 108 ff.

[44]See, among others, F. B. Ebersole, "Seeing Things," *Things We Know* (Eugene, Oregon: University of Oregon Books, 1967); Winston H. F. Barnes, "The Myth of Sense-Data" and G. A. Paul, "Is There a Problem About Sense-Data?" *Perceiving Sensing and Knowing,* ed. Robert J. Swartz (Garden City, N.Y.: Doubleday & Company, 1965); and J. L. Austin, *Sense and Sensibilia* (New York: Oxford University Press, 1964).

[45]See chap. 6, sec. II-B.

[46]See sec. III-B above.

[47]In chap. 6.

[48]Although not every philosopher would. Cf. A. D. Woozley, "Knowing and Not Knowing," *Proceedings of the Aristotelian Society* 53 (1952–53) reprinted in *Knowledge and Belief,* ed. A. P. Griffiths (London: Oxford University Press, 1967).

[49]*Summa Theologica,* II-II, q.2, a.10.

[50]In the philosophy of mind, philosophers have helped us see that what makes an emotion that emotion sometimes is not what we were likely to think. The difference

between indignation and annoyance or between shame and embarrassment lies as much or more in the social setting as in the feelings of the individual with the emotion. (See Errol Bedford, "Emotions," *Philosophical Psychology,* ed. Donald F. Gustafson (Garden City, N.Y.: Doubleday & Company, 1964). So too what makes faith faith involves much more than the feeling or attitude of the individual; it involves the social setting which includes the doubts of others.

[51]From Soren Kierkegaard, *Concluding Unscientific Postscript,* trans. David F. Swenson and Walter Lowrie. Copyright 1941 © 1969 by Princeton University Press. (Princeton: Princeton University Press, Princeton Paperback, 1968), pp. 179 and 180. Reprinted by permission of Princeton University Press and the American Scandinavian Foundation.

[52]Could God be thought of as love, then? If God is thought of as love, and only love, He is not being conceived in the traditional way. But could one who thinks of God in this way still believe in God? I think the answer depends upon the person's attitude. If he is reverent, worshipful, and trustful, that is one thing; if he is not, that is another. Suppose that there are two men, and that for both of them God is love (or Love), that is, love and only love, and each of them says that he believes in God. On the basis of this I think that we could straightforwardly say that neither believes in God in the *traditional* sense—that is, they do not think of God as Jews and Christians traditionally have. Now suppose that one is reverent toward God conceived thus, he worships Him and trusts in him, he stands in awe of what he sees as God's power in the world; perhaps he even prays. Say that the other man pursues a life of pleasure, or say that he leads a moral life, but in no way has a trustful or worshipful attitude toward God. On the basis of this difference I would be inclined to say that the first man believes in God—the God of the Bible—although he thinks of Him in his own way; and the second man does not believe in God, although he may draw moral inspiration from the Bible.

It might be said here that the first man who thinks of God as Love, and then worships him and prays to him, is confused; for one cannot meaningfully worship or pray to the abstract quality love, but only to the God in the traditional Biblical conception or, at any rate, something closer to it than love. If this is right, it would explain why philosophers and thinkers who have said that God is love have ended up not believing in God, for, not being confused, they would accept the implication that thinking of God thus rules out prayer, worship, and trust. In fact this implication may have prompted their conception of God as love. Even so, though, one can confusedly conceive of God as love and worship Him and pray to Him. The Kierkegaardian point amplified above is that what indicates belief in God is not the correctness or incorrectness, the confusion or lack of confusion, of the concept of God held by the believer; it is his attitude toward God—his relation to God, however he conceives of Him.

[53]Norman Malcolm, "Anselm's Ontological Arguments," *Knowledge and Certainty* (Englewood Cliffs, N.J.: Prentice-Hall, 1963), p. 161. Reprinted from *The Philosophical Review* 69 (1960). Also in *The Existence of God,* ed. John Hick (New York: The Macmillan Company, 1964). I think that Malcolm means by "atheist" someone who concludes that there is a God, but who has no *religious* belief in God. Alternatively, Malcolm conceivably could be saying that one might be convinced of the ontological argument's validity but still think the premises false, and so, not accepting the truth of the conclusion, remain a denier of God's existence. He is construed thus by Paul Henle in "Uses of the Ontological Argument?" *The Philosophical Review* 70 (1961). If this is what Malcolm meant, though, it is not clear why he says that the fool would stop saying in his heart "There is no God." How-

ever, whatever point Malcolm *meant* to make, the above quotation alerts us to the point I have made and wish to be noted here.

[54]That is, faith *need* not precede or accompany making a nonhypothetical discovery of a relationship of love to God, and so is not a condition for coming to know that there is a God. Although it may be that coming to have religious knowledge in *certain* ways presupposes faith. In chap. 5 we discussed the possibility of coming to see that there is a God via the question "Why should there be anything?" If such a discovery can be made through this question, then the question must be asked, and for it to be asked one may need to see the world as a place of awe. And to see the world thus *perhaps* one must already believe in God, or be on the edge of religious belief. If so then to come to know that there is a God *via this question* one must already believe or have faith, or be on the edge of it. But this is very different from faith being an absolute condition for the knowledge that there is a God or the knowledge that men stand in a relationship of love to Him.

Similarly, in chap. 9 we discussed the possibility that faith in the Bible may lead to religious knowledge, that is, the possibility that those who accept the Bible on faith may have come to know that there is a God through the Bible. But in such a case it is the Bible, not their faith, that tells believers that there is a God. To be sure, faith may be required for them to accept the Bible and to (possibly) come to know that there is a God through it. But, again, faith is not an absolute condition for such knowledge, as the possibility of a nonhypothetical discovery that there is a God makes clear.

appendix:
meaning

the falsification challenge

I

Not too many years ago Antony Flew voiced a challenge. His challenge was directed to religious believers and it was this: "What would have to occur or to have occurred to constitute for you a disproof of the love of, or of the existence of, God?"[1] It was Professor Flew's implicit argument that unless such a challenge could be met, an utterance like "There is a God" in fact denied nothing and so asserted nothing. (since the meaning of an assertion is the negation of its denial). One great merit of Flew's challenge was that it crystallised a malaise felt by many into a hard, pointed question. As a challenge this question elicited two basic reactions.

One reaction was: Flew's challenge cannot be answered; religious utterances deny nothing and do not qualify as genuine assertions. Having no assertive content they cannot be believed or disbelieved. However, they are important in other ways. They indicate a "blik" or express an intention to subscribe to a way of life.[2]

The other basic reaction was: Flew's challenge can be answered; religious utterances do deny something and so do qualify as genuine assertions. It was argued that the assertion that God loves men, for instance, denies the fact of pain or rather this fact counts against the assertion (but not decisively), and it was argued that the assertion that there is a God has a denial with eschatological content, if not content of a more accessible sort.[3]

II

Aside from these two reactions to Flew's challenge and their variants, there of course is another possibility: to challenge the challenge. This has rarely been done,[4] and it is this that I want to do here.

First it behooves us to become as clear as possible on just what Flew's challenge challenges the believer to produce. It asks "What would have to occur or to have occurred to constitute for you a disproof of the love of God?" A believer might reply straightforwardly that man's constant suffering for no reason would constitute for him a disproof of God's love for men.[5]

However, those with Flew's concern can argue that this will not do. What will count as suffering for no reason is not specified. One believer might consider the condition met when another did not. If the condition is specified (say a protracted third world war in which virtually every human being suffers), then we have what has been called a *psychological limit*.[6] It may be that many believers would cease to believe in God's love if such a world war were to occur, but others would or could persist in their belief. That is, many might be psychologically unable to continue believing in God's love given such a war, but others might continue to hold their belief. Such a war, then, cannot be a disproof of God's love. It does not constitute for believers a *denial* of "God loves men."

What Flew's challenge demands has been put this way: "an empirically determinable condition" which if it obtained would make, e.g., "God loves men" false.[7] It must be empirical and determinable, and it must be that if it obtains, the factual statement in question is false. Such a condition or its statement I will term an *"empirical denial."* Perhaps a paradigm case of a statement and its empirical denial would be the following: the statement "Smith has diphtheria" empirically denies that there are no diphtheria germs in Smith's throat.[8] Empirical denials, then, are to stand opposed to psychological limits. They are also to stand opposed to what might be called a *logical denial* or a *syntactical denial*. The statements "There is a God" and "God loves men" both have logical denials—namely "There is no God" and "God does not love men." These, however, are syntactically derivable. In a similar way we may derive a syntactical denial for "There are boobas," even though "booba" is a nonsense word. Nor can a statement's empirical denial be gotten simply by denying a necessary condition for the truth of that statement. That there is no Smith, for instance, cannot be the empirical denial of "Smith has diphtheria," even though if that condition did obtain, "Smith has diphtheria" would be false. If such a condition counted as an empirical denial, then at least some religious assertions clearly would have empirical denials, for at least some religious assertions have empirical necessary conditions for their truth. "God created men," for instance, has as a necessary condition that there are men; yet "God created men" would be one of the assertions challenged. One other word on what an empirical denial is not. "There is a God" might be thought to empirically deny the triumph of the Devil. But it does not, inasmuch as "the Devil" is no more an empirical term than "God" is.

III

Now that we are relatively clear on what Flew's challenge demands, we can challenge the challenge: Why, let us ask, should we be able to produce an empirical denial for a religious statement like "There is a God?" It is clear that as a matter of logic every statement including factual statements must have a denial, but this requirement is that a statement have a logical denial, not an empirical denial. (As Flew himself observes[9] the principle can be expressed in symbols: $p \equiv \sim \sim p$, i.e., syntactically.) And religious statements like "There is a God" do have logical denials. What is more, these logical denials can be filled out by reference to, e.g., the Bible. To say that there is no God is to say that the god of Moses and Abraham, of the old and new covenants, does not exist. That is, the logical denial of "There is a God" is not just a syntactical denial like "There are no boobas." "There are no boobas" cannot be filled out. So, considering that a religious statement like "There is a God" has a logical denial which is not just a syntactical denial, why should we be able to produce an empirical denial?

One with Flew's concern might give either of two replies to this question. The first is this: There is a principle or rule of language which states that every factual statement or assertion must have an empirical denial.

If this reply is made, it can be asked what support this principle or rule has. There can be no appeal to *logical* principles here as they require only that a factual statement have a logical denial (and as we have just seen, religious statements like "There is a God" do have logical denials that are not simply syntactical denials). Perhaps it will be replied that this rule *should* be adopted and will be by rational men. Aside from the persuasive flavor, what this comes down to is that they feel others as well should adopt this rule, and this is an admission that the rule is not a rule of language, but *their* rule of language. If, on the other hand, it is maintained that this principle is more than their own principle, one wants to know how it was established. If it is maintained that such a rule can be extracted from language, as some maintain, one wants to see the extraction.

The second reply seems to me to be stronger and much more subtle. It is

Flew's own reply, implicit in the reasoning behind his challenge, and it is this:[10] The negation of the denial of an assertion *means* the same thing as the assertion, and so if we can ask for the meaning of the assertion, we can ask what it denies. To ask what an assertion denies is to ask what would be incompatible with it, or what it empirically denies.

Certainly it is true that we do occasionally ask for the meaning of what people say or assert. So if this is all that those with Flew's concern presuppose, they seem to have proven their case. However, let us look carefully at what they have proven. Their reasoning is this: If we can ask for the meaning of an assertion (and we can), and if the meaning of an assertion is the negation of its denial (and it is), then we can ask what its denial (that which is negated) is. So far the argument is both cogent and innocuous. However, it remains both only as long as "denial" does not mean empirical denial, which is just what those reasoning in this manner must mean by "denial" to reach their conclusion. Meaning this, though, their reasoning is invalid, and it can be shown that their conclusion is false.

If it were true, an assertion's empirical denial itself denied would be that assertion's meaning. To see that this cannot be we need only consider the assertion "John loves Mary." It may be that this assertion denies that there is no John. But while the condition that there is a John is perhaps a necessary condition for the truth of "John loves Mary," its denial—that there is no John —cannot be this assertion's empirical denial. As was observed, a necessary condition which all would count as empirical can be specified for the truth of at least some religious statements, e.g., "God created man." So what is demanded when an empirical denial is demanded cannot be *just* the denial of an empirical necessary condition for the truth of the assertion. Even more certainly it cannot if the denial of an assertion's empirical denial is to be that assertion's meaning; for, to take the condition that there is no John, *its* denial (that there is a John) is not the meaning of "John loves Mary." We have as much reason to say that "John *hates* Mary" empirically denies that there is no John as we do to say that "John loves Mary" does, and it will be odd indeed if both these statements end up with the same meaning.

The empirical denial of "John loves Mary" must be different from and more specifically applicable than that there is no John. Perhaps the following condition will do, namely that John never shows any concern for Mary, that he is cruel to her and consistently denies any affection for her. But, again, the denial of this condition does not mean what "John loves Mary" means. For "John loves Mary, though this condition holds" is not self-contradictory. Perhaps most often it would be false, but it is not self-contradictory. Assume that when we say in some situation, "John loves Mary even though this condition holds, i.e., even though he never shows any concern for her, is cruel to her, and consistently denies any affection for her," we are wrong, and our statement is false. Still we know what would make our statement true;

we know what details to supply. If John were dying of some incurable disease and had resolved to alienate Mary for her own good by hiding from her his concern and affection and by being cruel to her, then in such circumstances, our statement would be true. Of course it should *never* be true if it is self-contradictory, as it would be if the condition itself denied were the meaning of "John loves Mary." And I suspect, regardless of the empirical condition specified, a story could be told in which, while the condition obtained, John nevertheless loved Mary.

Flew says that trying to find out what one would regard as counting against his utterance is one way of trying to understand it.[11] I think Flew is right; it is one way. But it is not a way that yields an empirical denial. Consider the following:

A asks: "What do you mean, she does not love you?"
B replies: "I mean she is not affectionate at all; she doesn't even care about my simple needs. I could starve as far as she is concerned."

Here B helps A understand his utterance—that is, what he means, by indicating what he is denying. But of course both A and B knew what is meant by "She loves me" and "She does not love me" before B gave this indication; both were acquainted with English. B was not indicating the meaning of what he said as one might to someone who did not know its meanig, e.g., a Frenchman; rather, indicating what he means here comes to indicating *why* he thought what he did. And in the light of a future disclosure—something that explains an intense preoccupation on her part—B can say quite rightly: "I was wrong, she does love me" and he can say this quite rightly even though she was not affectionate and did not care for his needs.

The situation is this, then: if those with Flew's concern are asked about the credentials of his challenge, they might make one of two replies. The first cites a principle of some sort, and is inadequate inasmuch as it raises the question of that principle's status and justification. The second reply is that Flew's challenge is simply a request for the meaning of religious statements. This reply, however, assumes what is false, namely that what a statement empirically denies itself denied is that statement's meaning.

IV

We should now try to winnow out what is right about Flew's challenge and also try to explain why it went wrong to the extent it did. The first shall be done in this section and the second shall be done in the next and final section.

Flew tells us that to assert something is necessarily equivalent to denying that it is not the case, a principle which he paraphrases as $p \equiv \sim \sim p$. In doing so he sells short his point. It comes out: an assertion must have a syntactical denial. He wants his point to be: an assertion must have an empirical denial. This it cannot be, but it can be more than that an assertion must have a syntactical denial, which the following demonstrates.

If someone announces with a pompous air that he believes that there are succubi on the Galápagos Islands, and we have the idea that he has said this only to impress us, we might ask him what succubi are. If he does not know, then in one very clear sense he literally does not know the meaning of what he said he believed. And this is so even though he can give us the syntactical denial of what he asserts and can say that it is not the case that there are no succubi on the Galápagos Islands. What he must be able to give us in some form is a logical denial that is more than a syntactical denial. This he would do if he were to tell us that he was denying there were no female demons who visit sleeping men on the Galápagos Islands. This filled-out denial, unlike the mere syntactical denial, conveys to us the meaning of his assertion because it conveys the meaning of "succubi." It does not convey to us the meaning of his assertion because it amounts to an empirical denial: succubi, he might add consistently, are completely undetectable.

What is right about Flew's challenge then is this: if someone says he believes something and knows what it is he believes, he should be able to give us its logical denial where that denial is not merely a syntactical denial. That is, he should be able to fill out the denial as was done, for instance, by replacing "succubi" with "female demons who visit sleeping men." But while this point seems right, it holds perfectly well for religious statements. As we have already observed, "There is a God" has a filled-out denial that the god of Moses and Abraham, of the old and new covenants, does not exist.[12]

Let us return briefly to the notion of a psychological limit. Earlier we noted that in a time of great suffering for mankind many believers might cease to believe in God. Their ceasing to believe, it was observed, might be explained in terms of a psychological limit being reached. To offer such an explanation—to say that a *psychological* limit was reached—suggests that believers cease to believe for irrational or nonrational reasons, as one might for no rational reason cease to believe that his friends care about him after several months of depressing weather. But it should be clear that most believers would cease to believe in God in a time of great suffering only if they thought of him as concerned with men—that is, only if they could offer what has been referred to as a "filled-out denial," which was filled out in a particular way. And further, they would cease to believe only if they saw, or thought they saw, an opposition between the world as it would then be and the world as it should be if such a God exists. The point here is not that believers ceasing to believe in such circumstances shows that there is no such God, but that their ceasing to believe shows that their belief is partly about the world.

To think that such believers must be able to specify what we have been calling an empirical denial for their belief to be about the world is—to put this point most forcefully—to make a mistake. It would not be a mistake only if 1) an empirical denial was necessary for an assertion to have meaning (or be an assertion) or 2) an assertion's empirical denial itself denied were its meaning. Proposition 1) needs to be proved or established to be accepted and, indeed, seems false in the light of, e.g. the case of loss of faith just noted. Proposition 2), as we have seen, is false.

V

Now let us try to see why Flew's challenge went wrong to the extent that it did. There seems to be one primary reason. It is this: Flew and those with his concern have unduly concentrated on hypotheses and the logical model of the hypothesis. A hypothesis is, almost by definition, a *tentative* statement which is to be *investigated*, and most often it is *explanatory* of some phenomenon. As such it is of value only if it is tied to a fairly clear method of verification or falsification. "Smith has diphtheria" is a valuable hypothesis and explanation of Smith's ailment, while "Smith is plagued by juju" is not, because while the first can be falsified by determining that there are no diphtheria germs in Smith's throat, the second cannot be falsified in any clear way. This being true, still the empirical denial of "Smith has diphtheria" cannot in all situations be that there are no diphtheria germs in Smith's throat. For if this condition holds, it does not always make "Smith has diphtheria" false: it would not if Smith had just gargled with some new highly effective gargle that temporarily eliminated all the diphtheria germs from his throat. Of course so long as no such gargle has been used, the testing of Smith's throat is perfectly adequate to determine if he has diphtheria. The point is that even so, this test condition is not an empirical denial of the statement in question, at least not in some situations. And notably this statement and this condition were earlier taken to be a paradigm of a statement and its empirical denial. Consequently a doctor can meaningfully say that Smith in his opinion has diphtheria even though there are no diphtheria germs in his throat without contradicting himself and even without being wrong. Although if a doctor were to frequently insist that his patients had diphtheria even when their throats were free of diphtheria germs, he might soon gain a reputation for being irrational. It might even be said that his diagnoses were meaningless in the sense that a quack's diagnoses are meaningless—namely, worthless and undependable.

The fact remains that hypotheses, including diagnoses, are tied to verification or falsification conditions in *something* like the way those with Flew's concern took an assertion to be tied to an empirical denial. And by concentrating on such a model, they came to expect too much (or too little) of assertions and particularly of assertions like "There is a God."

The believer who says that there is a God may not have tied to his statement a verification or falsification condition, but then most typically he is not offering a hypothesis. He is not tentatively explaining anything; he is affirming what he believes. (This is not to say that nothing counts against his belief that there is a God. Very much may under certain conditions. That is, just as it would count against a man's loving a woman if he showed her no concern *provided that* he had no good reason for not showing concern, so too evil would count against there being a God concerned with men *provided that* God had no redeeming purpose for men.) Of course if a believer is affirming his belief, he certainly does not want to be tentative. This is not an oddity of religious affirmation. When one man expresses his belief in another's ability or promise, the same holds. One is not offering a hypothesis in these cases but is affirming a relationship with another. This is a fact that philosophers such as Kierkegaard, Martin Buber, and Norman Malcolm have pointed to,[13] and it is this fact that Flew and others have failed to appreciate for what it is worth. The relationship that a believer affirms is or quite often is one of faith and trust. If one did impart the attitude appropriate to advancing a hypothesis to affirming a belief and a relationship of trust, the relationship would be subverted. One cannot affirm a relationship of trust by tentatively offering a judgment that is tied to a falsification condition. A French aristocrat imprisoned and awaiting the guillotine would not affirm his trust in the Scarlet Pimpernel if he soliloquised: "I believe that there is a Scarlet Pimpernel and that he will save me, and I will continue to believe it—unless he has not succeeded by 6:00 p.m." It may be prudent or rational to allow the Pimpernel only until 6:00 p.m. to save the man, but this is to say that it may be prudent or rational not to trust in the Scarlet Pimpernel while at the same time giving him a chance to effect a rescue.

So, given that the believer is affirming a belief and seeking to maintain a relationship of trust with God, it should not be surprising that the logic of his belief that there is a God, or of his belief that God loves men, is not that of a hypothesis. But this does not mean that he cannot say what his statement "There is a God" or his statement "God loves men" means or denies. He can give the logical denials of these statements—filled-out denials that are not just syntactical denials. He cannot give empirical denials, but then even a hypothesis apparently may not have an empirical denial. Nor does this mean that nothing in this world can count against his beliefs; things can count against them, and perhaps decisively. Lost faith attests to this.

Notes

[1]Antony Flew, "Theology and Falsification," *New Essays in Philosophical Theology,* ed. Antony Flew and Alasdair MacIntyre (New York: The Macmillan Company; London: SCM Press, 1955), p. 99.

[2]That religious utterances indicate a blik was contended by R. M. Hare in his contribution to "Theology and Falsification," *New Essays in Philosophical Theology,* pp. 99–103. That they indicate an intention to subscribe to a way of life was contended by R. B. Braithwaite in *An Empiricist's View of the Nature of Religious*

Belief (Cambridge: Cambridge University Press, 1955); reprinted in *The Existence of God,* ed. John Hick (New York: The Macmillan Company, 1964). For discussions of the reactions to Flew's challenge see William T. Blackstone, *The Problem of Religious Knowledge* (Englewood Cliffs, N.J.: Prentice-Hall, 1963), pp. 73–124; and Frederick Ferré, *Language, Logic and God* (New York: Harper & Row, Publishers, 1961), pp. 121–45.

[3]The first was argued by Basil Mitchell in his contribution to "Theology and Falsification," *New Essays in Philosophical Theology,* pp. 103–5. The second was argued by John Hick in "Theology and Verification," *Theology Today* 17 (1960): 12–31; reprinted in *The Existence of God,* ed. John Hick (New York: The Macmillan Company, 1964). At any rate this is the way Blackstone construes Hick's argument: Blackstone, pp. 112–16.

[4]It was done by George I. Mavrodes, "Bliks, Proofs and Prayers," *Pacific Philosophy Forum* 5 (1966): 49–54. Also see Gareth B. Matthews, "Theology and Natural Theology," *The Journal of Philosophy* 41 (1964).

[5]Cf. Paul R. Clifford, "The Factual Reference of Theological Assertions," *Religious Studies* 3 (1967): 344; and I. M. Crombie, "Theology and Falsification," *New Essays in Philosophical Theology,* p. 124.

[6]John Hick, *Faith and Knowledge,* 2d ed. (Ithaca, N.Y.: Cornell University Press, 1966), p. 167.

[7]Cf. Kai Nielsen, "On Fixing the Reference Range of God," *Religious Studies* 2 (1966): 16.

[8]Cf. John Wisdom, "The Logic of God," *Paradox and Discovery* (Oxford: Blackwell, 1965), p. 9.

[9]Flew, "Theology and Falsification," p. 98 n.

[10]Flew, "Theology and Falsification," p. 98.

[11]Flew, "Theology and Falsification," p. 98.

[12]This is not to say that all who believe in God would fill out what their beliefs denied in the same way, but it is not essential that they should. All that is essential is that "There is a God" have a denial that is filled out in some way. It should not come as news to anyone that men think of God in different ways or mean different things by "God."

[13]See, for instance, Soren Kierkegaard, *Concluding Unscientific Postscript,* trans. David F. Swenson and Walter Lowrie (Princeton: Princeton University Press, 1941), bk. 2, pt. 2, chap. 2, pp. 169 ff; Martin Buber, "Religion and Philosophy," *Eclipse of God* (New York: Harper & Row, Publishers, 1952), pp. 32–33; Norman Malcolm, "Is It a Religious Belief that 'God Exists'?" *Faith and the Philosophers,* ed. John Hick (New York: St. Martin's Press; London: Macmillan & Co., 1964), pp. 106–10.

B

more on the

falsification challenge

B

I

In his challenge to the religious believer, Flew asks him to specify what would count as a disproof for, e.g., "There is a God." A statement of such a specifiable condition I termed an "empirical denial." In Part A the concern was to show that a statement is a statement whether or not it has such an empirical denial. It was not to show that there are some statements which do not have an empirical denial; the concern was to show that it is not essential that they do. It was in connection with this point that the statement "John loves Mary" was discussed. But this very same example may indeed serve as an example of a statement for which, in certain complex situations, there is no empirical denial. That is, in some circumstances no matter what empirical conditions are specified, when the statement "John loves Mary" is made (if they are not merely denials of necessary conditions), they could obtain and still John might love Mary, as the developing situation would make clear. If the condition specified is that John is cruel to Mary and shows no concern for her, details could always emerge in such a situation to explain why, even though he loved her, he was cruel and showed no concern. And so on.

Flew has commented on statements similar to "John loves Mary" and their falsification in this complex sort of situation, and he makes an essential point which merits our attention.[1] He says that there nevertheless must be a set of presumably empirical conditions which would in the new circumstances that emerge show "John loves Mary" to be false. I think this is right. Certainly even in complex situations it will be true or false that John loves Mary. And if it is false, then tautologically the sufficient conditions for the falsity of "John loves Mary" in that situation will have been met, and presumably these conditions will be empirical. However, this is not to say that there is an empirical denial; that is, it is not to say that these conditions could have been specified in advance when the statement was made and when the full complexities surrounding John's love for Mary were not known and perhaps had not yet developed. In fact, it is to allow that perhaps they could not then have been specified. (Of course one can say that what is denied in even this situation is that John withholds affection from Mary except for good reason, and this is known in advance. However, this presumably will not be countenanced as an empirical denial for the same reason that constant suffering for no reason is not countenanced as the empirical denial of "God loves and is concerned for men"; neither is a specified empirical condition, it would be said.) This relates to the falsification challenge in the following way. The falsification challenge is asking *here and now* for a statement of the specified empirical condition which would show a religious statement, e.g., "There is a God," to be false. The implication of the challenge is that if this condition cannot now be specified (whether or not it can now be determined to be fulfilled), nothing is really now being asserted. What Flew's comments allow, then, is disastrous to the challenge: they allow that the falsification condition may not be clear at the time the statement is made and yet a genuine statement is made. Thus, if this is allowed, "There is a God" can now be an assertion by Flew's own view even if at this time no one can answer his challenge. By conceding this, Flew concedes the irrelevance of his challenge as a test for genuine statements.

Now to go on to another matter that Flew raised. It is perhaps less crucial to his challenge, but more noteworthy in the long run. In this admittedly complex business of how what we say relates to reality, there are a number of complicated areas, and Flew points out one of these which deserves some discussion. He observes that "no doubt a polymorphous notion like love does connect with ... empirical conditions in some fairly complex way."[2] But if so, he is pointing out, it still does connect with empirical conditions. This seems right. Further, I think that religious statements *taken as a class* present a kind of exception to what we might call a rule of understanding which emerges here. But this does not make them nonsense nor other than statements about what there is. The following explains why this is so.[3]

In some situations we can tell fairly easily whether John loves Mary. Sometimes, for instance, we can determine that John does not love Mary by determining that he is indifferent to her. In such instances there is no question of John's hiding his love for Mary or the like, and consequently his indifference is enough to establish that he does not love her. Similarly in many instances John's simply denying that he loves Mary is enough to establish that he does not. In such situations as these we may know all along what would show us that it is false that John loves Mary, and, therefore, in these situations or contexts the statement "John loves Mary" does have an empirical denial. That is, in these situations there is a known, specifiable condition that would show the statement "John loves Mary" to be false. This condition varies from context to context, to be sure (in one context it might be John being indifferent to Mary and in another it might be his abusing her), but still in such contexts "John loves Mary" does have an empirical denial. But also in some contexts it does not. That is, in some complex situations it will not be possible to state here and now what will show "John loves Mary" to be false. If both John and Mary are Dostoyevskian in character and their relationship is tortured as some human relationships are, it may be only sometime *after* we say that John loves Mary that we gain enough insight into their relationship to see what would show us that he does not. What would show us that he does not, we may discover, is that he *does* show her attention—something we could not have foreseen. Thus it appears that in some contexts "John loves Mary" has an empirical denial and in some it does not. At this point Flew might want to observe the following: All of this is right, but the only reason we can understand the statement "John loves Mary" in those complex situations where it has no here and now specifiable falsification condition (i.e., no empirical denial) is that we are familiar with situations in which the statement "John loves Mary" or cognates *do* have such a condition. Or, as this point might be expressed, our understanding of this statement in a context where it has no empirical denial is parasitic on our understanding of it or others in contexts where they do have an empirical denial, where we do here and now know what would show them false. I referred to this earlier as a kind of rule of understanding, and in its way, I think that it is right. It may be true that if we did not *sometimes* know to begin with what would make, e.g., the statement "John loves Mary" or its cognates false, we would never be able to understand such statements. If it is indeed right, then perhaps it expresses the connection with empirical conditions maintained by the statement "John loves Mary" in even those complex situations where the statement has no empirical denial. Also, it points out why one would feel that there is a difficulty with religious statements like "There is a God," "God is concerned with men," "God is merciful," etc. Since *all* such religious statements about God have no empirical denial, there are *no* religious statements upon which our understanding of those lacking an empirical denial can be dependent; so it seems no religious statement can be understood because none is ultimately connected to empirical conditions. However, there is a difficulty presented here only as long as religious statements are taken as a class, and that need not be done. That is, while it may be true that all religious statements about God's love, etc., are made in a complex situation and for this reason lack an empirical denial, it is not true that there are no clear statements upon which our understanding of them can depend. The statement "God loves men," for instance, is not only a religious statement but is also a "loves" statement. Thus "God loves men," like other "loves" statements in complex situations, can depend upon, e.g., "John loves his son," where this is a statement in a simple situation and where we know here and now what would show it false. And similarly "God is good" can depend upon "John is good" where this is a statement in a simple situation. And so on.[4]

II

Thomas McPherson in commenting on an earlier version of Part A has raised a number of points worth our pursuing.[5] First, he is concerned because I allow that evidence can count for or against the existence and love of God, which he feels it is wrong to do, at least as I have done it. Second, he feels that while there may be evidence for religious beliefs, it will be "internal" evidence. I shall discuss these in turn.

To allow that evidence can count for or against the existence and love of God is to concede too much—to give hostages to fortune—McPherson feels. McPherson's concern may be right. It is right if it is a concern with the picture that portrays the believer saying the opening lines of the Nicene Creed, "I believe in one God, Father Almighty, Maker of heaven and earth," as a bad superscientist offering a bad superscientific hypothesis. He rejects this picture as a mockery, as I do. However, I believe that he rejects too much. He not only rejects the idea that religious believers typically offer superhypotheses, but also the idea that there can be evidence for or against what the believer says when he says that there is one God, Father Almighty, Maker of heaven and earth. And I believe this should not be rejected.

One can be led to reject too much here by not considering the following.

1) One can affirm one's faith in, e.g., the love of another or in God's concern for one in many ways. However, inasmuch as one makes a tentative affirmation one does not affirm one's faith; rather one shows that one has no faith. Thus one cannot affirm one's faith in, e.g., the love of another by *tentatively* putting forward the view that the other loves one. A hypothesis is a tentative explanation or view of something. Thus, affirming one's faith in the love of another is not compatible with offering the hypothesis that the

other loves one. So too affirming one's faith that there is a God is not compatible with offering the hypothesis that there is a God.

2) However, one can make a statement which evidence will support or count against, without offering a hypothesis. One does so when he makes a statement without attempting to offer a tentative explanation or view of anything. This would be the case, for instance, if upon hearing that my father has been arrested for a serious crime, I cry out to those who have arrested him: "But he is innocent!" While I am not tentatively asserting this to explain anything or as a view to be investigated, there may be evidence for it, against it, or both.

3) Anyone can affirm his trust or faith in God or in another person *by* making such a statement, even if he cannot by offering a hypothesis. Thus one may affirm one's trust in another's love when he says "She loves me" (or "She *does* love me"), which may be true or may be false, of course. Far from an utterance being a performative ruling out its being a statement, which is what McPherson seems to think, almost every example of a speaker making a statement will be an example of his making that statement for some point; that is, of his doing something by making the statement, which makes it a performative.

4) Of course one *can* offer the hypothesis that there is a God. But if he does, he is not thereby affirming his faith. And most typically the latter, not the former, is the religious concern.

If these points are considered, what emerges is that, compatible with the believer affirming his faith in God, there *can* be evidence for (or against) there being a God, even though the believer is not putting forward the tentative view that there is a God on the basis of any such evidence.

We turn now to McPherson's second concern. Although McPherson is suspicious of allowing evidence to be relevant in any way to religious belief, he himself allows that "internal" evidence might have some relevance.[6] "Internal" evidence, I gather from McPherson's various remarks, is evidence 1) such that only the believer knows what constitutes it, 2) which would not convince a non-believer, and 3) which is not empirical. If I understand his concern regarding the relevance of "external" evidence for religious belief, it is again one I share: it is a concern with the picture of the believer as a kind of cosmologist with a world view that can be verified or falsified by anyone who has the time, technique, and proper equipment. But it is not clear to me that the distinction between "internal" and "external" evidence sheds any light on what is wrong with this picture.

In what follows I shall try to say why it is not helpful, and only half right, to characterise the evidence that can count for a religious belief as "internal" evidence (in the sense McPherson cites) and to briefly indicate what seems to me to be the role of evidence regarding, for instance, the belief that God is concerned for men. Hopefully in so doing I shall point out what is wrong about the picture of the believer as a cosmologist offering a world view to be investigated and established by neutral observers.

Far from evidence of God's concern being foreign to a religious person, it is often something he sees on every side. A believer may well thank God for much in his life and in the lives of others which he takes to be granted to him and to others through God's goodness. And those things for which he thanks God he sees as indications of God's concern and goodness. The believer may not seek evidence to shore up his belief in God's concern, but inasmuch as he is aware of indications of that concern, he is aware of what supports that belief. Does only the believer know what constitutes this evidence? I do not think so. The atheist may be able to correctly indicate what a believer would thank God for. The difference between the two is not that one knows what to point to and the other does not; the difference is that one sees what is pointed to as evidence of God's concern and the other does not. Nor need it be the case that the atheist never comes to see the indications of God's goodness for what they are; he might, and if he does, he might then come to believe in God. Conversions sometimes happen precisely when miracles are seen for what they are. McPherson wants to insist that evidence relevant to religious belief cannot convince a nonbeliever possibly because he is thinking of evidence as it is presented in the hypothesis verification model. It may be right that it is hopeless to try to prove to a non-believer that there is a God or that he is concerned for men by citing what he himself can point to but what he cannot see as indications of God's concern. A presentation of countless instances of what the believer sees as signs of God's concern, but what the non-believer cannot see as such, will not convince the non-believer. What he needs is not a presentation of such indications, but the eyes to see them for what they are. However, this does not mean that the indications of God's concern in the world and lives of men cannot convince the non-believer of that concern; it means only that they cannot before they are seen for what they are.

McPherson also suggests that the kind of evidence pertinent to religious belief is not empirical. Is this right? Certainly, if there are indications of God's concern, these indications are, or many of them are, in the world. But, on the other hand, they are not there for all to see as a tree shedding its leaves is there for all to see.

Is the evidence pertinent to religious belief empirical, then, or not? It is empirical in that it is there in the world to be seen by any who have eyes to see it; it is not empirical in that it cannot be seen by just anyone who has eyes in his head.

It seems, then, that the point of McPherson's suggestion that religious evidence is "internal" and not "external" is right, but the suggestion is wrong in its details. That is, to the extent that there may be evidence for religious beliefs, it will not be related to them as evidence is related to a cosmological hypothesis (or to any hypothesis). But the difference between these two species of evidence is not the difference between what McPherson calls "internal" and "external" evidence. Rather the difference is that the first may very likely not be seen for what it is—as indications of God's concern— while the other, once it is gathered, will plainly be evidence for or against the hypothesis in question. In terms of the categories of Chapter 1, the difference is that the first is nonhypothetical evidence and the second is hypothetical evidence.

Notes

[1]See Antony Flew, "The Falsification Response," *Religious Studies* 5: (1969).

[2]Flew, "The Falsification Response," p. 78.

[3]I have been helped greatly here by conversations with Donald F. Henze, although I am sure that he would not agree with me on every point.

[4]The problem of God predication at this point looms large in the minds of many, no doubt. They would want to point out that this analysis allows that "loves" is predicated of God in the same sense it is predicated of men. To be brief, so it does, but then so it is. If it were not, then truly we would be lost in our understanding of what we are being told when we are told that God is concerned for us and loves us as a Father. The problem of God predication is the subject of Part C of the Appendix.

[5]In Thomas McPherson, "The Falsification Challenge: a Comment," *Religious Studies* 5 (1969). In what follows I do not reply to McPherson's point that I do not distinguish between saying that p and $\sim \sim$ p are equivalent in meaning and saying that $\sim \sim$ p gives the meaning of p. The distinction McPherson points out is valid: often something equivalent in meaning does not give the meaning of what one says to someone else. Thus while "Au secours!" is equivalent in meaning to "Help!" it would not give the meaning of "Help!" to one who speaks only German. However, I do not think that any confusion regarding this distinction undercuts the argument I propounded to support the idea that assertions must have an empirical denial. If it does, so much the worse for the argument, which of course was not one I advocated as sound but one which I examined as a possible argument that a proponent of Flew's views might advance to support the falsification challenge.

[6]McPherson, "The Falsification Challenge: a Comment" p. 82. He says that "the view that reasons for religious belief are internal to the belief has been persuasively presented by such writers as Professor Peter Winch and Mr. D. Z. Phillips. From such a view it could be said that there is, in a sense, evidence for religious belief. . . ."

C

the problem of

god predication

C

I

Many religious thinkers and philosophers believe that saying something understandable about God requires giving the words one uses a special meaning. To meaningfully say that God *knows* what is in the hearts of men or *hears* prayers or *is concerned* for men, they think, is to use "knows," "hears," and "is concerned" in a special sense beyond the sense these words have when applied to mere men. The reasons thinkers want to say this are various; some are religious reasons, reflecting the desire not to limit God, and some are not, reflecting the suspicion that in the final analysis there can be no adequate meaningful concept of God. Whatever the reasons for this belief, though, it gives rise to a problem, the problem of God predication, which may be stated thus:

"Before we can understand statements about God, we have to know the sense of the terms predicated of God, e.g., 'knows' and 'is concerned.' But how do we determine their sense when they are predicated of God and not of men?" The problem, then, is one of *determining* the special sense—that is, the special *meaning* of such terms in their application to God.

Although philosophers have offered solutions to the problem of God predication, none has been recognized as successful. Aquinas' solution is the most famous—his doctrine of analogy—which asserts that we determine the sense of God predicates by a special kind of analogy.[1] I. M. Crombie has also offered a solution of a sort—however, he shifts his ground to do so. Crombie says that in fact we can never determine the special sense of God predicates but argues that "statements about God . . . are in effect parables, which are referred, by means of the proper name 'God,' out of our experience in a certain direction."[2] Unfortunately Aquinas' doctrine appears to be rather obscure. On the other hand, Crombie's view has the unhappy implication that the "religious man does not suppose himself to know what he means by his statements."[3] It is usually thought that to date not only these but virtually every effort to solve the problem of God predication has for one reason or another failed.

It seems evident that before God's existence can be proven or even discussed the sense of the predicates used to characterize God must be determined. And it seems equally clear that before the problem of evil can be solved the sense of "good" as it applies to God must be determined. While these propositions may seem clear and even self-evident, they are nevertheless false. They seem to be true only because it is taken to be clear that the problem of God predication is indeed a problem. At this point let me raise a prior question from the far side of the efforts to solve this problem and their failures: What reasons are there for thinking that God predicates must have some special sense different from the sense they have when predicated of men? That is, why should we think that there is a problem of God predication at all? Why do we not generally accept what Cardinal Newman said in regard to belief in the Trinty, that "Three, One, He, God, Father, Son, Spirit—are none of them words peculiar to theology, have all a popular meaning, and are used according to that obvious and popular meaning, when introduced into the Catholic dogma"?[4] It is with this forgotten question—why should we think that there is a problem of God predication?—and the reasons offered in reply to it that we shall be concerned in what follows.

Locating such reasons is not altogether easy, for very often philosophers who treat the problem of God predication start with the problem and not with the reasons why it is a problem, or, if they do offer reasons, they do not dwell on them.

Four main reasons for thinking that there is a problem of God predication are discernible. Generally they are intertwined when advanced, but they can be distinguished and treated separately. They are:

1) The terms predicated of God must have a special sense different from the sense they have when predicated of men because otherwise the statements made about God would be false.

2) They must have a special sense because otherwise God would be conceived of anthropomorphically and so delimited.

3) They must have a special sense because otherwise we would have an adequate concept of God using predicates in their ordinary sense and we can have no such adequate concept in this way.

4) They must have a special sense because otherwise God would be like men and He is to be completely unlike men in His activity. etc.

Each shall be treated in turn. What I hope to bring out is that none of these reasons succeeds in establishing the problem because each presupposes something that is either misconceived or is at least questionable.

II

We turn, then, to the first reason for thinking that there is a problem of God predication. It is this: the terms predicated of God must have a special sense, for otherwise the resulting statements about God would be false. In the *Dialogues Concerning Natural Religion* Hume has Cleanthes pose this dilemma to Demea:

> . . . if we abandon all human analogy . . . we abandon all religion and retain no conception of the great object of our adoration. If we preserve human analogy, we must forever find it impossible to reconcile any mixture of evil in the universe with infinite attributes.[5]

Paraphrased, the dilemma is this: when we say that God is good or loving, either we do not or we do mean by these terms what we mean when we say that men are good or loving; if the first is the case, we do not know what we mean; if the second is the case, since there is evil in the world, what we say of God is false.

Hume intends his dilemma to be an argument against saying anything about God, or at least about an infinite God. However, taken another way, it yields an argument and also the first reason for the necessity of determining a special sense for God predicates. That argument is that since statements about God employing terms in their ordinary sense would be false (the implication of the second horn of the dilemma), statements about God in order to have any chance to be true must employ their terms in a special sense. If this argument holds, then of course we are faced with the question: How is the special sense determined? That is, we are faced with the problem of God predication.

But are we in fact forced into the problem of God predication by the second horn of the dilemma? The first thing to note is that the truth of the second horn as it is formulated would at most necessitate that *some* terms require a special sense when predicated of God—for instance, "good" and "loving," but not "creates" or "gives." So at most the second horn would force us into a limited version of the problem of God predication. Another thing to note is that for the second horn to do even this a resolution of the problem of evil is assumed. That is, it is assumed that if there is evil in the world, God cannot be all-good. Someone who did not have the problem of evil, someone who had faith that God had a just purpose for the world's evil, then, would see no reason for the problem of God predication to arise at all, for he would not agree that the second horn of Hume's dilemma has the implications Hume ascribes to it. He would not agree that saying that God is good, when "good" means what is meant when it is said men are good, has the implication that what is said is false. In short, the problem of God predication arises here only for one who does not have faith in God's goodness, and it is tautological that if one does not think that God is good he will think that goodness cannot be truly predicated of God, except in a new sense.

I have presented this examination of the first reason for the problem of God predication in terms of Hume's dilemma and specifically in regard to the predicates "good" and "loving" because it seems to me that most often the first reason is supported in just this way by those who advance it. If one is going to argue that God predicates need a special sense because otherwise statements about God that contain them would be false, then he clearly should be able to show that statements about God that contain God predicates without a special sense would be false. The problem of evil appears to many to do this so far as "God is good" and "God is loving" are concerned.

It might be argued that a few other predicates require a special sense for the first reason. One such predicate is "personal." One might argue that as evil shows that "God is good" is false in the ordinary sense of "good," so certain considerations having to do with personal identity show that "God is a personal God" is false in the ordinary sense of "personal." Even Newman concedes that when God is said to be a personal God the meaning of "personal" cannot be the same as it is in reference to men.[6] It is not clear why he says this unless it is because, while God is loving, concerned, jealous, and demanding—all personal attributes—He is still immaterial; that is, He lacks a material body. If one thinks of a bodily criterion as the primary criterion for personal identity, then he will conclude that the notion of a person with no continuous material body is problematical and the notion of a person with no material body is incoherent.[7] Or if one thinks that a person is identical with his body and that survival of bodily dissolution is self-contradictory, then he is committed to saying that God who is immaterial cannot logically be a person in the ordinary sense of "person."[8] Perhaps Newman, unawares, was inclined to think along these lines. Today, this kind of solution to the problem of personal identity is thought of as rigorous and right-headed as it was in the past, and so would be taken as grounds for the conclusion that God cannot be personal in the ordinary sense of "personal." According to this solution, then, the statement "God is a personal God" must be false in the ordinary sense of "personal," and so if God is said to be personal it must be in a special sense and we will be faced with the problem of God predication at least as far as the predicate "personal" is concerned. But why should we accept this solution? And here again, as with the problem of evil, if one does not accept this solution the problem of God predication will not arise. At least not for the first reason.

My point is not that evil does not entail the falsity of "God is good" or that the meaning of "person" does not entail the falsity of "God is a personal God." Those points seem to me to be right, but they are here tangential. The main point I wish to make is that this first reason for the problem of God predication regarding "loving," "good," or "personal" (which are nearly the only predicates involved) presupposes particular resolutions of two knotty philosophical problems.

III

The second reason for thinking that God predicates must have a special sense is that, if they did not, God would be conceived of anthropomorphically and so would be delimited.

In a well known article already referred to Crombie asks the following in reference to "There is a God," "God loves us as a father loves his children," and "He shall come again with glory . . .":

> . . . is it not true that they appear to be statements to those of us who use them, because we deceive ourselves by a sort of conjuring trick, oscillating backwards and forwards between a literal interpretation of what we say when we say it, and a scornful rejection of such anthropomorphism when anybody challenges us?[9]

In another place Crombie says:

> What does a doctrine of creation amount to? If you think of God anthropomorphically, creation is all very well. He took some raw material, and by compounding and arranging it, gave it the properties we see around us; He now sustains it, and will one day put it on the bonfire. But if you think of God anthropomorphically, who made God?[10]

Clearly Crombie sees anthropomorphism as something believers should avoid. And as these passages bring out, if anthropomorphism is to be avoided, more God predicates than "personal," "good" and "loving" will have to be given a special sense: "creates" and "will come" are mentioned by Crombie. The list could be extended: "is wise," "commands," "punishes," "causes," and "moves" would be on it. In fact the second reason for thinking there is a problem of God predication pertains to every God predicate.

What is so objectionable about anthropomorphism, and what makes it a reason for the problem of God predication in the thinking of many, may be got at by examining the following dilemma: To say of God that he is a "first cause" or "will punish sins" or "commands us not to kill" is either to deal in human language and in human meanings or it is not. The first alternative comes to anthropomorphism; the second comes to agnosticism. On the first alternative "God" becomes merely a part of the natural order, and God's attributes are "reduced to the level delimited by human imagination." On the second alternative "causes," "moves," "is wise" and the like are emptied of meaning when predicated of God.[11]

As it stands, this dilemma argues for the impossibility of God predication, but, as with Hume's dilemma, it can be made over into an argument for God predicates requiring a special sense. When this is done it yields the kernel of the second reason for thinking that there is a problem of God predication. The revised argument is that God predicates cannot have the meaning they do ordinarily (in "human language") because if they did, God would be a part of the natural order and His attributes would be "reduced to the level delimited by human imagination." What makes anthropomorphism unacceptable is that it delimits God in such a way that He would no longer be more than a superhuman, spatially located and material.

Now if thinking of God in this way is indeed entailed by predicating, e.g., "is wise" of Him, then there is something radically wrong with saying that God is wise, or commands, or creates, or does or is anything in the sense in which we say these things of men. However, this entailment holds only if two assumptions are correct. One is that if we can meaningfully say that X is Y in the ordinary sense of "Y" we must be able to imagine X's Y-ness. The other is that if we can imagine X's Y-ness, then X's Y-ness is limited to what can be drawn from human experience. The first assumption is necessary if ordinary meanings of terms are going to reduce God's attributes to the level delimited by human *imagination*. The second is necessary if ordinary meanings of terms are going to reduce God's attributes to the level *delimited* by human imagination. It seems to me that both assumptions are wrong, or as wrong as they are right.

Consider the first assumption. It asserts that if we can meaningfully say of someone that he is wise, we must be able to at least imagine his wisdom. According to this principle, it is not necessary for us to have experienced his wisdom—that is, to have seen it exercised, just as it is not necessary for us to have seen a unicorn for us to meaningfully speak of such an animal; but it is necessary that we be able to imagine his wisdom just as we are able to imagine a unicorn. Thus if this principle were correct we could still meaningfully talk about a hypothetical wise man even though there were none, for we could imagine what a wise man would be like, just as we can now imagine what a horse with a narwhale's horn is like even though there are none. But unlike men, God is beyond imagination. He and His wisdom cannot be imagined, and so this principle asserts that His wisdom cannot be meaningfully spoken of—at least not with the meaning the term has when applied to men.

Is this right? In a novel by William Dean Howells the following exchange takes place:

> "I suppose it isn't well for us to see human nature at white heat habitually," continued Bromfield Corey, after awhile. "It would make us vain of our species. Many a poor fellow . . . has gone into battle simply and purely for his country's sake, not knowing whether, if he laid down his life, he should ever find it again, or whether, if he took it up hereafter, he should take it up in heaven or hell. Come, parson!" he said, turning to the minister, "what has ever been conceived of omnipotence of omniscience, so sublime, so divine as that?" "Nothing," answered the minister quietly. "God has never been imagined at all. . . ."[12]

Here, even though the minister admits and even insists that God and His attributes have never been imagined, he continues to speak of them, as he must if only to say that they have not been imagined. As a minister, though, he would of course speak of them in many connections. As a comforter he would remind his parishioners of God's mercy. As an exhorter he would remind his parishioners of God's omniscience, that He knows what is in their hearts. Clearly, the minister does not accept the first assumption—that is, the principle that if we can meaningfully speak of an X being Y we must be able to imagine X's Y-ness. And why should he accept it? If the exchange between Bromfield Corey and the minister concerned a nontheological matter, it would have been clear that all of us would reject this assumption.

Imagine that Bromfield Corey had said: "The suffering of humanity in the Middle Ages was great and extended to every facet of life. It was so detailed and ubiquitous that it is incomprehensible to one living in our age."

And suppose that the minister had replied: "It's true, we today cannot imagine the suffering of the Middle Ages."

Even if both were right, they would still be using the term "suffering" meaningfully and would still mean by it suffering.

It might be said at this point that there is a crucial difference between the suffering in the Middle Ages and God's attributes: while both cannot now be imagined, the suffering in the Middle Ages can *in principle* be imagined, but God's attributes cannot. It is not clear to me that this point is relevant, for the principle is that if we can meaningfully speak of the suffering in the Middle Ages, we must be able to imagine it now, not some time in the future. Of course the principle can be revised, but then it loses much of its initial plausibility. But, in any case, the point about the in principle imaginability of the suffering in the Middle Ages, as opposed to God's attributes, is dubious.

We are to accept such suffering as in principle imaginable because there is no logical reason why we could not be directly acquainted with that suffering, while there is a logical reason why we cannot be directly acquainted with God's attributes. But how could we be directly acquainted with the suffering in the Middle Ages? We live now, not then. True, we might read about such suffering and come to appreciate it keenly in this way, but then we can similarly read about God's mercy. Direct acquaintance must take a more immediate form: direct acquaintance requires our presence as perceiving agents. If so then the possibility of our direct acquaintance with the suffering in the Middle Ages requires nothing less than the possibility of time travel. Time travel, though, hardly seems intelligible. True, we can understand stories about time travel, such as H. G. Well's stories. To do so we depend upon the model of travel from one place to another. Similarly we can understand stories about an after life, in which we will be directly acquainted with God's attributes, by depending upon the model of waking from sleep. Time travel, then, can be entertained as a possibility. But it can be entertained only uncritically and with paradox. Any number of contradictions would be entailed by, for instance, my "travelling" to the Middle Ages: e.g., the possibility of my living and dying before my birth and my being my own antecedent. In the case of life after death we have no flat contradictions—only a mystery.[13]

It might be replied here that the suffering in the Middle Ages is imaginable in principle not because one can in principle travel in time to the Middle Ages but because one can in principle reproduce in the present the conditions of the Middle Ages; and it is for this reason that we can meaningfully speak of such suffering as suffering. But this argument concedes that direct acquaintance even in principle is not necessary to imagine God's mercy; all that is necessary is the in principle possibility of acquaintance with the same *kind* of thing. And one could accept this principle as it has now evolved and say that as the suffering of the Middle Ages can meaningfully be spoken of, so can God's mercy, for we are acquainted with the same kind of thing as God's mercy, namely the mercy of men. Though man's mercy differs notably from God's mercy in the matter of perfection, they are both the same kind of thing— namely mercy. Nothing in the principle rules this out. For that matter one might well claim, as many do, that we can be directly acquainted with God's mercy itself, and not just with the same kind of thing. Many have claimed an experience of God's mercy in this life. (Thus it can be argued that while time travel or some such thing is necessary for direct acquaintance with the suffering in the Middle Ages, life after death is not necessary for direct acquaintance with God's attributes.)

The second assumption is that if we can imagine X's Y-ness, then X's Y-ness is limited to what can be drawn from human experience. If we can imagine God as having wisdom, then His wisdom must be limited to what can be drawn from human experience. So in imagining God's wisdom we are limited to imagining Him only as wise as men are, or as wise as men can be imagined to be (which again is limited to our experience), and this makes God into a superhuman.

The minister in Howells' novel would perhaps also insist that we can not imagine God's wisdom. But his reason would be that there is something awesome and mysterious about it that is beyond our knowledge, and this inability would not prevent us from meaningfully speaking of God's infinite wisdom, nor would it make God meaningfully spoken of into a superhuman. The inability to imagine God's infinite wisdom that we now have before us, on the other hand, supposedly does entail the impossibility of meaningfully speaking of God's wisdom except as it reduces God to a superhuman. What is being thought of as the imagination here vis à vis this second assumption is rather different from what Howells' minister and the rest of us might suppose. And the operative reason why we cannot imagine God's wisdom as infinite has precisely to do with the way the imagination is being conceived. That way is basically that of Hume or Locke or at any rate is inspired by views associated with their epistemologies. What is supposed by this notion of the imagination is not only that some sense experience is necessary for imagination, but that in regard to God's wisdom, one's idea must be limited to what he has experienced through his senses. This notion is that to imagine something auditory is to have a faint echo of the sound in one's mind, and to imagine something tactile or olfactory is to revive a "copy" of the feel or smell in one's mind. Similarly, to imagine something visual is to have a mental picture or copy of it, and to have such a picture one must have garnered it or its elements through sense experience. God's wisdom is visual, since it certainly is not olfactory or tactile, etc. Thus if one can imagine God's infinite wisdom, he must have a mental picture of God as infinitely wise, but to have such a picture is to make God into a superhuman.

This picture of the imagination is obviously wrong. We can imagine what is visual (if it belongs to any of the senses) but non-picturable, and we can imagine the visual and picturable without mental pictures. We can imagine an infinite universe and infinite divisions of bodies, as well as infinite series of numbers, all of which cannot be pictured; or if they can be—and they can in a sense—so too can God's infinite wisdom. And when we respond to a friend's entreaty, "Imagine that you are lost in the Grand Canyon—what would you do?" and imagine that we are lost in the Grand Canyon, which is visual and picturable, we may have no mental picture whatsoever before our mind's eye. This view of the imagination is, in short, riddled with difficulties, and it is assumed by the second reason for thinking there is a problem of God predication. The point to be noted here, then, is that this picture of the imagination is assumed and this assumption is unexamined. Certainly many who advance the anthropomorphic reason for the problem of God predication and who would subscribe to the dilemma posed earlier in this section would question this notion of the imagination if they met it elsewhere. That they do not question it in this connection is a further indication that many start with the problem of God predication and not with the reasons why it is a problem.

Regarding the anthropomorphic reason for thinking that there is a problem of God predication, I think that we can draw these conclusions: Anthropomorphism is to be avoided only if it makes God into a kind of superhuman, material and spatially located. It was this notion of God that Crombie rightfully rejected when he rejected anthropomorphism. God would be made into such a superhuman by predicating, e.g., wisdom of him in the same sense it is predicated of men if the two assumptions we have discussed held. But one is simply wrong, and the other hinges on a dubious notion of the imagination. If, on the other hand, anthropomorphism means only that the predicates that apply to God apply to men with the same meaning, then there is nothing to be avoided as repugnant to religious sensitivity, for we have no reason to think that this *per se* makes God into a superhuman any more than we have a reason to think that our saying truly of dogs and men that they are hungry or clever makes dogs into men or men into dogs or limits a man's cleverness to that of a dog. (There is a sense in which we say that dogs are clever in a different sense from men—namely, where this comes to saying that dogs are clever in different *ways* from the ways in which men are clever, which is surely true. And if one were to say of a man that he was only clever in the sense a dog is, meaning only in the ways a dog is, clearly one would be derogating or limiting the man. But this does not mean that "clever" predicated of a dog *means* something different from "clever" predicated of a man, or that saying a man is clever and that he has a clever dog limits the man; it only means that dogs and men are clever in different ways.)

There is a further or alternative assumption in addition to the two noted and discussed which is linked to the anthropomorphic reason. I purposely did not draw it out and make it explicit, but perhaps it was obvious enough: it has to do with the connection between sense experience and meaning. It was not discussed above since it will be a chief concern in the next section.

IV

The third reason for supposing that there is a problem of God predication is this: God predicates must have a special sense because otherwise we would have an adequate concept of God using predicates in their ordinary sense, and we can have no such adequate concept in this way. One of the strengths of this reason is that it can rely upon religious believers themselves for support. Gaunilo, for instance, in his reply to Anselm, seems to concede that we can have no concept of God. In discussing this theme, Crombie has said the following:

We must acknowledge at once that in the ordinary sense we have no conception of the divine nature. We do not know God, and it would be absurd to claim that we know what kind of being He is. In so far as we use adjectives about Him ('omniscient', 'eternal' and so on) they do not enable us to conceive what it is like to be God. Omniscience is not infinite erudition, and what it is must be beyond our comprehension. And yet people, whether they be theists, atheists, or agnostics do normally suppose themselves to know what people are talking about when they talk about God. The critic, of course, has his own explanation of this fact. According to him, what makes people suppose that they can grasp the reference of talk about God is nothing more than the old anthropomorphic conception of a superhuman being somewhere above the sky. No civilized person believes there to be such a being, but the picture serves, in unsophisticated minds, to conceal from us that we do not know what we are talking about.[14]

The main argument for the no adequate concept reason runs this way: If God predicates had the meaning they have when applied to men, we would have an anthropomorphic concept of God as a superhuman; such a concept is ruled out as not adequate; thus we have no adequate concept of God using predicates in their ordinary sense; from which it follows that if we are to have an adequate concept of God, God predicates must be given a special sense which is yet to be determined. This argument is obviously closely related to that examined in section III; its main difference is that it turns solely on meaning and not on the imagination. In the same way this third reason is essentially the anthropomorphic reason with refined support. What requires examination here is the premise that if God predicates have their ordinary meaning, then our concept of God can only be of a superhuman. It is not clear that Gaunilo subscribed to this proposition, but Crombie does, and it is at the heart of the argument behind the no concept reason for there being a problem of God predication. The father of this premise may well be Locke or Hume. Hume thought that our concepts—that is, the meanings of all our terms that can stand as a proposition's subject or predicate—are ultimately derived from sense experience. The argument behind the third reason when it is expanded to include the Humian support of this linchpin premise may be put thus: Before we can talk meaningfully of God, we must have a concept of God, that is, the term "God" must have a meaning; to have a concept of God, we must have an idea of God; ideas are gotten from sense experience; we have no sense experience of God; therefore we can have no concept of God, unless we have a concept constructed from the ordinary meanings of predicates applied to God, like the constructed concept of a unicorn, which would then be a concept of a superhuman; but such a concept is inadequate; therefore we have no adequate concept of God using the ordinary meanings of predicates; from which it follows that if we are to have an adequate concept of God, we need to somehow impart a special sense to God predicates. Perhaps it is not surprising that one offering this argument would also conclude that no adequate special sense could ever be specified.

The assumptions discussed in the last section conjointly were that if X could meaningfully be said to be Y, then X's Y-ness could be imagined, and if imagined, X's Y-ness would be limited to sense experience. Here the assumption is: if "X" or "Y-ness" has meaning, that meaning is drawn from and limited to sense experience. In short what is assumed here is a form of what might be called the Humian theory of meaning.

I do not intend to argue at length against this theory of meaning. It is enough to mention the implications of such a theory that a man blind from birth could not meaningfully tell another the color of his hair and that we could not meaningfully speak of infinite divisibility or of vacuums or of magnetic fields.[15] So here too, in the support of the third reason for thinking that there is a problem of God predication, we find a dubious and unexamined assumption. Again, this is an indication that philosophers start with the problem and not the reasons for thinking that there is a problem. Now of course just as Hume's theory of meaning gave rise to and was displaced by versions of the positivist theory of meaning, so too the positivist theory in some form can do duty for the other in supporting the third reason or in arguing for the problem of God predication in another way.

We might get this argument, for instance: To speak meaningfully of God, we must have a concept of God—that is, the expression "God" must have a meaning; an expression is meaningless if it is *logically impossible* to point to samples of the sort of thing which the expression ostensibly signifies,[16] it is logically impossible to point to a sample of the entity God, unless we mean by "God" a natural object such as a superhuman; therefore the expression "God" has no meaning, unless our concept is of a natural object such as a super-human; but such a concept is inadequate; therefore we have no adequate concept of God; from which it follows that if we are to have an adequate concept of God, God predicates must have a sense yet to be imparted to them.

Or, ranging beyond the no adequate concept reason, the following sort of positivistic argument might be marshalled to support the problem of God predication: To factually assert anything, including that God is good or wise, one's putative statement must have an empirical denial; as they stand, religious statements (about God) do not have an empirical denial; therefore as they stand religious statements fail to assert anything; if they are under-stood as asserting that God is "good" or "wise" in the ordinary sense, that is, if ordinary empirical denials are stated, religious statements become real assertions, but false; from which it follows that if religious statements are to avoid being either (factually) meaningless or false, God predicates must have a special sense imparted to them.

Flew, who would subscribe to the first premises, might or might not advance this argument. In any case the demand for an empirical denial for real assertions hardly seems justified.[17] The various positivist criteria of meaning would, like the Humian criterion, rule out any special sense for God predicates that did not reduce God to a superhuman, or to some other natural object, which is to say that they would rule out any acceptable special sense. In other words, the positivist like the Humian would argue not only that it is necessary that God predicates have a special sense, but also that it is impossible. It is also evident that the positivistic argument has many advantages over the strictly Humian argument in that the theory of meaning it assumes is free of the oddities attached to the Humian view. To name an indicative matter, the version of the positivistic theory that covers terms (unlike the Humian) allows that the expression "vacuum" is meaningful.

Again my main purpose is not to argue that the third reason for thinking that there is a problem of God predication rests on a mistaken assumption. It is simply to point out that it rests rather heavily on an assumption that is itself open to some question. To argue that the various positivist criteria of meaning are mistaken, their ramified past would have to be exhumed, and it cannot be done here. The criticisms of these criteria are sufficiently docu- mented, I believe.[18] Suffice it to be made explicit that the no adequate concept reason for thinking that there is a problem of God predication is con- tingent on some form of positivist criterion; if not on a Humian theory of meaning.

V

We come now to the fourth reason. It is this: God predicates must have a special sense, because otherwise God would be like men. Crombie provides us with a statement of this reason and its logic:

> If you speak of the virtues of a certain sort of car, the word 'virtue,' being applied to a car, comes to mean something different from what it means in application to human beings. If you speak of hot temper, the word 'hot' does not mean what it means in the ordinary way. . . . When God is said to be jeal- ous, or active in history, it is felt that the word 'jealous' or 'active' must be being used here in a transferred sense. . . . The activity of God is presumably not like the activity of men (it does not make him hot or tired); to say then that God is active must involve modifying the meaning of the word.[19]

Crombie is citing here what might be called the logic of transferred sense. In one application it is that if the virtue of something (a sort of car) is not like men's, then "virtue" when predicated of that thing must have a transferred sense. In regard to God predication the logic is this: if a) God's activity is not like men's, then b) "active" when predicated of God must have a trans- ferred, special sense. This hypothetical, coupled with the truth of a) which seems clear to Crombie, of course entails b). While Crombie apparently

accepts this logic generally, he does not allow that it applies to God predication. It does not because it cannot; that is, he says that since we do not know
anything about one end of the transfer, namely God, no transfer of sense can
be made. He does not feel that all is lost, however. As was noted in section I,
he offers an alternative way of understanding religious statements about God.
But his way is shrouded with the unhappy consequence, already noted, that
the religious man does not suppose himself to know what he means by his
statements.[20]

What compelled Crombie to offer his alternative analysis, and what stands
behind the fourth reason for supposing that there is a problem of God predication, is what I called the logic of transferred sense, as it applies to God
predication. Clearly the fourth reason would hold if it were true that if a),
then b) *and* a) were true. Our question, then, becomes: Is it true that, if a)
then b), and, secondarily, is a) true?

Is a) true? Is it true that God's activity is not like men's? Crombie says
yes to this question: God's activity is unlike men's, for his activity in contrast
to men's does not make him hot or tired. Certainly it is true that this is a
difference between God's activity and men's. But does this make them unlike?
If they are unlike in this respect, they still may be alike in other respects.
For instance, God's and men's activities still may be alike in that they are
comprised of the same sorts of things: creating, communicating, listening to,
chastening. In spite of all that Crombie has pointed out, we may still say
that there is no difference between the activity of God and the activity of men
in this regard. Perhaps to simply assert that they are alike in being the same
kind of thing would be to beg the question regarding the validity of the fourth
reason, and that is not my point. My point is that even if Crombie is right
that God's activity and men's are unlike in the respect he points out, it does
not follow from this alone that they are unlike in the key respect of the kinds
of things they are.

But a) is true when expanded thus: God's activity is not like men's in the
respect that men's activity makes them tired while God's does not make Him
tired. Now the question is: Granted that this difference obtains, why does
it necessitate that "activity" have a different sense when predicated of God?
If a) as amended is true, why should we conclude that if a), then b)? The
answer can only be that if a) is true, then something essential to the meaning
of "activity" is lacking in God's activity, and so a new sense is required. Before
we ask if this is the case, let us strengthen the argument as much as possible.
The respect in which men's activity and God's differ is not simply that men's
activity happens to tire them, while God's does not happen to tire Him.
Rather God's activity does not tire Him because He is not the kind of entity
that can be said to tire (as a mathematical equation is not the kind of thing
that can be said to be irate). In this sense, God has one mode of activity and
men another. Now, does this difference mean that something essential to the
meaning of "activity" is lacking in the case of God's activity?

Such will be the case if it is essential to the meaning of "activity" that 1) that which is active tires or 2) that which is active may be said to tire.

In his book *Judaism: Development and Life* Leo Trepp writes:

> Daily observance is the pulse beat, supplying the individual Jew with the lifeblood of the divine. The Sabbath re-creates him, giving him the strength for meaningful daily living. It is linked to God's creative act itself (Genesis 2: 1-4). God rested from His work and hallowed the Sabbath. It is the only holy day ordained in the Ten Commandments, both in Exodus (20: 8-11) and in Deuteronomy (5: 12-15). But God needs no rest; the meaning of the term lies deeper. God ceased from making the world all by Himself; henceforth man must be His co-worker. As creator, God is the world's owner, and may ordain rest for those who toil in His domain. As we obey this command, we acknowledge God's ownership of the world and constitute ourselves not its master but its stewards.[21]

Trepp observes that although God the Creator rested, God needs no rest, for He does not tire. Yet even so, Trepp draws the implication from God being the world's creator that he is its owner. Other things being equal, creators own what they create. He understands the word "creator" to have its ordinary meaning despite the fact that God's act of creation cannot be said to have tired Him.

It may be doubtful to many that any being, including God, could create the world and not tire, but to affirm that God did just this, as Trepp does, hardly seems self-contradictory. This is also the case with saying that the question of tiredness does not arise with regard to God, which is what a believer might say to correct a child's question "How tired was God after creating the world?" Obviously, if it is not essential to the meaning of "activity" that that which is active can be said to tire (2) above), it will not be that that which is active tires (1) above). Is it self-contradictory or nonsense to say "God created the world but cannot be said to have tired from his act of creation"? It will be, if saying it is like saying that a man is a bachelor and then, some minutes later, saying that he is married; here someone has indeed contradicted himself, and one or the other assertion must be rejected. Also it will be if saying it is like saying "He is literally a bachelor and married" where no legal subtleties obtain and this is not simply a way of describing his attitude toward marriage. Here someone is apparently intentionally saying what is self-contradictory and nonsense (in the way self-contradictory expressions are nonsense). But it will not be if saying it is like saying that some men have the latent power to make the moon move just by thinking about it; here what is said is perhaps highly dubious and even farfetched, but it is not self-contradictory. (In fact it may not be so farfetched considering investigations into psychokinesis.)

Now I should think that saying "God created the world but cannot be said to have tired from his act of creation" is like saying "Some men have the latent power to make the moon move just by thinking about it." It may be dubious, but it is not self-contradictory. The speaker need not take back a part of his assertion to be consistent. He has not said two things separated by time which are mutually exclusive, nor has he intentionally said what is nonsense. If it is advanced that he has *un*intentionally said what is nonsense in the way a self-contradictory expression is nonsense, then one would want to see some reason for concluding this. The reasons are actually on the other side. First, that statement is made and understood by religious people. Second, it is understood enough by many who are not religious for them to reject it; although they may say "I do not believe it" or even "Impossible!" what is denied is understood and so is not ruled out as nonsense by the meanings of words, in contrast with what a married bachelor is, which is not understandable in this way and *is* ruled out by the meaning of words. In short, while a) as amended may be true, it is not true that if a), then b); while it may be true that God's activity is not like men's in the respect that men's activity makes them tired while God's does not make Him tired, it is not true that this being so, "active" when predicated of God must have a special sense.

It should be noted that the statement "God created the world but cannot be said to have tired from his act of creation" says nothing about *how* God created the world. The thought of those who say that God's activity must necessarily be tiring (or at least necessarily can be said to tire Him) is, perhaps, that God's activity is *bodily* activity. It may be that *bodily activity* necessarily is tiring. Granting this, why should we think that God's creation of the world, or any other activity of God, is bodily activity? Such an understanding of the Biblical stories seems naive in this day and certainly is not necessitated, although some philosophers have thought otherwise.

Both William P. Alston and Antony Flew offer reasons for thinking that there is a problem of God predication, which may be construed as variations of the fourth reason. They argue implicitly that because God is unlike men in some respect and that respect is essential to the meaning of a given predicate, or predicates, that predicate or those predicates must have a special sense when applied to God. Alston argues in terms of the predicates "speaks," "makes," "punishes," and "guides"; although he means to make a case for all such "action words." Flew states his case in terms of the words "father" and "he." Thus even if both offered good reasons they would not have established the problem of God predication generally. Their reasons hardly seem to cover the predicates "knows" or "understands," for instance. The same thing, of course, could be said about Crombie's argument.

Alston's concern is with "action words" as they pertain to God, and as such, his concern is close to Crombie's, which was with "activity" as it pertains to God. However, what Alston sees as essential to the meaning of such words is not that the specific activity tire one (or can be said to). In a collection of readings for introductory classes in Philosophy of Religion he says this: while God being immaterial can perform no bodily actions, "as we ordinarily use action words like 'speaks,' 'makes,' 'punishes,' 'guides,' the occurrence of bodily behavior is essential for their attribution."[22] Since God is immaterial and has no "bodily behavior," an action word predicated of God will require a special sense, he concludes. Apparently Alston assumes that an activity such as creating will necessarily be bodily activity or "bodily behavior." If Alston were right, it should always be self-contradictory or confused to speak of one making or guiding something with no bodily activity. If this were true it would be nonsense to investigate whether one can make a die come up a certain way with no bodily activity. But this is precisely the program of para-psychologists investigating psychokinesthetic phenomena. This is not to say that some human beings do have the power to influence rolling dice with no bodily activity, but it is to point out that investigations into this question are going on. And they would not be if it were self-contradictory or nonsense to suppose that some individuals possibly have the power. Consequently bodily activity is not essential to the meaning of action words, and we need not for this reason think that such words predicated of God require a special sense.

Flew, on the other hand, argues for the problem of God predication with the words "father" and "he." He rhetorically asks: "Could a father, in the ordinary sense of the word, be incorporeal, or a he be eternally sexless?"[23] He takes it that we will answer, "Of course not." However, Flew seems to have forgotten that there are fathers and then there are fathers. James Mill is the father of John Stuart Mill, but also Albert Einstein is the father of modern physics. Both senses are perfectly respectable and literal, both are listed in any good dictionary, but only the first requires that a father be sexual and so corporeal. The other sense, which is rather close to the sense of "creator," does not. So too with "he."

The fourth reason for thinking that there is a problem of God predication is like the first, and unlike the second and third, in that it is not a ubiquitous reason covering all God predicates. Rather it is a limited reason covering only certain God predicates, depending on its statement. This means that the fourth reason cannot very well establish by itself the problem of God predication generally. It also means that each of its different forms must be judged on its own merits and answered in terms of the particular predicates and the particular essential element cited. Most often, though, the essential element cited is something that has to do with having a body—getting tired, bodily activity, having a sex—and the predicates cited are, consequently, limited to a certain range. This being true, the considerations raised here should cast serious doubt on the fourth reason.

VI-A

Is there a problem of God predication? Do we have any enduring reason to think that God predicates cannot have the same sense they have when predicated of men? It seems that we have not. Upon examination none of the four main reasons cited to establish the problem of God predication stands up as an independent reason. At best these reasons are contingent upon questionable resolutions of knotty philosophical problems, such as the problem of personal identity, or the correctness of such philosophical doctrines as the positivist theory of meaning, resolutions and doctrines antithetical to religious belief in their own right. It may be that if one accepts these doctrines and resolutions, then *he* has the problem of God predication. But there is some question about the correctness of these views. Thus, it will be an established problem only when, e.g., the positivist theory of meaning in some form is seen to be right, or the Flew or the Penelhum resolution of the problem of personal identity is seen to be right. In the absence of any other reasons for thinking that there is a problem of God predication we may conclude that there is no conclusive reason not to think Newman is right: God predicates are our quotidian terms applied to God in their common, understood sense, and there consequently is no problem about their special sense.

Of course if there are other reasons for supposing that there is a problem of God predication, then these reasons will have to be weighed before we can finally conclude that Newman was right. However, we should be careful lest we accept the old reasons as new reasons. As was observed in section I but not stressed, the four reasons examined are often intertwined. We saw in our examination of the third reason how it might be argued that there is no adequate concept of God because the only concept there could be is anthropomorphic. And we saw how it might be argued that there is no adequate concept because religious statements (e.g., "God is good") are either false or "factually meaningless." Also it could be argued that God is not like men because this would make statements like "God is good" false or "factually meaningless," and that God is not like men because if he were he would be anthropomorphic, and so on. All these are permutations of the old reasons and offer no genuinely new reason for supposing that there is a problem of God predication. Also, we might note that one can argue from no adequate concept of God to the necessity of a special sense for God predicates, or one can argue the other way from the inadequacy of the ordinary sense for God predicates to no adequate concept of God; it seems to go one way as well as the other.

VI-B

Not only should we conclude that there is no conclusive reason for thinking that there is a problem of God predication, but if there were such a problem, it would be ruinous to faith in God. Religious belief would, of course, be nonsense or close to it if God predicates had *no* sense. But it would also be ruinous if God predicates had a sense *different from* their ordinary sense.

Believers are consoled and heartened when told of God's concern and mercy precisely because of the meaning of "concern" and "mercy." If these terms mean something else when predicated of God, then they have no reason to take heart. True, the special sense to be determined might be something that could yet give them hope. But, if there were a problem of God predication and God predicates did require a special sense, then in no case should believers take any consolation from being told that God is *merciful;* for until the special sense of "mercy" was determined, they could not know what was meant, and after it was determined, their consolation, if any, would not come from the meaning of "mercy."

This point seems to escape many writers on God predication. Michael Novak in his *Belief and Unbelief* writes:

> From the point of view of philosophical understanding, however, the crucial issue is how we are to understand the key words "omniscient," "omnipotent," "person," "moral agent," and "good," when (1) we use them of men, and when (2) we use them of God. If we think that the key terms are to be used in the same way for God as for man, . . . then manifestly God does not measure up to human standards; he is cruel, sadistic, or simply nonexistent. But if our understanding of the key terms does not lead us to use them in the same way for God as for man, what, then do we mean when we use these terms? How can we use ordinary words in extraordinary ways?[24]

Novak then goes on to say that what is needed is a new conception of God, that is, a determination of the special meanings of his "key words" as they apply to God. Novak allows that there is a problem of God predication for a variant of the first reason. He is a Catholic philosopher and in allowing the problem he is following Aquinas. However, he is unlike Aquinas in being oblivious to the just noted implications of there being a problem—the implications of, e.g., "mercy," "good" and other God predicates not meaning what they ordinarily mean. Aquinas saw the difficulty and attempted to avoid it by saying that God predicates are neither univocal nor equivocal; that is, while they do not have the same sense they have when predicated of men, they do not have a different sense either. A dark saying, but at any rate a recognition of the difficulty.

Perhaps one reason that Novak does not feel the difficulty here is that he almost immediately tells us what it means to say that God is good, namely, "that he is the source of honesty, friendship, creativity—of those instincts and dispositions that follow upon fidelity to understanding,"[25] which makes God the source of what Novak concludes is the good for man.[26] But the main reason that Novak does not feel the difficulty is that he unconsciously allows "good" predicated of God to mean what it means when predicated of men and not what he has defined it to mean. Thus he argues that God is good, even though he does not prevent evil because God has drawn those who suffered to himself their fundamental good.[27] That is, he argues that God is yet good because of his special purpose. He does *not* argue, as he should, that God is good even though He does not prevent evil (suffering) because not preventing evil is perfectly compatible with his definition of God's goodness.

VI-C

Finally let us observe several things that religious people are inclined to say that appear to leave them with the problem of God predication.

The first we have already noted. It is what the minister in Howells' novel says: we cannot imagine God. Or it is what a believer says in awe before God's majesty: no man can imagine God's power or His love. As we have already observed, this inability to imagine God or his attributes does not entail that we cannot speak of God's love or power and mean love or power. To think otherwise is to assume a connection between imaginability and ordinary meaning that does not exist.

Also we noted that some religious people have seemed to say that we have no adequate concept of God. Gaunilo, for one, seemed to say this. I think that it may be noteworthy, though, that Gaunilo was a philosopher. Further, if we look at the context in which Gaunilo says what he does, we will find that his concession is not what it might appear. Criticizing Anselm's argument, he says:

> I, so far as actual knowledge of the object [a being than which none greater can be conceived], either from its specific or general character, is concerned, am as little able to conceive of this being when I hear of it, or to have it in my understanding, as I am to conceive of or understand God himself: whom, indeed, for this very reason I can conceive not to exist.[28]

What Gaunilo is saying is that he has little understanding of God; he is not in a position to appreciate all that God is. Clearly, he does not mean that he cannot meaningfully speak of God, for one point he wants to make is that he can meaningfully doubt God's existence, which entails that he can meaningfully speak of God. Also, presumably, Gaunilo would allow that God is merciful—even if he could not conceive of (in the sense of fully understand) his mercy.

Third, religious people sometimes say outright that the ordinary meanings of their words are not adequate for God's attributes. Often they say this in praising or thanking God. Thus one might say: "The words that we have cannot adequately express the goodness of the Lord." While such proclamations may indeed have formed a great part of the theological motivation for hypothesizing that God predicates have a special sense, nevertheless a second look at them should make it clear that they should not have. The point of such utterances is that God's goodness, for instance, is so great that it defies expression. Note that it is God's goodness that is said to be so great that it defies expression. That is, it is the *extent* of God's goodness that defines expression. To describe God's goodness adequately is impossible—that is the point. But for this point to be preserved it is essential that God's goodness *be* goodness. Consequently such utterances do not give any basis to the view that God predicates have a special sense, and so they do not give rise to the problem of God predication; rather their point requires that there should be no such problem and that, e.g., "goodness" predicated of God should mean just that: goodness.

Another thing which is sometimes said by religious people that we ought to observe and disarm is exemplified by the following: "What the Bible means by 'God's activity' is never what we mean by 'men's activity.'" If anything entails the problem of God predication, it seems that this statement should. Yet, though this statement may very well be true, it does not entail that God predicates have a special sense.

The above statement might mean either of two things. First it might mean that the term "activity" has one meaning when men's activity is spoken of and another when God's activity is spoken of. If this were meant, then the problem of God predication would indeed be entailed, but this is not meant. What is meant is the second thing that the statement might mean, namely, that what the Bible refers to as God's activity is never what we refer to as men's activity. And this does not entail the problem of God predication. It does not do this any more than the possibly true statement "What some seventeenth-century Englishmen meant by (referred to by) 'travel' is not what some contemporary Englishmen mean by (refer to by) 'travel,'" entails that "travel" has two different meanings. This statement would be true if some seventeenth-century Englishmen referred only to travel by foot, horseback, or coach, and some contemporary Englishmen refer only to travel by jet or car. And this is perfectly compatible with "travel" meaning one thing for both sets of Englishmen. All that the statement's truth requires is that the two sets of Englishmen exclusively refer to different modes of travel. So too, all that the truth of the religious statement requires is that God's activity consist of modes of activity different from men's activity, so that when God's activity is referred to, certain modes of activity are referred to, and when men's activity is referred to, other modes are referred to. This would be the case if God's activity could not be said to be tiring, while man's activity could be said to be tiring. (The significance, or lack of significance, of the fact that men cannot perform God's modes of activity we have already discussed in section V.) This point applies to more than God's and man's activity. Regarding God's concern, love, mercy, and other personal attributes, God's mode of each attribute is different from man's mode of that attribute. Thus while God loves us as a Father His love is completely unfaltering as no earthly father's love is, and similarly for the other attributes.[29]

It is perhaps appropriate as well as instructive to end by noting something said by a man who was at once a religious man and a philosopher. It is this, said by Spinoza:

> But in philosophy, where we clearly understand that to apply to God the attributes which make a man perfect, is as bad as to want to apply to a man those words which make perfect an elephant or an ass, these ["desires," "is affected with weariness," "is affected with pleasure"] and similar words have no place; and we cannot use them here without thoroughly confusing our conceptions. Therefore speaking philosophically we cannot say that God demands something from someone, or that something wearies or pleases him, for all these are human attributes, which have no place in God.[30]

In this passage Spinoza seems concerned about belittling God. This, it seems to me, is a religious concern—the same that is evinced when, in praising God, it is said that words cannot express God's majesty. However, the implication that seems to reside in this passage is *not* 1) that God is loving and good, but more so than men (infinitely so—which is the religious conclusion), but 2) that we cannot say that God is loving or good, or apply to him any other attribute that men have. And 2), of course, leaves us with the problem of God predication. It is not abundantly clear that Spinoza in fact meant to accept 2) and not 1), for elsewhere he speaks of God's will[31] and of God's decrees,[32] which 2) would seem to rule out. But, although Spinoza may have wavered between 1) and 2), to the extent that he opted for 2) he allowed the problem of God predication entry. As I hope it has emerged, he did so needlessly.

Notes

[1]*Summa Theologica,* I, q. 13, a. 5. *Basic Writings of Saint Thomas Aquinas,* edited and annotated by Anton C. Pegis (New York: Random House, 1945). © 1945 by Random House, Inc.

[2]I. M. Crombie, "Theology and Falsification," eds. Antony Flew and Alasdair MacIntyre (New York: The Macmillan Company; London: SCM Press, 1955), p. 124.

[3]Crombie, "Theology and Falsification," p. 128.

[4]John Henry Cardinal Newman, *An Essay in Aid of A Grammar of Assent,* ed. Charles Frederick Harrold (New York: Longmans, Green and Co., 1947), p. 96, pt. 1, chap. 5, sec. 2. Used by permission of David McKay Company, Inc.

[5]*Dialogues Concerning Natural Religion,* pt. 11.

[6]Newman, *loc. cit.*

[7]Cf. Terence Penelhum, "Personal Identity, Memory, and Survival," *The Journal of Philosophy* 56 (1959): 805–903.

[8]Cf. Antony Flew, "Death," *New Essays in Philosophical Theology,* p. 269.

[9]I. M. Crombie, "Theology and Falsification," *New Essays in Philosophical Theology,* p. 110.

[10]I. M. Crombie, "The Possibility of Theological Statements," *Faith and Logic,* ed. Basil Mitchell (George Allen & Unwin, 1957), p. 63.

[11]This dilemma is drawn from one posed or cited by Frederick Ferré in his *Language, Logic and God* (New York: Harper & Row, Publishers, 1961), p. 68, in connection with which he cites E. L. Mascall, *Existence and Analogy* (London: Longmans, Green and Company, 1949) p. 87.
It is not clear that Crombie would subscribe to the dilemma in this or any formulation; we shall return to Crombie's views about anthropomorphism when we turn to the third reason for thinking that there is a problem of God predication, which, as we shall see, is closely related to the second reason.

[12]William Dean Howells, *The Rise of Silas Lapham* (New York: Collier Books, 1962). © 1962 by the Crowell-Collier Publishing Company, p. 182.

[13]Although some philosophers might tend to disagree with this. Cf. Antony Flew, "Death," *New Essays in Philosophical Theology,* pp. 261 ff.

[14]I. M. Crombie, "The Possibility of Theological Statements," *Faith and Logic,* p. 55.

[15]At least so Hume seems to have thought. See his *Treatise* and *Enquiry Concerning Human Understanding.*

[16]John Passmore, *Philosophical Reasoning* (New York: Charles Scribner's Sons, 1961), p. 87.

[17]See Part A. Also cf. this argument's dilemma with Hume's in sec. 2 above.

[18]See Carl Hempel, "Problems and Changes in the Empiricist Criterion of Meaning," *Semantics and the Philosophy of Language,* ed. Leonard Linsky (Urbana, Illinois: The University of Illinois Press, 1952); and Alvin Plantinga, *God and Other Minds* (Ithaca, N.Y.: Cornell University Press, 1967), pp. 156–68.

[19]I. M. Crombie, "Theology and Falsification," *New Essays in Philosophical Theology,* p. 120.

[20]Crombie, "Theology and Falsification," pp. 120–28.

[21]From *Judaism: Development and Life* by Leo Trepp. © 1966 by Dickenson Publishing Company, Inc., Belmont, California. Reprinted by permission of the publisher.

[22]William P. Alston, ed., *Religious Belief and Philosophical Thought* (New York: Harcourt Brace Jovanovich, 1963), p. 223.

[23]Antony Flew, *God and Philosophy* (New York: Harcourt Brace Jovanovich; London: Hutchinson, 1966), p. 38.

[24]Michael Novak, *Belief and Unbelief* (Mentor-Omega. New York: The New American Library, 1965). © 1965 by Michael Novak, p. 137.

[25]Novak, *Belief and Unbelief* p. 145.

[26]Novak, *Belief and Unbelief* p. 144.

[27]Novak, *Belief and Unbelief* pp. 145–46.

[28]Gaunilo, "In Behalf of the Fool," *The Ontological Argument,* ed. Alvin Plantinga (Anchor Books. Garden City, N.Y.: Doubleday & Company, 1965). © 1965 by Doubleday & Company, Inc., p. 9.

[29]Cf. John King-Farlow, " 'Could God be Temporal?' A Devil's Advocacy," *Southern Journal of Philosophy* 1 (1963): 25.

[30]A. Wolf, trans. and ed., *The Correspondence of Spinoza* (London: George Allen & Unwin, 1928; New York: Russell & Russell, 1966), Letter 23, pp. 190–91.

[31]Wolf, Letter XIX, p. 149.

[32]Wolf, Letter XXI, p. 179.

selected bibliography

Books

ALTIZER, J. J., and HAMILTON, WILLIAM. *Radical Theology and the Death of God.* Indianapolis: The Bobbs-Merrill Company, 1966.

AQUINAS, St. THOMAS. *Summa Theologica,* Second Part of the Second Part. *Basic Writings of St. Thomas Aquinas,* II. Edited and annotated by Anton C. Regis. New York: Random House, 1945.

BAILLIE, JOHN. *The Sense of the Presence of God.* New York: Charles Scribner's Sons, 1962.

BAMBROUGH, R. *Reason, Truth and God.* London: Methuen & Co., 1969.

BLACKSTONE, WILLIAM T. *The Problem of Religious Knowledge.* Englewood Cliffs, N.J.: Prentice-Hall, 1963.

BRAITHWAITE, R. B. *An Empiricist's View of the Nature of Religious Belief.* Cambridge: Cambridge University Press, 1955. Reprinted in John Hick's *The Existence of God.*

BROWN, S. C. *Do Religious Claims Make Sense?* New York: The Macmillan Company, 1969.

BUBER, MARTIN. *Eclipse of God.* New York: Harper & Row, Publishers, 1952.

BURTT, G. A. *Types of Religious Philosophy.* rev. ed. New York: Harper & Row, Publishers, 1951.

CALVIN, JOHN. *Institutes of the Christian Religion,* bk. 1, chap. VII. *Calvin's Institutes,* I. Translated by Henry Beveridge. Grand Rapids, Michigan: Wm. B. Eerdman's Publishing Company, 1962.

EBERSOLE, FRANK B. *Things We Know.* Eugene, Oregon: University of Oregon Books, 1967.

FERRE, FREDERICK. *Language, Logic and God.* New York: Harper & Row, Publishers, 1961.

FLEW, ANTONY. *God and Philosophy.* New York: Harcourt Brace Jovanovich; London: Hutchinson, 1966.

FLEW, ANTONY, and MACINTYRE, ALASDAIR, eds. *New Essays in Philosophical Theology.* New York: The Macmillan Company; London: SCM Press, 1955.

FREUD, SIGMUND. *The Future of an Illusion.* Translated by W. D. Robson-Scott. New York: Doubleday & Company, n.d.

GILKEY, LANGDON. *Naming the Whirlwind: The Renewal of God-Language.* New York: The Bobbs-Merrill Company, 1969.

GILL, JERRY H., ed. *Essays on Kierkegaard.* Minneapolis: Burgess Publishing Company, 1969.

GRIFFITHS, A. PHILLIPS, ed. *Knowledge and Belief.* London: Oxford University Press, 1967.

HEPBURN, RONALD W. *Christianity and Paradox.* New York: Pegasus; London: Watts, 1958.

HICK, JOHN, ed. *The Existence of God.* New York: The Macmillan Company, 1964.

_____. *Faith and Knowledge.* 2d ed. Ithaca, N.Y.: Cornell University Press, 1966.

_____, ed. *Faith and the Philosophers.* New York: St. Martin's Press, Inc.; London: Macmillan & Co., 1964.

HIGH, DALLAS M. *Language, Persons and Belief.* New York: Oxford University Press, 1967.

_____, ed. *New Essays on Religious Language.* New York: Oxford University Press, 1969.

HOOK, SIDNEY, ed. *Religious Experience and Truth.* New York: New York University Press, 1961.

HUDSON, W. D. *Ludwig Wittgenstein: The Bearing of His Philosophy Upon Religious Belief.* Richmond, Virginia: John Knox Press; London: Lutterworth Press, 1968.

HUME, DAVID. *Dialogues Concerning Natural Religion.* Edited by Norman Kemp Smith. 2d ed. London: Thomas Nelson and Sons, 1947.

HUXLEY, T. H. *Selections from the Essays of T. H. Huxley.* Edited by Alburey Castell. New York: Appleton-Century-Crofts, 1948.

JAMES, WILLIAM. *The Varieties of Religious Experience.* New York: Random House, Modern Library, n.d.

KANT, IMMANUEL. *Critique of Pure Reason.* Translated by Norman Kemp Smith. New York: St. Martin's Press, Inc.; London: Macmillan & Co., 1964.

KAUFMAN, G. D. *Relativism, Knowledge and Faith.* Chicago: The University of Chicago Press, 1960.

KAUFMANN, WALTER. *Critique of Religion and Philosophy.* Garden City, N.Y.: Doubleday & Company, 1961.

KIERKEGAARD, SOREN. *Concluding Unscientific Postscript.* Translated by David F. Swenson, completed after his death and provided with an introduction and notes by Walter Lowrie. Princeton: Princeton University Press, 1941.

_____. *Fear and Trembling.* Translated by Walter Lowrie. Princeton: Princeton University Press, 1941.

_____. *Philosophical Fragments.* Translated by David F. Swenson. Princeton: Princeton University Press, 1962.

KING-FARLOW, JOHN. *Reason and Religion.* London: Darton, Longman & Todd, 1969.

LEWIS, H. D. *Our Experience of God.* Muirhead Library of Philosophy. London: George Allen & Unwin, 1962.

LOCKE, JOHN. *An Essay Concerning Human Understanding,* II, bk. IV. Collated and annotated by Alexander Campbell Fraser. New York: Dover Publications, 1959.

MACINTYRE, ALASDAIR. *Difficulties in Christian Belief.* London: SCM Press Ltd., 1959.

_____, ed. *Metaphysical Beliefs,* 2nd ed. London: SCM Press, Ltd., 1970.

MACINTYRE, ALASDAIR, and RICOEUR, PAUL. *The Religious Significance of Atheism.* New York: Columbia University Press, 1969.

MALCOLM, NORMAN. *Knowledge and Certainty.* Englewood Cliffs, N.J.: Prentice-Hall, 1964.

MARTIN, C. B. *Religious Belief.* Ithaca, N.Y.: Cornell University Press, 1959.

MATSON, W. *The Existence of God.* Ithaca, N.Y.: Cornell University Press, 1965.

MAVRODES, GEORGE I. *Belief in God.* New York: Random House, 1970.

McPHERSON, THOMAS. *The Philosophy of Religion.* London: D. Van Nostrand Company, 1965.

MITCHELL, BASIL, ed. *Faith and Logic.* London: George Allen & Unwin, 1957.

MUNITZ, MILTON K. *The Mystery of Existence.* New York: Dell Publishing Co., 1968.

NOVAK, MICHAEL. *Belief and Unbelief.* New York: The New American Library, Mentor-Omega, 1965.

PASSMORE, JOHN. *Philosophical Reasoning.* New York: Charles Scribner's Sons, 1961.

PHILLIPS, D. Z., ed. *Religion and Understanding.* Oxford: Blackwell, 1967.

PLANTINGA, ALVIN. *God and Other Minds.* Ithaca, N.Y.: Cornell University Press, 1967.

————, ed. *The Ontological Argument.* Garden City, N.Y.: Doubleday & Company, Anchor Books, 1965.

PRICE, H. H. *Belief.* Muirhead Library of Philosophy. London: George Allen & Unwin, 1969.

RAMSEY, IAN T. *Religious Language.* London: SCM Press, 1957.

SANTAYANA, GEORGE. *Reason in Religion.* vol. III of *The Life of Reason.* New York: Collier Books, 1962.

SMITH, NORMAN KEMP. *The Credibility of Divine Existence.* Edited by A. J. D. Porteous, R. D. Maclennan, and G. F. Davie. New York: St. Martin's Press, 1967.

SMITH, RONALD GREGOR. *The Doctrine of God.* London: Collins, 1970.

Talk of God. Royal Institute of Philosophy Lectures, vol. II, 1967–68. New York: St. Martin's Press, Inc.; London: Macmillan & Co., 1969.

TOULMIN, S. *An Examination of the Place of Reason in Ethics.* Cambridge: The Cambridge University Press, 1961.

TREPP, LEO. *Judaism: Development and Life.* Belmont, California: Dickenson Publishing Company, 1966.

VAN BUREN, PAUL. *The Secular Meaning of the Gospel.* London: SCM Press, 1963.

WISDOM, JOHN. *Paradox and Discovery.* Oxford: Blackwell, 1965.

————. *Philosophy and Psychoanalysis.* Oxford: Blackwell, 1953.

WINCH, PETER. *The Idea of a Social Science and its Relation to Philosophy.* London: Routledge and Kegan Paul, 1958.

WITTGENSTEIN, L. *Lectures and Conversations on Aesthetics, Psychology and Religious Belief.* Edited by Cyril Barrett. Berkeley and Los Angeles: University of California Press, 1966.

————. *On Certainty.* Edited by G. E. M. Auscombe and G. H. von Wright. Translated by Denis Paul and G. G. M. Auscombe. Oxford: Blackwell, 1969.

WOLLHEIM, RICHARD, ed. *Hume on Religion.* New York: The World Publishing Company, 1964.

ZUURDEEG, W. F. *An Analytical Philosophy of Religion.* Nashville: Abingdon Press; London: George Allen & Unwin, 1959.

Articles

ALDRICH, VIRGIL C. et al. "Symposium: Are Religious Dogmas Cognitive and Meaningful?" *The Journal of Philosophy* 51 (1954).

ALLEN, DIOGENES. "Motives, Rationales on Religious Beliefs," *American Philosophical Quarterly* 3 (1966).

ALLEN, R. E. "The Ontological Argument." *The Philosophical Review* 70 (1961).

ALLISON, HENRY E. "Faith and Falsifiability." *The Review of Metaphysics* XXII, 1969.

ALSTON, WILLIAM P. "The Ontological Argument Revisited." *The Philosophical Review* 69 (1960).

ANDERSON, ALLAN W. "Faith, Truth, and Religious Knowledge." *Pacific Philosophy Forum* 5 (1967).

ARNER, DOUGLAS. "On Knowing." *The Philosophical Review* 68 (1959).

ARNETT, WILLARD E. "Santayana and the Poetic Function of Religion." *The Journal of Philosophy* 53 (1956).

ATTFIELD, R. "Non-tentative Religious Beliefs and Rationality." *Sophia* 9 (1970).

AYERS, ROBERT H. "Theological Discourse and the Problem of Meaning." *The Canadian Journal of Theology* 15 (1969).

BAILIFF, JOHN D. "Religious Discourse and Existence." *Pacific Philosophy Forum* 5 (1967).

BURNHEIM, JOHN. "The Concept of Religious Experience." *Sophia* 6 (1967).

CAHN, STEVEN M. "The Irrelevance to Religion of Philosophical Proofs for the Existence of God." *American Philosophical Quarterly* 6 (1969).

CAMERON, J. M. "R. F. Holland on 'Religious Discourse and Theological Discourse.'" *The Australasian Journal of Philosophy* 34 (1956).

CHARLESWORTH, M. J. "Linguistic Analysis and God." *International Philosophical Quarterly* 1 (1961).

CLARK, MICHAEL. "Knowledge and Grounds: A Comment on Mr. Gettier's Paper." *Analysis* 24 (1963).

CLIFFORD, PAUL R. "The Factual Reference of Theological Assertions." *Religious Studies* 3 (1967).

COBURN, ROBERT C. "The Hiddenness of God and Some Barmecidal God Surrogates." *The Journal of Philosophy* 57 (1960).

————. "A Neglected Use of Theological Language." *Mind* 72 (1963).

COPLESTON, F. C., S. J. "The Philosophical Relevance of Religious Experience." *Philosophy* 31 (1956).

COX, DAVID. "A Note on 'Meeting.'" *Mind* 60 (1951).

————. "The Significance of Christianity." *Mind* 59 (1950).

CROMBIE, I. M. "Theology and Falsification." *New Essays in Philosophical Theology*. Edited by Antony Flew and Alasdair MacIntyre. London: SCM Press, 1955.

————. "The Possibility of Theological Statements." *Faith and Logic*. Edited by B. Mitchell. London: George Allen & Unwin, 1957.

DUFF-FORBES, D. R. "Faith, Evidence, Coercion." *Australasian Journal of Philosophy* 47 (1969).

————. "Reply to Professor Flew." *Australasian Journal of Philosophy* 40 (1962).

————. "Theology and Falsification Again." *The Australasian Journal of Philosophy* 39 (1961).

EBERSOLE, FRANK B. "Perfection and Existence." *Things We Know.* Eugene, Oregon: University of Oregon Books, 1967.

————. "Whether Existence is a Predicate." *The Journal of Philosophy* 60 (1963). Reprinted in a more recent form as Chapter XII of his *Things We Know.*

EWING, A. C. "Awareness of God." *Philosophy* 40 (1965). Reprinted in his *Non-Linguistic Philosophy.* London: George Allen & Unwin; New York: Humanities Press, 1968.

————. "Religious Assertions in the Light of Contemporary Philosophy." *Philosophy* 32 (1957). Reprinted in his *Non-Linguistic Philosophy.* London: George Allen & Unwin; New York: Humanities Press, 1968.

FINDLAY, J. N. "Can God's Existence Be Disproved?" *Mind* 57 (1948). Reprinted in Antony Flew and Alasdair MacIntyre's *New Essays in Philosophical Theology*; also in J. N. Findlay, *Language Mind and Value.* New York: Humanities Press; London: George Allen & Unwin, 1963; and in Alvin Plantinga's *The Ontological Argument.*

FLEW, ANTONY. "Falsification and Hypothesis in Theology." *The Australasian Journal of Philosophy* 40 (1962).

————. "The Falsification Response." *Religious Studies* 5 (1969).

————. "Theology and Falsification" (Symposium). *University* (1950-51) (no longer published). Reprinted in Antony Flew and Alasdair MacIntyre's *New Essays in Philosophical Theology.*

FRANKLIN, R. L. "Necessary Being." *The Australasian Journal of Philosophy* 35 (1957).

GILL, JERRY H. "God-Talk: Getting on With It: A Review of Current Literature." *The Southern Journal of Philosophy* 6 (1968).

————. "J. L. Austin and the Religious Use of Language." *Sophia.* VIII, 1969.

————. "Kant, Kierkegaard and Religious Knowledge." *Philosophy and Phenomenological Research* 28 (1967). Reprinted in his Essays on Kierkegaard.

————. "The Tacit Structure of Religious Knowledge." *International Philosophical Quarterly* 9 (1969).

————. "Wittgenstein and Religious Language." *Theology Today* 21 (1964).

GLASGOW, W. D. "Knowledge of God." *Philosophy* 32 (1957).

GOTKURDEL, K. G. and KING-FARLOW, JOHN. "Über Formal Entscheidbare Sätzenkonjunktionen der Principia Theologica und Verwandter Systeme." *Analysis* 30 (1970).

GRANT, C. K. "From World to God?" (Symposium). *Proceedings of the Aristotelian Society*, supplementary vol. 41, 1967.

HARE, PETER H. "Religion and Analytic Naturalism." *Pacific Philosophy Forum* 5 (1967).

HARE, R. M. "Theology and Falsification." (Symposium). *University* (1950-51) (no longer published). Reprinted in Antony Flew and Alasdair MacIntyre's *New Essays in Philosophical Theology.*

————. "Religion and Morals." *Faith and Logic.* Edited by B. Mitchell. London: George Allen & Unwin, 1957.

HARTLAND-SWANN, J. "What is Theology? (A Reply to Professor Lewis)." *Philosophy* 29 (1954).

HAYNER, PAUL C. "Analogical Predication." *The Journal of Philosophy* 55 (1958).

HENLE, PAUL. "Uses of the Ontological Argument." *The Philosophical Review* 70 (1961).

HENZE, DONALD F. "Faith, Evidence, and Coercion." *Philosophy* 42 (1967).

————. "Language-Games and the Ontological Argument." *Religious Studies* 4 (1968).

HEPBURN, RONALD W. "From World to God." *Mind* 72 (1963).

HERBERT, ROBERT. "Puzzle Cases and Earthquakes." *Analysis* 28 (1968).

HICK, JOHN. "Faith and Coercion." *Philosophy* 42 (1967).

————. "God As Necessary Being." *The Journal of Philosophy* 57 (1960).

————. "Sceptics and Believers." *Faith and the Philosophers*. Edited by John Hick. New York: St. Martin's Press; London: Macmillan & Co., 1964.

————. "Theology and Verification." *Theology Today* 17 (1960). Reprinted in John Hick's *The Existence of God* and, in a revised form, in his *Faith and Knowledge,* Chapter VIII.

HOLLAND, R. F. "Religious Discourse and Theological Discourse." *The Australasian Journal of Philosophy* 34 (1956).

HOLMES, ARTHUR F. "Philosophy and Religious Belief." *Pacific Philosophy Forum* 5 (1967).

HORSBURGH, H. J. N. "The Claims of Religious Experience." *The Australasian Journal of Philosophy* 35 (1957).

————. "Mr. Hare on Theology and Falsification." *The Philosophical Quarterly* 6 (1956).

————. "Professor Braithwaite and Billy Brown." *The Australasian Journal of Philosophy* 36 (1958).

HUBER, CURTIS E. "Professions of Faith and the Problem of Meaning." *Pacific Philosophy Forum* 5 (1967).

HUDSON, W. D. "On Two Points Against Wittgensteinian Fideism." *Philosophy* 42 (1968).

HUGHES, G. E. "Has God's Existence Been Disproved? A Reply to Professor J. N. Findlay." *Mind* 57 (1949). Reprinted in Antony Flew and Alasdair MacIntyre's *New Essays in Philosophical Theology.*

HUTCHINGS, P. Æ. "Necessary Being." *The Australasian Journal of Philosophy* 35 (1957).

JONES, J. R. and D. Z. PHILLIPS. "Belief and Loss of Belief: A Discussion." *Sophia* 9 (1970).

KEKES, JOHN. "The Sceptical Challenge to Rationality." *Metaphilosophy* 2 (1971).

KENNY, A. "God and Necessity." *British Analytic Philosophy*. Edited by Bernard Williams and Alan Montefiore. New York: The Humanities Press, 1966.

————. "Necessary Being." *Sophia* 1 (1962).

KING-FARLOW, JOHN. "Cogency, Conviction, and Coercion." *International Philosophical Quarterly* 8 (1968).

————. " 'Could God be Temporal?' A Devil's Advocacy." *The Southern Journal of Philosophy* 1 (1963).

————. "Religion, Reality, and Language." *Pacific Philosophy Forum* 5 (1967).

KRAFT, J. "Religion, Experience and Metaphysics." *Ratio* 1 (1957).

LEVIN, DAVID MICHAEL. "Reasons and Religious Belief." *Inquiry* 12 (1969).

LEWIS, H. D. "The Cognitive Factor in Religious Experience (Symposium). *Proceedings of the Aristotelian Society,* supplementary vol. 29, 1955.

————. "Contemporary Empiricism and the Philosophy of Religion." *Philosophy* 32 (1957).

————. "What is Theology?" *Philosophy* 27 (1952).

LLEWELYN, J. E. "Three Conceptions of Faith." *The Journal of Philosophy* 61 (1964).

MACINTYRE, ALASDAIR. "Is Understanding Religion Compatible with Believing?" *Faith and the Philosophers.* Edited by John Hick. New York: St. Martin's Press; London: Macmillan & Co., 1964.

————. "The Logical Status of Religious Belief." *Metaphysical Beliefs.* Edited by A. MacIntyre. London: George Allen and Unwin, 1957.

MALCOLM, NORMAN. "Anselm's Ontological Arguments." *The Philosophical Review* 69 (1960). Reprinted in John Hick's *The Existence of God,* in Alvin Plantinga's *The Ontological Argument,* and in Norman Malcolm's *Knowledge and Certainty.*

————. "Is it a Religious Belief that 'God Exists'?" *Faith and the Philosophers.* Edited by John Hick. New York: St. Martin's Press; London: Macmillan & Co., 1964.

————. "Knowledge and Belief." *Mind* 61 (1952). Reprinted in his *Knowledge and Certainty.*

————. "On Knowledge and Belief." *Analysis* 14 (1953).

MARTIN, C. B. "A Religious Way of Knowing." *Mind* 61 (1952). Reprinted in Antony Flew and Alasdair MacIntyre's *New Essays in Philosophical Theology;* also in his *Religious Belief,* in a revised form as Chapter V.

MATSON, WALLACE I. "Bliks, Prayers, and Witches." *Pacific Philosophy Forum* 5 (1966).

MATTHEWS, GARETH B. "Theology and Natural Theology." *The Journal of Philosophy* 61 (1964).

MAVRODES, GEORGE I. "Bliks, Proofs, and Prayers." *Pacific Philosophy Forum* 5 (1966).

————. "God and Verification." *The Canadian Journal of Theology* 10 (1964).

McCLENDON, JAMES W. "Religion and Language." *Pacific Philosophy Forum* 5 (1967).

McCLENDON, JAMES W. and SMITH, JAMES M. "Saturday's Child: A New Approach to the Philosophy of Religion." *Theology Today* 27 (1970).

McKinnon, Alastair. "Unfalsifiability and the Uses of Religious Language." *American Philosophical Quarterly* 2 (1965).

McPherson, Thomas. "Assertion and Analogy." *Proceedings of the Aristotelian Society.* New Series, 60 (1959-60). Reprinted in his *The Philosophy of Religion.*

————. "The Existence of God." *Mind* 69 (1950).

————. "The Falsification Challenge: a Comment." *Religious Studies* 5 (1969).

Miller, John F. III. "Theology, Falsification and the Concept of Weltanschauung." *The Canadian Journal of Theology* 16 (1970).

Mitchell, Basil. "The Justification of Religious Belief." *Philosophical Quarterly* 2 (1961).

————, "Theology and Falsification." (Symposium). *University* (1950-51) (no longer published). Reprinted in Antony Flew and Alasdair MacIntyre's *New Essays in Philosophical Theology.*

Moore, G. E. "Is Existence a Predicate?" *Proceedings of the Aristotelian Society.* supplementary vol. 15, 1936. Reprinted in Alvin Plantinga's *The Ontological Argument* and in *Logic and Language.* second series. Edited by A. Flew. Oxford: Blackwell, 1959.

Nielsen, Kai. "Can Faith Validate God-Talk?" *Theology Today.* 20 (1963).

————. "Eschatological Verification." *The Canadian Journal of Theology* 9 (1963).

————. "God and Verification Again." *The Canadian Journal of Theology* 11 (1965).

————. "In Defense of Atheism." *Perspective in Education, Religion, and the Arts.* Contemporary Philosophic Thought: The International Philosophy Year Conferences at Brockport, vol. 3. Albany, N.Y.: State University of New York Press, 1970.

————. "The Intelligibility of God-Talk." *Religious Studies* 6 (1970).

————. "On Fixing the Reference Range of God." *Religious Studies* 2 (1966).

————. "On Believing that God Exists." *The Southern Journal of Philosophy* 5 (1967).

————. "The Primacy of Philosophical Theology." *Theology Today* 27 (1970).

————. "Wittgensteinian Fideism." *Philosophy* 42 (1967).

————. "Wittgensteinian Fideism: A Reply to Hudson." *Philosophy* 44 (1969).

Penelhum, Terence. "Divine Necessity." *Mind* 49 (1960).

————. "Is a Religious Epistemology Possible?" *Knowledge and Necessity.* Royal Institute of Philosophy Lectures, vol. 3, 1968-69. New York: St. Martin's Press; London: Macmillan & Co., 1970.

————. "On the Second Ontological Argument." *The Philosophical Review* 70 (1961).

————. "Religion and Philosophical Sophistication." *Pacific Philosophy Forum* 5 (1966).

Phillips, D. Z. "From World to God?" (Symposium). *Proceedings of the Aristotelian Society.* supplementary vol. 41, 1967.

————. "Philosophy, Theology and the Reality of God." *The Philosophical Quarterly* 13 (1963).

————. "Religion and Epistemology: Some Contemporary Confusion." *The Australasian Journal of Philosophy* 44 (1966).

————. "Religious Beliefs and Language-Games." *Ratio* 12 (1970).

————. "Wisdom's Gods." *The Philosophical Quarterly* 19 (1969).

PLANTINGA, ALVIN. "A Valid Ontological Argument?" *The Philosophical Review* 70 (1961).

PRICE, H. H. "Belief 'in' and Belief 'that.'" *Religious Studies* 1 (1965).

————. "Faith and Belief." *Faith and the Philosophers.* Edited by John Hick. New York: St. Martin's Press, 1964.

————. "On Believing—A Reply to Professor R. W. Sleeper." 2 (1967).

PRIOR, A. N. "Is Necessary Existence Possible?" *Philosophy and Phenomenological Research* 15 (1955).

RAINER, A. C. A. "Necessity and God: A Reply to Professor Findlay." *Mind* 58 (1949). Reprinted in Antony Flew and Alasdair MacIntyre's *New Essays in Philosophical Theology.*

RAMSEY, I. T. "Contemporary Philosophy and the Christian Faith." *Religious Studies* 1 (1965).

ROTH, MICHAEL. "A Note on Anselm's Ontological Argument." *Mind* (1970).

RUSSELL, BERTRAND. "Mysticism and Logic." *Mysticism and Logic.* Garden City, N.Y.: Doubleday & Company, n.d.

SAUNDERS, JOHN TURK and CHAMPAWAT, NARAYAN. "Mr. Clark's Definition of 'Knowledge.'" *Analysis* 25 (1964).

SCHMIDT, PAUL F. "Is There Religious Knowledge." *The Journal of Philosophy* 55 (1958).

SHAFFER, J. "Existence, Predication and the Ontological Argument." *Mind* 71 (1962).

SLEEPER, R. W. "On Believing." *Religious Studies* 2 (1966).

SMART, J. J. C. "The Existence of God." *New Essays in Philosophical Theology.* Edited by Antony Flew and Alasdair MacIntyre. New York: The Macmillan Company; London: SCM Press, 1955.

SMITH, CONSTANCE. "Knowledge of God." *Philosophy* 33 (1958).

SMITH, JOHN E. "The Experiential Foundations of Religion." *The Journal of Philosophy* 55 (1958).

SWANSON, J. W. "Religious Discourse and Rational Preference Rankings." *American Philosophical Quarterly* 4 (1967).

TAYLOR, RICHARD. "A Note on Knowing and Belief." *Analysis* 13 (1953).

————. "Rejoinder to Malcolm." *Analysis* 14 (1953).

THOMPSON, SAMUEL. "Tradition, Revolt and Reconstruction in Philosophy of Religion." *The Review of Metaphysics* 13 (1959).

TOMBERLIN, JAMES E. "Is Belief in God Justified?" *Journal of Philosophy* 67 (1970).

TRETHOWAN, DOM ILLTYD. "In Defense of Theism—A Reply to Kai Nielsen." *Religious Studies* 2 (1966).

————. "Mr. Henze on Faith." *Philosophy* 42 (1967).

WAINWRIGHT, W. J. "Religious Statements and the World." *Religious Studies* 2 (1966).

WARD, J. S. K. "Existence, Transcendence and God." *Religious Studies* 3 (1968).

WEISS, PAUL. "Religious Experience." *The Review of Metaphysics* 17 (1963).

WERNHAM, JAMES C. S. "Eschatological Verification and Parontological Obfuscation." *The Canadian Journal of Theology* 13 (1967).

WHITELEY, C. H. "The Cognitive Factor in Religious Experience" (Symposium). *Proceedings of the Aristotelian Society.* supplementary vol. 29, 1955.

WINCH, PETER. "Understanding a Primitive Society." *American Philosophical Quarterly* 1 (1964). Reprinted in D. Z. Phillips' *Religion and Understanding.*

WISDOM, JOHN. "Gods." *Proceedings of the Aristotelian Society* 45 (1944-45). Reprinted in his *Philosophy and Psychoanalysis,* and in *Logic and Language.* First Series. Edited by Antony Flew. Oxford: Blackwell, 1960.

————. "The Logic of God." *Paradox and Discovery.* Oxford: Blackwell, 1965. Also in John Hick's *The Existence of God* under the title, "The Modes of Thought and the Logic of God."

YOLTON, JOHN W. "Professor Malcolm on St. Anselm, Belief and Existence." *Philosophy* 36 (1961).

ZABEEH, FARHANG. "Ontological Argument and How and Why Some Speak of God." *Philosophy and Phenomenological Research* 22 (1961).

index